A SNIPER'S JOURNEY

A SNIPER'S JOURNEY

THE TRUTH ABOUT THE MAN BEHIND THE RIFLE

GARY D. MITCHELL WITH **MICHAEL HIRSH**

FOREWORD BY DOUGLAS VALENTINE

NAL
CALIBER

NAL Caliber
Published by New American Library, a division of
Penguin Group (USA) Inc., 375 Hudson Street,
New York, New York 10014, USA
Penguin Group (Canada), 90 Eglinton Avenue East, Suite 700, Toronto,
Ontario M4P 2Y3, Canada (a division of Pearson Penguin Canada Inc.)
Penguin Books Ltd., 80 Strand, London WC2R 0RL, England
Penguin Ireland, 25 St. Stephen's Green, Dublin 2,
Ireland (a division of Penguin Books Ltd.)
Penguin Group (Australia), 250 Camberwell Road, Camberwell, Victoria 3124,
Australia (a division of Pearson Australia Group Pty. Ltd.)
Penguin Books India Pvt. Ltd., 11 Community Centre, Panchsheel Park,
New Delhi—110 017, India
Penguin Group (NZ), cnr Airborne and Rosedale Roads, Albany,
Auckland 1310, New Zealand (a division of Pearson New Zealand Ltd.)
Penguin Books (South Africa) (Pty.) Ltd., 24 Sturdee Avenue,
Rosebank, Johannesburg 2196, South Africa

Penguin Books Ltd., Registered Offices:
80 Strand, London WC2R 0RL, England

First published by NAL Caliber, an imprint of New American Library,
a division of Penguin Group (USA) Inc.

ISBN 0-451-21652-0

Set in Berkley
Designed by Ginger Legato

Printed in the United States of America

PUBLISHER'S NOTE
While the author has made every effort to provide accurate telephone numbers and Internet addresses at the time of publication, neither the publisher nor the author assumes any responsibility for errors, or for changes that occur after publication. Further, publisher does not have any control over and does not assume any responsibility for author or third-party Web sites or their content.

The ideas, procedures, and suggestions contained in this book are not intended as a substitute for consulting with your physician. All matters regarding your health require medical supervision. Neither the author nor the publisher shall be liable or responsible for any loss or damage allegedly arising from any information or suggestion in this book. The opinions expressed in this book represent the personal views of the author and not of the publisher.

For my wife,
Ellen,
who has remained by my side
as I live with the memories that haunt me daily;
and for my parents,
Gladys and Alexander

—Gary D. Mitchell

For my mother,
Essie Hirsh,
and for all the mothers who have known the anguish
of sending their children off to war

—Michael Hirsh

FOREWORD

by Douglas Valentine

G ary Mitchell, at the age of nineteen, became an assassin for the U.S. government, and that experience affected him for the rest of his life. *A Sniper's Journey* is a fascinating and often tragic story about a young man's struggle to survive under perilous circumstances. It's a story of a grown man's quest to find peace of mind.

The drama began in June 1969, when Gary found himself in an infantry outfit in central South Vietnam. The war was raging. Nearly ten thousand GIs were killed that year. It was the second-deadliest year in a war that claimed fifty thousand American lives. The situation was desperate. The people in charge were willing to do anything to win.

Under these dire circumstances, Gary became a sniper and was plunged into a world of deadly intrigues and wrenching emotional conflicts that remain unresolved today. But he wasn't used as infantry snipers are currently being used in Iraq. He wasn't positioned on a rooftop, in radio contact with his commanders, carefully selecting and picking off insurgent snipers in modern "hit-and-run" urban warfare.

As Gary explains, "This was a preplanned assassination, and in comparison to combat, I had plenty of time to think about it, to decide whether it was something I was willing to do."

In Gary's case, anonymous men, probably employed by the CIA, used him to assassinate unsuspecting people from a distance, while he was in hiding. The people he killed never heard the report from his rifle.

The great irony of A Sniper's Journey is that Gary Mitchell had no idea whom he was working for on his sniper missions. He didn't know about the Phoenix Program while he was in Vietnam. He didn't learn about it until thirty years later. But it is very likely that Mitchell's sniper missions were part of Phoenix.

Created in 1967 by the CIA, Phoenix was designed to "neutralize" the people in the shadow government that ran the insurgency in South Vietnam. To "neutralize" meant to kill, capture, or make to defect. Robert Komer, the CIA officer initially in charge of Phoenix, imposed a quota of eighteen hundred neutralizations per month on the people running the program in the field. In 1969, Phoenix neutralized 19,534 people. Of those, 4,832 were killed. By the time the war was over, the CIA estimated that Phoenix had killed some twenty thousand people. The Vietnamese put the number at over forty thousand.[1]

The Phoenix Program in 1969 had some six hundred American military men, and fifty CIA officers in Saigon, and at region, province, and district headquarters.[2] They had no forces of their own, but could reach into any unit and grab anyone they needed. If they wanted to "search and destroy" a village that was thought to harbor guerrilla leaders, they could send in a regular army battalion to do the job. They could call in a B-52 attack on a remote village, if that village was thought to harbor an important individual in the shadow government.

But search-and-destroy missions and five-hundred-pound bombs did little to win the hearts and minds of the Vietnamese. So Komer told his Phoenix staff "that he wanted a 'rifle shot' approach—a

---

1 "Phoenix 1969 End of Year Report" (Saigon, February 28, 1970, Headquarters, United States Military Assistance Command, Civil Operations and Rural Development), p. 6.

2 Hearing on the Nomination of William E. Colby (Committee on Armed Services, U.S. Senate, July 2, 20, 25, 1973), p. 172.

sniper's attack, not a shotgun approach" against the people managing the insurgency.[3]

There you have it from the horse's mouth. The crux of the Phoenix concept was using snipers to assassinate the leaders of the Viet Cong insurgency.

Which is why expert shooters like Gary were in hot demand in 1969.

Understanding Phoenix is essential in putting what Gary Mitchell did in its proper historical context. Otherwise, what you're about to read seems almost unbelievable.

Gary's coauthor, Michael Hirsh, knew that I had written a book about the Phoenix Program, and that Professor Alfred W. McCoy described it as "the definitive account." Published in 1990, it took five years to research. It is based on interviews with the CIA officers who created and ran the program, including the first Phoenix chief, Robert Komer, and his successor, William E. Colby, who managed the program from 1969 to 1971. Colby would serve as director of Central Intelligence from 1973 to 1975.

In simple terms, the Phoenix Program had two tiers: tactical and strategic. On the tactical level—from the 240 districts down to several thousand hamlets—its purpose was the political control of people. To this end, everyone in South Vietnam was registered in a national ID program. Everyone was investigated, and those deemed to be Viet Cong supporters were entered into a computerized blacklist. People who were not actively opposing the VC were considered sympathizers and put on the blacklist, too.

The blacklist enabled the people running Phoenix to conduct a massive dragnet across South Vietnam. This was the purpose of the tactical lower tier.

There were forty-four provinces in Vietnam. A province was like

---

3   Douglas Valentine, *The Phoenix Program* (New York, William Morrow & Company, 1990), p. 131.

a state in the United States. A district was like a county. The CIA ran Phoenix at the province level and above.

If a tactical-level VC suspect was "at large," the Phoenix district adviser notified his CIA boss in the province capital. At this point the CIA sent a counterterror team, often Green Berets or Navy SEALs, to neutralize the suspect. If the VC suspect could not be captured and brought to the Province Interrogation Center, he or she was killed.

Neutralizations at the strategic level required more careful planning and execution than at the tactical level. For example, Buddhists composed the vast majority of the Vietnamese population, and many Buddhists held positions of power in business and government. The Saigon government could not be seen to be repressing Buddhists who opposed U.S. policies, so the CIA neutralized troublesome Buddhists in ways that ensured "plausible deniability."

One way of ensuring plausible deniability was to use expendable army snipers like Gary Mitchell to assassinate important people who were otherwise untouchable.

All CIA assassinations meet this "deniability" criterion. They must be deniable by the expendable people who carry them out, as well as those who plan them.

Phoenix veterans tend to despise the word *assassin,* because many of their targets were not military personnel. People on the blacklist included union organizers, doctors, lawyers, schoolteachers, and even Buddhist monks. Some of these people were secret members of the shadow government that ran the insurgency. Others were nationalists opposed to U.S. policy. Some were victims of mistaken identity, or falsely accused, or targeted by corrupt officials for failing to pay bribes.

The CIA bosses chose the targets, and CIA assassins don't like thinking, as one spook put it, that Phoenix was "the greatest blackmail scheme ever invented: 'If you don't do what I want, you're VC!'"

To admit that Phoenix was an assassination program would mean that the people who created it and ran it, and those who served as its assassins, might someday be labeled war criminals. Which is a powerful enough motive for everyone involved to deny that the program ever assassinated anyone.

But what else do you call a carefully selected "targeted kill" of a key individual by a sniper?

In *A Sniper's Journey*, you will learn about unbelievable things that not only were possible, but routine during the Vietnam War.

Don't be surprised to learn that the same thing is happening today. As reported in *Newsweek*, U.S. Special Operations assassination teams are being deployed in Iraq to effect what they call "the Salvador Option."[4] The Salvador Option was an extrapolation of the Phoenix Program, conceived and often managed by the same people.

Christopher Dickey, in his book *With the Contras*, spoke about the training manual given to the CIA contract officers who ran the death squads in El Salvador. He describes it as "a little book with a cover in the blue and white of the Nicaraguan flag. The graphic motif was rows of heads with large holes through them. Targets. It looked as if they were targets for snipers."[5]

That training manual was created by and for people in the Phoenix Program.

A Sniper's Journey is a complete war story because it acknowledges that the war doesn't always end when your tour of duty is over and you go back to the real world. For some veterans like Gary Mitchell, the war rages on forever, because the realization has surfaced that they did things they weren't supposed to do. And the only way they can find any peace of mind is to tell their story.

Alas, there are many prohibitions against doing that. For a person of conscience, it is hard to write about killing people. In this respect, *A Sniper's Journey* is not just a story of a young man's lost innocence;

---

4   Michael Hirsh and John Barry, "The Salvador Option," *Newsweek*, January 14, 2005.
5   Christopher Dickey, *With the Contras* (New York, Simon & Schuster, 1985), p. 256.

it's about a grown man's endless quest for validation. For no matter where Gary Mitchell journeys in search of a tangible connection to his past, there is no evidence of his ever having been a sniper.

There never will be. Finding documented proof of covert operations is like going to the local Mafia boss for the inside scoop on crime. It's not going to happen.

The military and CIA spend billions of dollars learning how to manipulate people. The process starts with breaking down a young person's personality and rebuilding him as a killing machine. The moral prohibitions the recruits have learned at home, in school, at church, about right and wrong, are replaced with new taboos. It's like being sworn into a secret society and swearing never to reveal its secrets. The soldiers come out of boot camp able to do things that, under normal circumstances, they would never consider.

Initially, a soldier is taught to feel no remorse, so that he functions as part of the machine. Years later, when he finds himself grappling with nightmares and shame, the taboos prevent the soldier from telling what he has done. The skeletons stay in the closet.

But sometimes the machine breaks down, and people like Gary Mitchell emerge from the wreckage to tell their stories. In Gary's case, it's taken more than three decades. Sometimes it happens sooner, as in the case of the whistle-blower among the MPs at Abu Ghraib.

No matter how long it takes, the government is prepared to discredit those who go public, who attempt to puncture the balloon of plausible deniability. Spooks and soldiers who have engaged in similar activities emerge from the shadows to discredit the renegades who speak out or stumble into the public limelight.

Some people will say that Gary Mitchell's story doesn't ring true. Certified snipers will insist that the CIA didn't need to borrow regular army guys. The Green Berets and Navy SEALs who volunteered for assassination missions will be the most vitriolic in their criticism.

They knew what they were getting into. They signed nondisclosure statements and are subject to fines and imprisonment if they break the code of silence. Their careers and reputations are at stake.

Even if Gary Mitchell were to find the people who guided him on his sniper's journey, they would disavow him. Witness what happened when a Navy SEAL revealed that former Nebraska senator Bob Kerrey had participated in the murder of over a dozen innocent Vietnamese civilians. Witness the criticism heaped upon Hugh Thompson, the man who single-handedly stopped the My Lai massacre. The list goes on and on, but the outcome is always the same: The lone whistle-blower is invariably discredited.

A Sniper's Journey is a warning to Americans that their government is more powerful, more manipulative, and more ruthless than they could ever believe.

Living with this problem is the challenge of Gary Mitchell's life. Writing *A Sniper's Journey* is the cathartic act that sets the record straight. It is a story of self-realization and healing, told without bitterness, about things we need to know.

With the assistance of coauthor Michael Hirsh—who served as an army combat correspondent in Vietnam—Mitchell finds redemption by telling what happened. Mike Hirsh adds his own unique blend of humor, compassion, and experience, and helps Gary tell his story without being apologetic. They tell it with candor and a sense of time and place that turns the unimaginable into a lesson about truth. It is a lesson that helps us understand and cope with the great uncertainties, sorrows, and mysteries of living in such tumultuous times.

Douglas Valentine is the author of *The Hotel Tacloban* (a widely acclaimed account of life in a Japanese POW camp), *The Phoenix Program*, *TDY* (an action/adventure novella about the CIA's involvement in international drug smuggling), and *The Strength of the Wolf*, a nonfiction book about the early years of federal drug law enforcement. A sequel,

FOREWORD

The Strength of the Pack, about the origins of the DEA, is forthcoming in 2006 through the University Press of Kansas. Mr. Valentine is the author of many articles about the war on terror, which are easily accessible on the Internet.

THE RULES

In 1969, the CIA's highest official in South Vietnam, future Director of Central Intelligence William Colby, issued the following "instruction":

The PHOENIX program is one of advice, support and assistance to the GVN (Government Viet Nam) Phuong Hoang program aimed at reducing the influence and effectiveness of the Viet Cong Infrastructure in South Viet Nam. . . .

Operations against the Viet Cong Infrastructure include the collection of intelligence, identifying these members (of the Viet Cong), inducing them to abandon their allegiance to the Viet Cong and rally to the government . . . and, as a final resort, the use of military or police force against them if no other way of preventing them from carrying on their unlawful activities is possible. Our training emphasizes the desirability of obtaining these target individuals alive and of using intelligent and lawful methods of interrogation to obtain the truth of what they know about other aspects of the Viet Cong Infrastructure. U.S. personnel are under the same legal and moral constraints with respect to the operations of a Phoenix character as they are with respect to regular military operations against enemy units in the field. Thus, *they are specifically not authorized to engage in assassinations* [italics mine] or other violations of the rules of land warfare, but they are entitled to use such reasonable military force as is necessary to obtain the goals of rallying, capturing, or eliminating the Viet Cong Infrastructure in the Republic of Viet Nam.

INTRODUCTION

My wife, Ellen, and I had a rule: Holiday time is ours and ours alone. Call us on the phone—we don't answer. Knock on our door—we're not home. It's been that way almost from the time we got married—second marriages for each of us—back in 1981 when we were both soldiers stationed in Germany. I forget how the tradition started, but it seemed to work for us.

At least I thought it did. But hey, I'm a guy; how am I supposed to know what a woman is thinking? What seemed like the beginning of the end, or maybe it was the end of the beginning of our relationship, happened on Christmas Day in 1996. We were home alone in Los Angeles, and had spent Christmas Eve with Ellen's family. Of course, when we headed for home, it was with a large bag of leftovers—turkey, rolls, stuffing, the works—which we planned to eat while watching a Christmas movie on television.

You're probably wondering what all this has to do with what I've called *A Sniper's Journey*. Trust me and hang in there for a minute; it's all part of the road I'm traveling.

Late in the afternoon Ellen was in the kitchen warming up the leftovers and I came in to help. I had been a little edgy and snapped at her a couple of times over nothing. Nowadays, I would recognize the signs and know what was coming. But at that time—not a clue.

I was trying to open a package of dinner rolls, the kind that's heat-sealed in cellophane, and I just couldn't find the seam. Finally, in frustration and anger, I screamed a couple of expletives and threw the rolls onto the counter.

I'll let Ellen tell it from her perspective, because this book isn't just about me and how the killing I did and the dying I saw affected me. It's about us, our relationship, and how my experiences in the army impacted our marriage.

"I was standing there, watching Gary struggle with the package of rolls. I watched the change begin to show on his face. He was even beginning to sweat a little bit, and then he started cussing, and the entire demeanor of his body went from casually relaxed to tense and stiff in an instant. His face became hard, and then he slammed the rolls onto the counter.

"If you've never seen a transformation like that, or even if you have, it's scary to watch. As soon as he threw the rolls I said, 'Gary, what the hell is the matter with you?' And that did it. That's all it took. He started screaming and yelling at me. What had been the beginning of a very pleasant afternoon had suddenly turned—as it had so many times in the past—into this horrible nightmare. At that point, anything I said or did was just fuel for the fire that was burning inside of him."

I told you her perspective would be worth hearing. Okay, I was completely out of control by that time. There was nothing she could do or say that was going to defuse my rage. I was, for lack of a better term, totally and completely insane at that moment. She told me to calm down, and that was really the wrong thing to say to me. Of course, anything she said would have been the wrong thing. "Calm down, listen to what you're saying, take a deep breath." It was all wrong.

I looked at her and raised my fist like I was going to hit her, and even in the state I was in, I knew better than to actually do it. So I slammed my fist onto the counter so hard that the impact caused a couple of glasses to fall over.

Ellen recalls, "When he made his hand into a fist and actually started to draw back, I thought that he was really going to let me have it. I couldn't even see my Gary in the face that was glaring at me. I took a couple of staggering steps backward just at the time that he slammed his fist into the counter.

"I immediately started to cry, and the tears did what words never could do. It was like throwing a glass of cold water in his face. I could see his face just crumple; all the rage and anger drained out. He reached for me, instantly saying, 'I'm sorry, I'm sorry. Oh, my God, I'm sorry!'

"When he moved toward me, I backed up a couple of more steps and stared at him, wondering who the hell this person is.

"I said, 'That's it! I've had enough! No more! Get some help, *now,* or get a lawyer.'"

When I realized what I had done, scaring Ellen so badly that she broke down into tears, I was shocked and ashamed. Ellen was the light of my life. I honestly believe that if she hadn't come into my world when she did, I might have done what a lot of Vietnam vets have done—killed myself. Ellen has always been willing to talk with me, cry with me, or hold me as I cried. She had never criticized, passed judgment, or withdrawn in horror. But now—this.

At that moment I was scared, angry with myself, and embarrassed; I felt like every bit of the ass that I had been a few moments before. Ellen was just standing there, trembling and crying. The more she cried, the more her body was racked by the sobs. I reached out and she backed away, and at that moment I wanted to die; I really did.

I begged her to forgive me, and she kept backing farther away. All kinds of thoughts went through my mind. *Will she ever kiss me again? Will she ever trust me again? My God, what will I do if she actually gets a lawyer?*

She said, "Please don't touch me." I went outside and sat on the patio. I didn't know what to do. After a while she came outside, and calmly but firmly said, "I'm not kidding. I've had enough. You get some help. This is not open to debate."

At that point, if she'd asked me to shoot myself, I'd have gladly done it. But she said, "Gary, I love you. I've done everything I can, but nothing seems to work. I will not put up with this anymore."

So now you've got some idea of where my story is going. Getting there hasn't been—as they used to say—"half the fun." When I finally saw a psychologist for the first time, she listened as I described the nightmares and episodes of violence, the periods of misery, the inability to leave my war experiences behind. And she asked me to write them down, to write a journal of my memories and nightmares. And that's what *A Sniper's Journey* is—a telling of the events that shaped my life, as I now remember them. The journey began in Granbury, Texas, moved on to Vietnam, where I was used as an always-get-the-job-done sniper, through a twenty-four-year army career that took me from buck private to chief warrant officer with an American advisory group to the Saudi Arabian National Guard in the first Gulf War. It's a journey that continues to this day, because, as those who suffer from it—and those who love them—know all too well, the battle we fight with post-traumatic stress disorder (PTSD) is ongoing. My hope is that the servicemen who are now fighting another war, and the families who will welcome changed men and women home from that war, can learn from my experience and deal with the emotional trauma that war inevitably causes before it tears them and their families apart.

—Gary D. Mitchell
Los Angeles, California
November 11, 2005

CHAPTER ONE

Let's Join Up

In February of 1968 I was eighteen years old, one of eighty-eight kids in the senior class at the only high school in Granbury, Texas, thirty-seven miles southwest of Fort Worth. I had the world by the tail and a tiger in my tank. I was convinced beyond the shadow of any doubt that I was hipper and, quite frankly, much more intelligent than many of those around me, especially my parents. While they hadn't yet reached older-than-dirt status, at sixty-three and fifty-eight, respectively, my father and mother seemed ancient to me. They'd had fourteen children, eight of whom had died in infancy. All that life experience gave my parents the confidence to believe that they knew what was best for me. I was convinced they were wrong.

Granted, this certainty about who I was and what I was capable of deciding for myself was relatively newfound. Like most boys moving into their late teens, I'd been testing the limits; but under the watchful eyes of just about every adult in Granbury, there wasn't a whole lot I could get away with. Talk about taking a village . . . Granbury kids were the poster children for the concept.

Consider our chat about me joining the army. It happened one evening at the dinner table. Our family custom was to watch the *CBS Evening News* with Walter Cronkite and get our nightly measure of combat footage from an obscure little country in Southeast Asia called Vietnam before adjourning to the kitchen for our evening meal.

Before eating, my father would always say a prayer of thanks, which he always concluded with a request to protect America's service members, especially those over in Vietnam. My family was given to honoring our military. Fact is, from World War II forward for half a century, my parents had almost continually had one of their children in the service. My oldest brother, Leon, had been an army infantryman fighting in Europe. Another brother, Harrell, served in the Marine Corps during the Korean War. And another brother, Howard, was on active duty in the air force and was about to retire just as I was signing up. Much to what I'm sure was the relief of my mother, my sisters Barbara and Ruth never entered the service.

I came from a generation that, as children, watched John Wayne, Audie Murphy, Jimmy Stewart, Glenn Ford, and others give fantastic movie performances in which they always died heroically, not suffering terribly from their wounds, and in general, glorifying warfare. We also tuned in to TV series such as *Combat!* with Vic Morrow, and *Twelve O'Clock High* with Robert Lansing that portrayed the heroics of war, but gave little indication of the mental and physical suffering.

So I figured it shouldn't have come as a surprise to Mom and Dad when I said, "I think I'll join the army."

My father didn't miss a beat: "No, you're not, either."

I was eighteen; I was graduating from high school. I thought I should be able to decide my own future. I puffed out my boyish chest and asked, "Why not?"

Dad's answer was simple. "Because I said you're not, that's why— eat your supper."

Rather than heeding his warning, I said, "I'm old enough. I don't have to have your permission to join. I can do it if I want to, and you can't stop me."

My mom looked shocked, but she made no comment. However, the look on her face indicated that the family was going to soon need the services of a good funeral director, because she was quite sure that my father was going to kill me.

He looked at me with his face showing a hurt and anger that parents experience when the children they've raised from infancy begin to assert their independence. But to my surprise, he didn't even raise his voice when he said, "Okay, but you'll be making a mistake, and you'll regret it if you do," and without another comment, he continued to eat his dinner.

For the rest of the evening I couldn't think of anything other than the fact that my dad thought I'd be making a mistake. Surely someone with my level of worldly experience and intelligence could make up his own mind without parental guidance. After all, it wasn't a life-or-death decision—or so it seemed to me then. I was just considering joining the army for three short years. Absurd as it may sound, the fact that the army was smack in the middle of an armed conflict really didn't cross my mind.

Why? Because Granbury, Texas, population three thousand, had been only slightly touched by the war. One young man whose sister-in-law was in my high school class had died, and two others, one of whom was my cousin, had been seriously wounded. The entire town—like much of the country—was still somewhat naive about the growing conflict. The fact that we could see the war nightly on our television screens didn't make it any more real to us than *Gunsmoke*. We had our few who found ways to avoid the draft, but for the most part, the young men being drafted served, and a number elected to volunteer. And with those few exceptions, all returned home safely and resumed their lives.

That night I tossed and turned a lot, awakening in the morning to the realization that I was now even angrier at the comments my father had made than I'd been at dinner. I always drove to school with a friend named Steve, and we usually stopped at a small store and bought a Coke to drink on the way. On this morning, the entire time we were in the store and then on the way to school I groused to him about the way my father had dismissed my decision. I repeated the argument that hadn't had any impact on my dad. "Hey, I'm eighteen. I'm old enough to be drafted. Why shouldn't I join the army? Isn't it the thing you should do, especially during a war?" (Decades later, I can see that this argument was inconsistent with my ability the previous evening to ignore the fact that the army was fighting a war in order to convince my parents—and myself—that a three-year enlistment carried no inordinate risks. The only way to explain it—I was a hormonally driven teenager; logical thinking and deductive reasoning weren't necessarily part of the package.)

I was whipping myself into a fiery rage that can only be experienced by a child on the cusp between adolescence and adulthood. The very idea that I could make a mistake—how dared he? During the remainder of the drive to school, I moaned and groaned about the situation. Just as we pulled up, I said, "Let's skip school. I'm going to join the army!" My friend didn't even turn the car engine off; he simply turned the corner and headed toward Fort Worth.

The recruiter welcomed us warmly—after all, he was getting a gift that all recruiters wished for: a free recruit, a walk-in, a warm body that would be graduating from high school in only three months, and old enough that he didn't need his parents to sign.

I took the tests, passed them without difficulty, and allowed myself—no, demanded—to be scheduled for a physical examination. The following week I skipped school again and went to the Armed Forces Entrance and Examination Station (AFEES). There I took more intelligence and aptitude tests and then faced the battery of medical exams one must pass in order to enter the armed forces.

I passed every test and examination they administered and was sent to see a counselor to select my job in the army. For no reason that I can recall, I wanted to be a truck driver, but according to the counselor, training classes for that MOS (military occupational specialty) were filled. As an alternative, he offered me a job as a mechanic, which I accepted, signed the papers, and then headed back home to Granbury.

Now there was only the little matter of telling my parents that against their best advice I had joined the army. Suffice it to say that the conversation did not go well. My father was infuriated that, in a rebellious state, I would ignore his opinion and enter the military—especially in the midst of an armed conflict. In retrospect, what was weighing on his mind was that he and my mother had been through this twice before, a fact that I didn't bother to take into consideration. Mom didn't say much, but my father went into full lecture mode. He talked about kids rebelling, going against parental wishes, thinking they knew more than the people who raised them from birth.

It was not a pleasant conversation for someone who was under the delusion that he was a grown-up. If I thought I could have gotten away with it, I would have stood up to him and declared my adulthood, but I had to put all my mental energies into shielding myself from the verbal flak that my dad was sending in my direction. The unpleasantries lasted about an hour, and it was pretty much one-way. He was sermonizing from the mountaintop, and I was down below, and you know what they say about what flows downhill.

In the end, he accepted that it was out of his hands and simply said, "You're a man, now; you'd better take care of yourself. It would kill your mama if something happened to you." I understand now that it would have hurt him just as much as it would have hurt my mom.

My high school graduation ceremony took place on May 24, and I had three final weeks of civilian life before I reported for induction in mid-June. There was no point in looking for a three-week job, so I just roamed around town trying to capitalize on the newfound status I was enjoying as a high school grad as well as an incipient man in uniform. Because my father was already drawing his Social Security, I got a small monthly check. It was only about eighteen dollars, but that was a lot more in 1968 than it is now. Gas back then was just thirty-four cents a gallon, a McDonald's burger with fries and a shake was only sixty-three cents, a pack of Marlboros was half a buck, and a ticket to the movies was a dollar. With the money burning a hole in my pocket, I drove around town in my '65 Ford pickup trying to chase girls. My problem was that I was a bit like the dog that liked to chase cars—if he caught one, he probably wouldn't know what to do with it. I'd managed to lose my virginity a few months before graduation, and I was hopeful that it marked the start of a new era in the social life of Gary D. Mitchell. But that comes under the heading of "the best-laid plans of mice and men often go awry." *Unlaid* would be more like it.

Perhaps it's time to change the subject and talk about religion instead.

The last church service I attended in Granbury took place the day before I departed for active duty, and it was especially touching, even for a worldly-wise eighteen-year-old. The pastor talked about my joining the army and how patriotic an act that was. Then he offered a special prayer for my protection in this new endeavor. Protection? Despite the warning my father had given me I still didn't have a clue. But several of the men in the church were WWII and Korea veterans, and we even had one WWI veteran, and they knew what was coming.

The next morning I said good-bye to my parents. Dad was stoic, while Mom shed a few tears. Through it all I was trying not to bawl and squall like a ten-year-old. My friend Steve volunteered to deliver me to the recruiting station on what would be my last morning as a civilian for a couple of dozen years. Neither one of us said much on the hour-long drive. When we finally arrived, we shook hands, I took my little gym bag from the backseat, and he drove away with barely a nod of good-bye.

I reported to the recruiter and he put me, along with several other enlistees, on a bus to Dallas, where we spent the night in the lap of luxury at the Texas Hotel. The following morning we went to the Armed Forces Examination and Entrance Station (AFEES), had a quick medical screening to make sure we were still fit to fight for our country, and then took our oath of enlistment. Then, with a kid who'd taken Junior ROTC in high school acting as our platoon sergeant, we were put on a bus to Fort Polk, Louisiana. Many hours later we arrived at the reception station at Polk, where the pejorative term *trainee* was embedded in my vocabulary forever. It was a term of disrespect that we all grew to hate. By the end of basic training, I would rather have been called a son of a bitch than a trainee.

CHAPTER TWO

Combat

You remember the movie *Private Benjamin* with Goldie Hawn? "There must be some mistake," she said, looking around the basic-training barracks for the first time. "I joined the army with the condos." Somehow I think that Private Benjamin and I must have had the same recruiter, a guy who was willing to fudge the truth and hide the fine print if it would get me to sign on the dotted line.

I wasn't looking for condos; I signed up to be an army mechanic. That's even what they trained me to be, but they also sent me to advanced infantry school. I did get to play with army trucks for a short time in Korea, but there was a war going on, and I was told the infantry couldn't fight it without me. When I got word that I was going to Vietnam to be part of the 1st Air Cavalry Division (Airmobile), I went right down and had a conversation with my first sergeant. What a mistake that was.

I showed him my enlistment contract. He showed me the fine print: ". . . will be trained as a mechanic." "Did we train you as a mechanic?" he asked.

"Yes, First Sergeant."

"Well, what are you complaining about, soldier? We did what we said we were going to do. You're trained." My next stop was the army's Jungle Warfare School on Okinawa.

A month later, there I was, assigned to B Company, 2nd Battalion, 7th Infantry, the famed Garry Owen Battalion, living in a hooch in the general vicinity of Phuoc Vinh in central South Vietnam. And now here I was, ten days after arriving in country, gearing up to go out on my first combat patrol, a night ambush. I was carrying an eighty-pound rucksack, an M-60 machine gun, and several ninety-round belts of ammo, a pretty good load for a now-nineteen-year-old kid who weighed less than 140 pounds dripping wet. And dripping wet was my current condition. Not because it was raining, but because sweat was pouring off me in buckets. Some of it was because I hadn't yet acclimated to the heat and humidity, but mostly it was unadulterated fear on a scale heretofore unimaginable to a kid fresh out of small-town Texas. Until now, my biggest fears fell into two categories: dating related and father related. There had been the possibility of being turned down for a date by a girl I had the hots for in my high school class, or meeting her father if she happened to say yes—both were problematical. Having my father find out from the town cop that he'd caught me with a case of beer in the backseat had once been terrifying. But now all that was kid's stuff. No matter how much my father had yelled at the time, I lived through it.

I couldn't say that about the next few hours in the jungle. Since I hadn't been around long enough to build up the "it just doesn't matter" emotional armor that the old guys seemed to have, all I could do before we headed for the perimeter of the base camp was tote up the things I was afraid of.

I was afraid I might die, or worse, suffer a debilitating wound. I was afraid I might screw up and compromise the mission. I was afraid I might freeze under fire, or show fear. I was afraid I might wet my pants—or worse. Underlying it all, even though I didn't actually understand it yet, was that I was afraid I might let my buddies down. That one doesn't really rise to a conscious level until you've been under fire several times, 'cause it takes a while for you to figure out that what soldiers fight for is not a cause, not an ideology, not even a country. In a place where a skinny kid named Gary Mitchell has, absurdly, become an instrument of American foreign policy, all a guy really fights for is his buddies. Someday, if I survive it, I figure that I can put on a DAV or Legion or VFW or VVA cap and speak about the nobility of going into battle for my country, but back then, that wasn't what drove me.

It's not an original thought, but anyone in uniform who's been in a war comes to that understanding, while those who haven't been there still talk about glory on the battlefield—a nice concept on a large scale, but meaningless when death might be one bullet away. And contrary to popular belief, in a war where both sides are often shooting at targets they never see, the bullet that gets you doesn't even need to have your name on it; "to whom it may concern" will do the job.

As we left the base camp for the spot where we were going to establish an L-shaped ambush, I kept thinking that it didn't make sense for them to give me, the FNG (military slang for Fucking New Guy), the machine gun. The guy with the M-60 is the one who needs the steadiest nerves and who has to be able to maintain fire discipline. Unless the squad gets into a fight where the only way out is for everyone to let fly in an effort to suppress the enemy, you don't want to be just blasting away. And truth be told, I didn't know how I'd handle the weapon if things got ugly.

By the time we arrived at the ambush site and set up, it was so dark I couldn't see my hand in front of my face. I was dying for a cigarette, but that was out of the question. My head hurt, my mouth was dry, and I had stomach cramps.

The headache could have been from the weight of the helmet. The dry mouth could have been because we hadn't had any water for a while—drinking from a canteen makes noise, and the sound of swishing water carries a long way in the jungle at night. Or the cotton-mouth might have been nerves. The stomach cramps could be a result of the heat, or from not having adjusted to humping all of that weight, or from the infamous malaria pills that were known to cause diarrhea in the most seasoned guys. Frankly, given how my gut felt, I was praying that the phrase *scared shitless* had some basis in fact, because the alternative could be really ugly.

A thousand questions ran through my mind, all of them unanswerable. The biggest one was, Will we actually end up in a firefight tonight, or will it be a dry run? My squad leader had placed everyone in position, and we all were supposed to know where our squadmates were located, the field of fire we were supposed to cover, and where we were not supposed to fire unless our position was being overrun.

Time seemed to stand still. I glanced at the glow-in-the-dark face on my watch. 2230—10:30 P.M. We had been in position for just over an hour. Without contact, we would remain here until dawn and then hump back to our base camp. The thing everyone seems to worry about on a night ambush is falling asleep, but as frightened as I was, I don't think I could have fallen asleep on a bet. Every sound in the trees caught my attention; my imagination began to play tricks on me. If I could have just spoken to the nearest guy, it would have helped. Or smoked a cigarette, or had something to eat, or a cup of coffee. Not a chance.

We couldn't even slap at the bugs that were munching away at any exposed skin they could find. So much for the army's insect repellent. Well, maybe that's not fair. I figure without it they would have at least chewed off an ear or two. When I had reached the point that I thought I could not be more miserable, it started to rain. Of course, I couldn't move to get my poncho, so I got wet. If I had been any wetter I would have drowned. I remembered my mother saying to me when I was a kid that I didn't have enough sense to come in out of the rain. The thought made me smile for just a second. If she could see me now.

It was about midnight, and time seemed to slow down even more. Pure misery, coupled with fear, was almost more than a nineteen-year-old could stand. And then it happened. The noise came from directly in front of me! It was slowly moving straight at me! I wanted to yell to the guy hidden a few yards away, but I couldn't. I wanted to ask the squad leader what to do, but I couldn't. None of the field problems in advanced infantry training (AIT) had taught me how to deal with a situation like this. I wasn't supposed to talk, and I absolutely wasn't supposed to shoot unless the squad leader gave the signal to fire, but something was coming straight at me. *What do I do? I just can't sit here and wait to die.*

My temples were throbbing so hard I was sure the enemy could hear them. If they couldn't, it was only because my beating heart was so loud it drowned them out. I had to do something! Whatever was out there was getting closer! The other guys had to hear it, but there was no way for me to confirm that. What if they'd fallen asleep? We could get wiped out while I was waiting for the signal to fire. At the very least, could I allow an opportunity for an ambush and squad body count to pass?

I made an instant decision to spray and pray, cutting loose with the M-60. After hours of sitting there in the dark like a blind man, listening to natural sounds like buzzing insects and hard rain, smelling wet jungle smells, the eruption of full automatic fire was a shock to all the senses.

The larger shock came when my squad leader started yelling, "Cease fire, cease fire!"

My training had been very effective. My aim had been true. The problem was, the only body our squad would be counting that night was the water buffalo I had killed. The squad leader figured it was passing through on its way to the stream about two hundred yards behind us.

I had compromised our position. We had to return to our base camp. If I had a tail, it would have been between my legs. But worst of all, the other squad members were really harassing me about my first combat kill. I'd become "Ol' Deadeye Mitch." And just when

I thought it couldn't get any worse, it did. I was going to have to face our platoon sergeant. You've heard about a fate worse than death? Suddenly I understood what that expression meant. Now I was really scared.

Since the squad leader appeared so upset, I could only imagine what the platoon sergeant—or his boss, the lieutenant who was our platoon leader—might do. This could go all the way up to the first sergeant or company commander. I'd disobeyed a direct order not to fire unless instructed to do so. They could court-martial me for that. How would I explain it to my father? All my older brothers had been in the service; but my dad had not been in the service. They'd all been honorably discharged. Now I was going to change all that. Everyone back in Granbury would know. What was that expression—death before dishonor? That's where my head was on the way back into the base camp.

We arrived at base camp about 0430—4:30 A.M.—and my squad leader brought me into the platoon sergeant's tent. For what seemed like hours we endured an ass reaming that covered infractions ranging from incompetence, through wasted time and ammunition, to the danger everyone had been placed in because the enemy could have ambushed us once I revealed our position. I was almost in tears.

All of a sudden the platoon sergeant looked in my direction and burst into the most surprising laughter I've ever heard. My squad leader cracked up, too. I was standing there, red-faced and still unsure of what to do. Finally, the senior NCO said, "Welcome to Vietnam, Mitch. Go get some sleep." Just as I reached the door, he said, "Mitch, this one's on me. Don't let it happen again—understand, soldier?"

I left, cleaned my weapon, restocked my ammunition, and finally had that cigarette and cup of coffee.

It really didn't take long for me to fall into the routine of combat operations. Routine pretty much came to mean boredom punctuated by occasional moments of terror, which is to say that I was still fairly uncomfortable on patrols. I was now a rifleman, but like everyone else, carried a few belts of ammunition for the machine gun.

Early one morning we were returning from an all-night ambush where we'd made no contact, and rather than work our way around the edge of a small rice paddy, someone made the choice to go across it. I'd learned by now that rice paddies were great ambush locations—for us and the enemy—but none of us questioned the decision. Maybe it was the fact that we knew there was a lukewarm meal and dry cots waiting for us that prompted us to take the shortcut. And we almost got away with it.

We were three-quarters of the way across when the first shot rang out, causing us to dive into the water and take cover behind the paddy berms, while blasting the wood line in an effort to keep the bad guys down. What we had to quickly figure out was where the shot came from. It would have been easier if he had sprayed a clip in our direction. But this guy—if there was only one; we couldn't be sure—wasn't a novice. Each time he threw a shot at us, it came from a different location. Because we couldn't find him, we couldn't get up and move.

Then the pace picked up a bit. We now had at least two shooters—one from the front and one from the right flank, and their aim was getting better. One of my squad members was hit, and the medic had to try to get to him. But every time he made a move in the direction of the wounded man, another shot would ring out. After a while it seemed as though the enemy was toying with us, since they never actually hit the medic, just kept him pinned in place.

After a few more minutes, the shooter to our flank got lucky and scored a direct hit on the radio. Now we had no way of communicating, or getting air or artillery support or reinforcements from the base camp, which was less than four kilometers away.

It had become obvious that the shooters were much better than we had initially given them credit for. Their plan was to shoot and move, shoot and move. Without exposing ourselves we could do nothing, and doing nothing was not going to get us out of there. One of the ways you break an ambush is to start firing and run toward the enemy. Not only does it force them to take cover, but it turns static targets—us—into moving ones. The plan our squad leader devised would have us rush the area to our front, where we suspected one of the enemy fighters was still located. While we were doing that, the medic could get to our wounded guy. This would put the medic and his patient in a precarious position, because while the rest of us would be inside the wood line, the two of them would still be fully exposed in the rice paddy.

One negative thing about battle plans is that the bad guys don't have to sign off on them. When we charged the wood line, the two shooters suddenly became many. Two more of my buddies were wounded on the way, but we were able to drag them into the wood line with us. Now we had to do something to pull the enemy's focus from the medic and his patient. My squad leader decided that a couple of us would race back to the medic and help him drag our partner in, while the rest of the squad did all in their power to burn up their weapons with rapid fire.

Lucky me, I was chosen along with a buddy to make the run to the medic. We took off our rucksacks and the extra machine gun ammunition, and waited for the squad members to start firing so we could move. This was one of those moments when I thought my folks might have a shot at collecting on my life insurance. The opposing force had already proven to us that they were a well-coordinated unit that had been professionally trained. They knew what they were doing and how to get the most out of their location. They also had evened the odds by taking out our radio; it was us against them, and would stay that way unless we got very lucky.

On the squad leader's signal, all hell broke loose. Our guys were firing as fast as they could, and we were running as fast as we could, zigging and zagging, trying to provide the least shootable target. The guy with me was slightly wounded. Just a small flesh wound on the shoulder that grazed him more than it hit. Later, he told me it felt like a bee sting. Miraculously, we were still alive when we reached the medic. Our problem now was that any fool would know what the next step was, and we'd long since stopped thinking that the enemy was a fool. The squad was going to start shooting again, and we were going to try to get the medic and our casualty back to the wood line.

That's when we got lucky. While we were waiting for the shooting to start, a Cobra gunship happened to fly over. Of course, they had no idea what was going on. The squad leader fired a red star cluster (a signal pyrotechnic) in the general direction of the aircraft. It wasn't near enough to endanger the bird, but close enough to get the pilot's attention. The most beautiful sight I had ever seen was that of the Cobra banking to check out what was going on.

In its own way, the arrival of the gunship was both good and bad news. If the pilot knew where our lines were, and where the enemy was, no problem. But if he had to guess—big problem. Cobras are equipped with miniguns that are most unforgiving when they start shooting. How did we solve the problem without a radio?

The squad leader yelled that he was going to pop white smoke grenades to mark his location, and he wanted one of us to throw red smoke toward the enemy. That meant we had to toss two grenades, because the medic had seen fire from one area, and the wounded in action (WIA) had seen fire from another.

I yelled back that we'd throw ours as soon as he threw his. Each of us had pulled the pin on a grenade, and held the spoon in place until we saw the white smoke. The only thing that made me think this plan might work was that the Cobra was lazily drifting back and forth, watching us, and waiting. No question that the pilot could see us; he just didn't know where the rest of our guys were at and didn't want to take any chances firing until he was certain.

The instant we saw the white smoke pop, we threw our reds and dropped as deep into the water as we could get without drowning ourselves. The Cobra banked and started a campaign of deforestation all around the red smoke. When the gunship started shooting, the squad also started firing. We jumped up, each grabbed an arm, and began dragging the wounded man to the wood line as fast as we could move. I know it was painful, and he groaned the whole way, but we kept going. It was one of the longest eighty meters I had ever run.

As soon as we got into the woods, we could hear other aircraft coming in our direction, obviously summoned by the gunship pilot. The whole episode was over in minutes. We got our wounded onto a Dustoff that would take them to the nearest medical facility, and we regrouped to move on back to our base camp.

By the time I had been in Vietnam about a month I'd participated in a number of firefights, quite a few ambush patrols, and several reconnaissance-by-force missions that everyone described by the much less politically correct title of *search and destroy*.

Up to that time I had not knowingly taken the life of another human being. Don't get me wrong—I'd fired my share of rounds with every intent to kill as many of the enemy as I could, but I'd never actually seen someone I'd fired at die. On this warm and clear afternoon, that fact, along with my life, was destined to change.

We were preparing to cross a stream, always a dangerous part of any movement. While in the water, you have nowhere to go if you are fired upon. Before the squad crossed, my buddy walking point and the squad leader were watching the opposite bank as well as the surrounding area, attempting to locate anything out of the ordinary. Not seeing anything, they waved us forward. But just as the point man stepped into the stream, the Viet Cong sprang their ambush from the opposite bank. Why the enemy began firing before we were all in the water, I don't know, but their mistake was our good fortune. Maybe it was their turn to have a nervous FNG screw up their ambush. Sometimes you catch a break.

The point immediately jumped out of the stream and into the underbrush uninjured, and all of us began to return fire. During the firefight, one of the VC rose up slightly into a position where I could plainly see him. Since my arrival in country, my shooting skills and instincts had been honed significantly, so without thinking I fired a short burst of three or four rounds from my M-16.

Everything suddenly changed into slow motion. All of the sounds were muffled, as if they were coming from a great distance away. I could see his body twitch with the impact of each round in his torso. It almost appeared that he looked directly at me as he slowly fell backward onto the bank, and then his crumpled body edged into the shallow water, dead. We were so close, I was sure I could see the light in his eyes change when life as we know it departed his body.

The firefight continued for what seemed to be an eternity, although thinking back I know it was just a few short minutes before the VC pulled back and disappeared into the woods. We carefully crossed the stream, passing right next to my first combat kill. I could hear my buddies' enthusiastic praise as I came across the stream. "Damned good," said one. "Right on, Mitch," said another. A third pumped his fist and cut loose with a loud "All riiiiiight!!" I almost tripped stepping out of the stream because I couldn't take my eyes off of the man lying there. He wasn't just a gook or a slope or a dink or a VC. He was a human being, and I had ended his life. Purposefully and intentionally. I came to Vietnam a kid, and now I was a killer. The squad leader must have gotten a good look at my face, because he grabbed my arm, helped me step out of the stream, and asked, "Mitch, you okay?"

Of course I answered, "Yeah, fine, just missed my step." But on the way back to our base camp I couldn't get out of my mind the sight of the dead man lying in the water where we left him. I kept replaying the firefight in my head. I must have watched myself fire that burst of rounds twenty times. Outwardly I tried acting as if nothing were bothering me, but internally I was wrestling with what soldiers throughout the ages have agonized over. Against everything I'd been taught as a child, I had taken another life. I'd heard other guys in the same circumstances rationalize it with pat phrases like "It don't mean nothing" or the all-purpose "Sorry 'bout that." Maybe for them that stuff worked. But it wasn't doing the job for me.

Once we arrived at the base camp, we cleaned our weapons, re-stocked our ammunition, and then had some time to eat, rest, and write letters. I remember that the inactivity was horrendous for me. I tried to write but couldn't concentrate, so I didn't finish the letter. After all, how do you tell your parents that you killed someone? I went over to the mess tent and got a cup of coffee, wishing I could drink a few beers, but we were scheduled to go out again shortly after sunset. Finally I walked down to the end of the tents next to a bunker and sat down on the ground. I was staring at the perimeter, looking at absolutely nothing, when I heard a voice say, "Are you all right?"

I looked up and it was my squad leader. I suddenly realized that I had tears running down my cheeks. Having been through it himself, and with other young men in the squad, he knew what I was feeling, the conflicting emotions I was experiencing. His comment was simple. "It won't get any easier, but you will learn to live with it. Nearly everyone goes through the same thing you're going through right now. They just don't admit it. We've gotta move out in about two hours, so you've got a little time to work things out in your mind. If things go right tonight, you might have to do it again. I need to know that you can."

Without another word, he reached into his pocket, took out a pack of cigarettes, shook one loose, and offered it to me. Then he pulled out his Zippo, lit it for me, and walked away, leaving me alone with my despair. I took a deep drag, exhaled, then tossed the smoke on the ground, put my head down on my knees, and silently sobbed. My innocence was gone, lost at the edge of a stream ten thousand miles from home. At that moment, I had no way of knowing what it meant for my future—but I knew that deep inside, I'd changed.

War takes place at the extreme ends of a continuum—it's either dull and boring, or filled with more excitement than one could possibly imagine. And it can go from one extreme to the other faster than the speed of light. There are exceptions to this rule, however, moments where you actually have time to consider that you're being put into a situation where death is a distinct possibility. What's still a mystery to me is that when I was in one of those situations, I chose to move forward rather than play it safe.

Consider a patrol we were on about a week after my first kill. We had been out for a couple of days when the point found the opening to a tunnel. This was very unusual, because they were normally so well camouflaged that unless you knew exactly what you were looking for, you'd almost have to fall through the entrance in order to find it. This led my squad leader to believe that it could be one of only two things: either Charlie had heard us coming and left very quickly, or it was a trap. Personally, I didn't have a clue which it was, but I did know that this would probably lead to a very exciting day for one unlucky SOB.

We called for engineer support because they usually took care of tunnels. No help available. We called for ARVN (Army of the Republic of Vietnam) engineer support. No help available. We couldn't just blow the tunnel entrance and move on, because within hours after we were gone, the VC would have dug it out and it would be fully functional. Tunnels had been known to lead to underground field headquarters, hospitals, supply storage areas, and more. Experience had taught us that tunnels usually provided all kinds of information for our intelligence folks, so we couldn't just leave it without sending someone down.

When the squad leader started looking up and down the squad, I knew what was coming. I weighed less than 140 pounds and was five feet ten inches tall. Unfortunately, I was the smallest guy on the patrol. I willed myself to grow three inches and gain forty pounds, but before my will could win the battle with nature, he looked at me and said, "Mitch, do I have a deal for you." I was volunteered. Eventually I would grow to a height of six feet and weigh two hundred pounds, but the future would do me no favors on this day. Suffice it to say that I was more than a little upset.

Tunnels were terrifying. We'd actually had classes on them where we learned they could hold all kinds of nightmarish things: water traps, ambushes, and explosive booby traps. The only thing certain about going into a VC tunnel was the uncertainty of what you might face.

I stripped off my ruck, took off my fatigue jacket, and, feeling buck-naked wearing just a T-shirt and pants, prepared to go in. In one hand I had a borrowed .45-caliber pistol with one nine-round magazine and one additional round in the chamber. In the other I held a flashlight. I stood silently at the entrance as my larger buddies tied a rope around my waist. If I got myself blown up or shot in an underground firefight, the theory was that they could drag my body out without having to send anyone else down to get what was left of me.

I could see my squad leader keeping his eyes on me as I was preparing for the ordeal, and strangely, it wasn't the first time I'd noticed he was watching me closely. I also had the same feeling I'd had on my first patrol. I was scared shitless and realized that I had absolutely no control over what was about to happen. *Pure terror* is an inadequate term to describe the feelings I was experiencing. At a time like that you're doing about thirty things at once. You pray. You try to plan what you will do if something happens. You hope the medic is as good as you think he is, and you try to show your buddies that you have no fear. All the while they're being helpful and encouraging, you know that deep down, they're relieved that it's you and not them going down that hole.

When I was as prepared as I was going to be, the squad leader radioed command that "we" were ready to proceed. My unspoken question was: *What we? Does he have a mouse in his pocket?* If ever there was an "I" mission, this was it.

Command gave the okay to proceed, and two of us moved about

twenty meters to the tunnel entrance. If I dropped in the hole and it blew up, only my rope handler and I would get blown to pieces. Just before I climbed down, I paused to offer a silent but heartfelt prayer that went something like this: *God, forgive me of all my sins, and have mercy on my soul. God, don't let me die. God, don't let me screw up. God, don't let me be maimed—go ahead and let me die instead. God, don't let me show my fear so much that I pee my pants in front of everybody.* I figured that just about covered all the eventualities, and the rope handler was urging me to get moving. So I did.

As soon as you enter a tunnel, the temperature becomes cooler and the humidity drops noticeably. The smell is musty. You strain to listen, but the only sound is your heart beating so loud you're sure it would keep you from hearing the snap or click of a booby trap. Then again, it might be just as well—at least if you didn't hear it you wouldn't know that you were about to die.

After crawling about twenty feet in, I found the first booby trap. It was one of our own grenades, buried with the pin pulled. It had just enough dirt to hold the spoon in place, but if you crawled over it, your movement would cause it to roll, permitting the spoon to pop. I gently lifted the grenade, ensuring that the spoon did not pop, and backed up to the entrance. I yelled, "Grenade," threw it in the opposite direction of the squad, and dropped back into the hole.

I resumed crawling, passed the spot where I'd found the grenade, and began looking for the next booby trap. The training manuals say that it should be at or near the entrance to a chamber or group of chambers, so as I moved I kept sweeping the walls, floor, and ceiling with my flashlight. Having the light was simultaneously a blessing and a curse. It meant I could see where I was going, but it also meant that if there was anyone else down there, they could easily see me coming. I continued moving the flashlight around and noticed that about fifteen inches in front of my face there was a stick or root hanging from the ceiling of the tunnel. I was just about to stretch my hand out to push it aside, when the root moved!

I froze in place. Roots don't move. When I aimed the light at the thing, I noticed several more just like it, hanging from the ceiling to within about four inches of the floor. Then it hit me: They were snakes! *Dear God, what do I do now?* They were too low to crawl under, and the tunnel was too narrow for me to go around them. A silent but deadly booby trap.

Vietnam was home to a variety of poisonous snakes, including cobras, kraits, and the fabled bamboo vipers, which GIs referred to as "the two-step," because the rumor was that if you're bitten, you'll fall dead before you can take two steps. I'd spent a lot of time in the outdoors growing up in Texas, and never got comfortable with snakes. So to come face-to-face with them in a tunnel where the VC had hung them from the ceiling on very fine threads was, for me, a too-close encounter of the worst kind.

I backed out of the tunnel and reported my findings to the squad leader, who told me to make a cup of coffee while they figured out what to do. We couldn't just toss a grenade into the tunnel, because there'd be no way of knowing that it had killed them all, and the ones that survived might be loose in the dirt. The explosion might also cave in the tunnel, and that wouldn't make the intelligence people very happy.

There really seemed to be only two solutions: Try to burn them out, or get them out by hand. Given that I've always had an uncontrollable fear of snakes, burning them out was my choice. Actually, sending someone else down to deal with the problem was my first choice, but that didn't seem to be an option. Have I mentioned how nice it is to be needed? I was not a happy camper.

Then we began to worry that if I went down there and burned them out it might use up all the oxygen in the tunnel. This brought us back to square one: getting the snakes out by hand. My squad leader said that I could take my time figuring it all out, as long as I was ready as soon as I finished my coffee.

I began running the problem over in my head. There were at least half a dozen snakes down there hanging from the ceiling. Was that all of them? Were there any just crawling around waiting for me? There was only one way to find out. Go back and see.

We got a stick about eighteen inches long and fashioned a loop at the end of it with commo wire. It was a homemade version of something I'd seen on *Wild Kingdom*, but the TV snake wranglers were getting the big bucks for taking chances with poisonous snakes. I never saw anything about this in my recruiting sergeant's office. And there was certainly nothing about it in the papers I signed that guaranteed me training as a mechanic. Maybe someday, if I survived this experience, I'd get to hide under the hood of a deuce-and-a-half. But not right now.

Back down the hole I went, this time maneuvering with a pistol, flashlight, and the snake catcher. I put the loop around the first snake. This was not an easy task, since the snake was wiggling and I was shaking. I tightened the loop, and then the snake really started wiggling. Between its wiggling and my shaking, the string came loose from the ceiling of the tunnel. It was now too late to change my mind. Hoping the snake could not wiggle out of the loop, I started backing out of the tunnel. That's when I realized that I had no plan in the event it got loose. I didn't know whether the species was inclined to attack or flee—and at what speed. Fortunately the noose held, and I made it out of the tunnel with the snake. I released it, and another member of the squad killed it as soon as my loop was clear.

Five more times I made this journey, crawling through the tunnel, lassoing a deadly snake, and then backing out. How long did it all take? Days. Weeks. Months. Not really, but it sure felt like it. Finally, with all the known snakes gone, I had to make one last trip into the tunnel to determine what was in there.

I made it past where the grenade had been, past where the snakes had been, and almost to what, at first, looked like the end of the tunnel. But then it made a ninety-degree turn to the right. What could be next? Another grenade booby trap? More snakes? A couple of VC undercover B-girls on R & R from 100 P Alley in Saigon asking me to buy them Saigon tea?

Would you believe none of the above? The tunnel made that right turn and opened into a large chamber. A large, very empty chamber. No cache of weapons or ammunition. No medical facilities. No sleeping or cooking facilities. No battle plans for the invasion of Saigon. No . . . nothing. I'd crawled over a grenade, handled snakes, and almost died of heart failure to find an empty chamber!

I went back outside and reported to the squad leader that the only thing there was an empty chamber. We blew the tunnel entrance and returned to our base camp, where military intelligence was waiting to speak to us. They kept telling me I had obviously screwed up, that I had missed something. Finally, for the first time but certainly not the last time in my army career, I spoke my mind, suggesting that if they were so certain that there was something of value to be found in that tunnel, they could get off their dead asses and look for it themselves. My squad leader didn't even flinch when I said it.

Thus far I'd managed to come through every combat mission I'd been on without injury. That was a good thing, but I couldn't shake the thought that it was only a matter of time before I got my turn.

About 0600 on a relatively cool morning, I finally got an assignment that was a bit closer to what I'd signed up to do. We were going on a resupply convoy for ammunition, food, repair parts, fuel, and the ten thousand other things that are needed to fight a war and keep the troops going—and based on the fact that I'd driven a truck some while I was in Korea, I was assigned to drive.

We were headed to the giant army base at Long Binh, a three- or four-hour trip down a heavily traveled road that was swept by the engineers every morning for newly planted mines. After driving for about an hour and a half, we stopped for sandwiches and hot coffee. We also got briefed on the fact that our route took us past a rubber plantation where several convoys had recently been ambushed. The intelligence raised the pucker factor, but compared to being on a foot patrol through enemy territory, driving a deuce-and-a-half seemed like a piece of cake. We grew even more confident when the convoy made it completely through the plantation area without incident. But it seems that in a combat zone, even when you're out of the woods, you're not out of the woods.

We were passing a convoy outbound from Long Binh when it happened. A command-detonated mine exploded under one of the last trucks in the oncoming group just as it was passing the vehicle I was driving, which was pretty much in the middle of our convoy. When a huge mine designed to take out a tank or a truck goes off, the explosion consumes all of the oxygen in the immediate area. For a second or two that seems like a lifetime, you can't breathe. You're also being banged around as the energy from the blast throws everything outward. Then you get part two of the blast—the implosion, where everything including oxygen gets sucked back in.

I wasn't sure what hit me. Could have been a small piece of shrapnel from the truck they tried to blow up, or a small piece of rock flying out of the hole where the mine had been buried. Whatever it was, it punctured the scalp above my left ear, traveled between the scalp and skull, and exited at the crown of my head. Judging by the amount of blood pouring from the wound, I thought half my head was gone. It didn't compute that I couldn't actually be consciously thinking about how badly I'd been hit, yet have suffered a fatal head wound. I just knew I was dead!

My first instinct was to reach up and touch it, but I was afraid to. Who knew what I'd be dipping my hand into? Would I have to try to push my brain, or at least what was left of it, back into my head? Then it dawned on me that the explosion may just have been the opening shot in a full-scale attack on the convoy. When we were briefed early that morning, we'd been told to keep moving if anything happened. You didn't want to stop and sit in a potential kill zone. I knew that if I paused to deal with my injury, I'd be blocking the trucks behind us, and it would give the enemy a perfect opportunity to wipe us out.

So while constantly smearing away the blood that was pouring down my face, I kept driving, praying that we'd be able to stop before I bled out or ran off the road, whichever came first. About two miles down the road, my prayers were answered when the convoy commander ordered a halt to check for damaged vehicles and wounded personnel.

Remarkably, I was the only one in the entire convoy who'd been injured. The medic checked me over, said I would live, put a pressure bandage on the entrance and exit wounds—and we continued on to Long Binh. I don't think I've ever had a headache like that one.

When we arrived at the staging area, the medic used the convoy commander's jeep to take me to the 120th Medical Evacuation Hospital. They cleaned me up, X-rayed my head, and put a single suture on the exit wound. Then they released me to full duty. I would have never believed that so much blood could come pouring out of such a tiny, relatively minor wound. The only meds they gave me to take were aspirin for the headache, and they told me that if it persisted for more than twenty-four hours, to go see our battalion surgeon.

When we returned to the staging area and reported to the convoy commander that I wouldn't be needing a body bag after all, he took one look at me and made what I thought was a brilliant command decision: On the convoy back to base camp, I'd be riding shotgun. I don't know whether or not he could actually see it, but I was shaking so badly that I'm not sure I could have operated the clutch, so he got no argument from me.

The trip back was uneventful. When we arrived, the medic took me over to the battalion's medical platoon and asked our own doc to look me over. He gave me two days of limited duty, during which I had time to reflect on the irony that thus far, I'd survived jungle firefights without a scratch but nearly managed to get myself blown up while driving a truck, which is pretty close to what I signed up to do.

CHAPTER THREE

Marksmanship School

I'd learned a lot during my first few months in combat, but most of all I learned that just about anything you do, including nothing, can get you killed. Therefore, in the interest of survival, any legitimate opportunity to avoid combat operations is one that should be embraced. Just getting an afternoon off because your congressman is coming to visit is cause for soaring morale. That probably explains the reports that the politicians brought home about how everybody they met was in great spirits. Hell, we get pulled off the line, get clean fatigues, a shower, real food instead of Cs—life is good.

So in early August, when my squad leader takes me to see the platoon sergeant, and this E-7 tells me they're sending me away for a week to attend a specialized marksmanship course, I'm happier than a possum in the middle of a May rainstorm. I actually allow myself to smile when he says he likes what he's been hearing about me, especially that I don't panic under fire like some of the FNGs. But what I'm thinking is, anything that'll make me shoot better will improve my chances of going home to Texas.

Next morning around 0630, when my buddies in B/2/7 were moving out on another operation, I grabbed my M-16 and hauled a duffel bag with enough clothing for a week down to the airstrip. I tried not to seem too impressed when I discovered they'd brought in a Huey just for me. The flight to Long Binh was quick and uneventful, and when we got there, the crew chief pointed to a hole in the fence, and a tent just beyond it.

I checked in and found a bunch of other guys who'd also been selected for the marksmanship training. Eventually there were thirty of us, and they hauled us in trucks to a secluded area—it took a while to get there, so I'm not even sure if it was on the base or not—where we were told to stash our gear quickly and report back to a pair of staff sergeants who would be our instructors.

I could tell that these two guys had been around. And they were old. Okay, so maybe *older* is a better way to put it. I was nineteen; if they were thirty, they looked ancient to me. Looking back, I guess they might have been between thirty and forty, which made them three days older than dirt, and it was God's little joke that they had lived that long. I thought it was odd that they had no unit patch on their fatigues, but they did have U.S. ARMY and a name tag above the pockets, so I didn't think much of it at the time.

Their spiel was in the same vein as the one given to me by my own platoon sergeant. "You've all been selected because you shoot relatively well and you kept your head together under fire." They said their mission was to teach us to become better shooters with our M-16, and that we'd "learn some special things with an M-14." They never once used the term *sniper,* not that first day, nor five days later when I completed their course.

It was almost noon when they finally got started. The first briefing began with a warning: "Anybody who doesn't give a hundred and ten percent, we'll put you on the first bird out of here." There's nothing they could have said that would have motivated me more. It was a matter of self-preservation. If I go back, I go out on patrol; here, I don't have to. They were giving me an excuse not to be dead. I wasn't about to turn them down.

We spent that first afternoon cleaning our own M-16s. We tore them down till there was nothing left to tear down. We cleaned everything, even the outside, because that's what they wanted us to do. I hadn't cared if it was rusty on the outside. The way I looked at it, a little rust made for better camouflage. And as long as the bolt carrier and all the moving parts were moving the way they were supposed to, it wasn't going to jam. We knew that from experience. All thirty of us had been in country for several months, all combat veterans. We were probably equally divided between PFCs and spec 4s, maybe a couple of buck sergeants.

But our experience in the field suddenly wasn't important. The sergeants had their own rules for their own games, and they were serious about them. Even today I still don't understand the meticulous effort to clean the stock and grip, but I didn't want to go on patrol, so I would've spit-shined the thing if they told me to. During the next couple of hours, the sergeants were constantly coming around, making sure that we were doing what we were supposed to do. Finally my rifle parts passed inspection, and one of them said, "Okay, oil it; reassemble it."

We were assuming that since this was a marksmanship school, they'd want to get us onto the firing range as quickly as possible. Once again, that thing about "never assume anything" came into play. Instead of shooting, they had us reading. Everyone received a dog-eared copy of the "Army Marksmanship Manual," and from late afternoon until lights out, they had us in our tents reading it. We were far enough off the beaten path that there were no electric lights in the tents, but they'd thoughtfully provided lanterns. And, of course, there was the usual bitching. "Why are we reading this thing again? I know about a sight picture, and a cheek-stock weld with the 16 and a thumb-cheek weld with the M-14." We all knew about leading a moving target, and that if the wind was blowing perpendicular to the path of the bullet, you had to adjust your sight. These were basics. But, again, if it's a choice between spending an evening reading a training manual or spending it out on ambush, I'll take the book. Hell, I'll take the whole library.

Early the next morning, after a gourmet breakfast of C-rats and coffee, they hauled us out to what turned out to be a pretty decent firing range. They'd used concrete construction pipes set in the ground to simulate foxholes, and beside each hole they'd marked off a prone firing position. We began firing at fixed silhouettes twenty-five meters out. Hitting the target wasn't the object; what they wanted us to do was to try to tighten our shot groupings. It was the kind of precision shooting that nobody bothered with in the field with an M-16. Aiming? Shot group? I vaguely remember that from training. I was used to just squeezing off a few rounds and hoping one hit. So it took me a while to get back in the mode of a Texas rabbit hunt, where hitting a small target with a single shot actually mattered. The instructors kept pacing behind us, chain-smoking like steel-mill chimneys, and saying, "Stabilize your breathing." I don't think any of us knew what they were talking about. Did they want us to hold our breath and shoot? They didn't clarify. Just, "Stabilize your breathing. It makes the weapon shake." I didn't ask, and I don't think anyone else did, either.

Finally I put three shots in the target tight enough that the sergeant's quarter-size metal disk covered them, and I was moved to the fifty-meter targets. Tight shot groups were still the task, and when I succeeded there, I went on to one hundred meters, then two hundred, and finally to 250 meters, still with the M-16.

When they moved us to the drop-down targets three hundred meters out, all they wanted us to do was hit it, where didn't matter. It didn't take long before we discovered that if you could hit the dirt in front of the target, it would kick up and knock it over. But I didn't do that too often, because I found that even at that distance, which is about three football fields plus another ten yards, I was a pretty good shot. They wanted us to be able to hit it consistently—and they defined that as eight rounds out of ten. If you couldn't do that, you were gone, and on that first day a couple of guys got sent home.

We went back to the tents, cleaned our weapons, and enjoyed

a good night's sleep. We had no way of knowing it was the last full night's sleep we were going to get until the course was over.

The next morning everyone was issued a standard M-14, and we started working in teams of two on the twenty-five-meter targets, zeroing our weapons. One guy would take his turn as the shooter, while the other served as spotter, using a scope to give ranges, and to report hits and misses. Then we'd switch. By the end of the day we were back at the three-hundred-meter target. Just before darkness fell, we stopped shooting, ate our C-rations, and did some smoking and joking. Then they took us back out to the twenty-five- and fifty-meter ranges for night fire. When it started raining I remember thinking, *Okay, that's it for tonight*. But it wasn't. We just kept shooting.

When I was with my unit, I'd been in firefights at night and in the rain. But that's a completely different kind of shooting. Spontaneous. Not analytical. On a firing range it's a new experience. The rain and moon create shadows on the target. The targets look different in moonlight than they do in sunlight. The standard military silhouette target looks larger at night; somehow the moonlight magnifies it, especially those sixties-era white targets with black circles. I had expected them to give us some instruction before turning us loose for night firing, but I guess they wanted us to figure out what we could for ourselves.

The next morning was when the sergeants began teaching us technique. I remember them saying that because the targets look larger than they actually are, we have to take this into consideration when aiming. If the downrange target looks two inches tall, it's probably only an inch and three-quarters. That doesn't sound like much of a difference, but at three hundred meters, a quarter of an inch is critical. If you're off by that much, you're either going to miss completely, or it won't be a good hit. It was after that lecture that we were introduced to the scope.

Even though I'd first learned to hunt at the age of twelve, it was always with plain iron sights on the barrel of a rifle. I'd never even looked through a scope. So when they mounted it on my M-14 and handed the rifle back to me, it was a revelation. The target was right there, almost on top of me. They helped us zero the weapons, and that's when shooting became more than just instinct. Suddenly there was math involved. They started with the adjustments that raise or lower the impact point at three hundred meters. Those are little pick marks on vertical lines in the scope. Raise the weapon to put the next pick mark on the target and the bullet will strike two and a half, three inches higher. Once we got that worked out in our heads, they showed us how similar adjustments in aiming moved the strike point left or right. That was more thinking than I was used to doing with a loaded rifle in the bush, and they told us that this was just the beginning, because there were mathematical adjustments we'd have to learn to compensate for distance—shooting five hundred meters with a scope zeroed for three hundred, for example—and for angle—firing uphill or down—as well as over water.

Where I had been used to a solid cheek weld to establish a sight picture through the peep-and-open steel sights, I had to adjust in order to properly use the scope. You didn't want your eye up against the rear element of the scope, because that prevents a full sight picture. Conversely, you didn't want your shooting eye to be so far from the rear of the scope that you're seeing too much space around the scope. It's a matter of trial and error, and yes, experience. The key to the whole thing is a proper thumb-cheek weld that consistently puts your eyeball in the same position behind the scope. That, and the stock placed solidly in the pocket of your shoulder, so that you're physically locked to the weapon. Without that cheek weld, it's possible that when the rifle kicks back, it will move independently of your head, and the scope could smack you right in the eye. With a proper weld when you pull the trigger, you move back as one unit— your body, your cheek against your thumb, and the rifle.

For the remainder of that day, through much of the night, and into the next day, all we were doing was shooting, shooting, and shooting. We left the scopes zeroed at three hundred meters, but were aiming at targets as far as five hundred meters out. They'd given us a little spotter scope that they taught us to use, but since we were shooting at known distances on the range, it wasn't something we came to rely on during the course.

On the final day, the class was down to thirteen guys. Seventeen had already been sent home because they just couldn't do the job. Now they were having us practice on targets seven hundred meters out. Eight hundred meters is half a mile. During all my time in country, there hadn't been an opportunity to engage targets that could be seen that far away. But it never dawned on me that I was being trained to find those types of targets and kill them. I was so naive that I was still invested in the notion that this was marksmanship school, and if it made me a better shooter, it improved my chances of seeing Texas again.

Once the instructor thought I was comfortable shooting at seven-hundred-meter targets with the M-14, he pulled a switch. I got into the foxhole and fired at all the range distances with the scoped 14. Then the instructor would take that rifle and hand us our M-16 with open sights, and have us fire from 50 to 250 meters. And then they'd have us switch again. They were trying to see if we could adjust quickly between the two rifles. It took practice, but I didn't have any real trouble with it.

Next came my final exam. I started with the M-16 and fired on all the ranges, 50, 100, 150, 200, 250, and 300 meters. Then I switched to the M-14. At five hundred meters, you had to have four hits out of four. When I got up to seven hundred meters, the E-6 told me I was expected to have one hit out of two shots. Then he said, "Okay, only one person has hit this target today. Let's make it two." So I fired the first round, and it hit. He reached over and patted me on the back and said, "See if you can do it again." So I fired, and I hit again. He said, "Son, I believe you could shoot a gnat off an elephant's ass without disturbing the elephant. Get off my range. We're through here."

I went back to their little admin tent with my M-14 and my personal M-16, cleaned both weapons, and turned in the 14. The clerk wrote down my name and Social Security number (which had replaced service numbers), and said, "Okay, go back to your unit." That was it. I looked around at the other guys coming off the range and realized the ones who didn't make the cut had only one rifle, the M-16 they brought with them from their unit.

Most nineteen-year-olds aren't terribly introspective. Never during the time I spent at the shooting school did I wonder why I was learning how to hit a target nearly half a mile away, when that kind of opportunity had not presented itself on any of the combat ops I'd been in with the 2/7. It didn't dawn on me that they'd just trained me to become a sniper; during the weeklong school, no one had ever used that term. I guess I was pretty naive and trusting of my superiors. I had been around long enough to become cautious, but not yet cynical about what was being said and done. One thing I was sure of was that as a spec 4 in an infantry squad, it didn't matter why I was being told to do something. Figuring out the reason for it was well above my pay grade. The other thing was that I certainly hadn't been around long enough to comprehend that everything that's done in the military is done for a reason. As an individual, I might not understand the reason if it were explained to me, and chances are, it was never going to be explained to me at all. But there's always a reason, and at that stage in what would turn out to be a twenty-four-year army career, I didn't question it.

When I reported back to my platoon at company headquarters, I walked into the orderly room and the clerk said, "Hey, Mitchell, how you doin'?".

I said, "I got through it; I'm here."

He said, "Yeah, you were gone the whole week, so I know you got through it." And with that, life immediately returned to what we considered normal: guard duty, patrol, this and that detail. Guys in my squad asked where I'd been, and I told them I'd been sent for marksmanship training, to learn how to shoot better. Nobody had told me not to talk about it; there was nothing spooky about it. I came back a better shooter than when I'd left, and that made me feel a bit more confident. For the time being, that was a good thing.

CHAPTER FOUR

The Old Man Wants to See You

L ife returned to normal following my return from marksmanship school. We'd go out on patrols, engage the enemy—or not—return to base camp to rest, refit, and recuperate for as long as we could, and then do it all over again.

It was clear that in our area of responsibility in South Vietnam, we were fighting a classic guerrilla enemy. Today the label du jour is *insurgent,* but making any Vietnam-Iraq comparisons tends to get political, so for the moment I'll just tell you about how it was in my first war.

The division's intelligence officers had grown increasingly concerned about a small village not far from the base camp that they believed was hiding, supporting, and sheltering Viet Cong guerrillas who were routinely harassing other villages as well as staging occasional attacks on our troops. Something had to be done about it, and Company B/2/7 got the assignment.

It all began with a daylight patrol in an area about three kilometers from the village. From a grunt's point of view, daylight patrols were not a good thing. We could be seen leaving the base camp by innocent-looking civilians just tending to their rice paddies who could spot us coming and spread the word. There was no stealth involved—and maybe that was part of the plan. I don't know. In fairness, I should hasten to add that we weren't terribly fond of night patrols either, because even with the one or two starlight scopes available to us, we were still out there in the dark. And as I learned on my first one that ended with the unfortunate demise of an enemy water buffalo, sitting quietly in one place, no talking, smoking, eating, laughing, or scratching for hours on end wasn't especially comfortable. I suppose had I been a student of Zen Buddhism I could have profitably used the enforced quiet time to meditate, but I had this crazy thing about not wanting to get killed, so remaining silently overamped on adrenaline was my only real choice.

I should also mention that having now spent more than two months in country, I'd adopted the attitude of the typical infantryman: "It just doesn't matter." That applied to everything related to life and death. See the bodies that your squad killed. It doesn't matter. Watch the medics zip a buddy into a body bag. It doesn't matter. Sure, you get a twinge in your gut, but you have to go on, so you don't even realize that the gut twinge comes from an invisible knife blade being stuck into your psyche and twisted, just a little. Just enough so that you're briefly aware of a pain, but you automatically make it go away. You have to. It's the only way to keep going. You don't let anything affect you, or more correctly, you don't allow anything to affect your job performance. *Xin loi.* Sorry 'bout that. It just doesn't matter.

But back to this daytime patrol. As we crossed the base camp perimeter, the squad leader gave the order to lock and load. We all jammed a magazine into our weapons, chambered a round, and put the rifle on safe. I always had the feeling that my blood pressure went up a few notches as the round slammed home, probably because it meant we were outside the protective womb of the base camp and now had only one another and our radio for support.

In our single-file line I was second, behind the point man. If he went down, my job was to take point and continue leading the patrol. In short order and without incident, we arrived at the area we were assigned to sweep. Halfway through on our second pass, Charlie made known his objections to our presence. We were ambushed.

It was clear almost from the beginning that the VC attacking us were not prepared for a large-scale fight. We took no incoming mortar rounds, and the sporadic rifle fire aimed our way hit no one. The squad's response was massive firepower, and the VC chose to break contact and run. We trailed them like a posse in hot pursuit of the bad guys, and our running firefight led us right to the edge of the suspect village, where the enemy shooters disappeared.

Even though this was not an out-of-the-ordinary experience for grunts in Vietnam, it was especially difficult because it reminded us that we weren't able to easily distinguish friendlies from enemies at close range. There were no white hats and black hats in our version of the Wild West; face-to-face everyone claimed to be our friend. If I heard "VC numbah ten, GI numbah one" one more time, I swore I'd kill someone. Who knew that I'd soon have the chance to make good on that oath?

By radio we informed the CO what had happened, and he directed other squads to join up with us and surround the village. Once we moved in, the village elders, who told our interpreter that we were obviously mistaken, because there were no Viet Cong in their village, met us formally. "VC numbah ten . . ." I refused to hear it. I could feel my level of hostility climbing in direct proportion to the quantity of bullshit that was being hurled in our direction. I'd get that itchy feeling on the back of my neck, and could tell that it would take more than a couple of Tums to neutralize the acid that was pouring into my stomach. At some point I suppose it dawned on me that deliberately antagonizing a bunch of adrenaline-hyped, homesick, armed-to-the-teeth American teenagers was, at best, an incautious thing for the village elders to do.

But they persisted in claiming that there were no strangers in the village—and we insisted that since we chased VC into the village, if there were no strangers among them, then the village must be VC.

Not understanding Vietnamese as spoken by our interpreter (an ARVN sergeant who seemed like he was on our side), I'm not sure that our argument was presented in such logical fashion. It didn't matter. The elders continued to deny the charge. They really had no other choice.

If it was a VC village, then they fully supported the operations of the local guerrillas, many of whom were probably fathers and sons from this very village, and they couldn't divulge who the VC were or where they were hiding. On the other hand, if it was a village that supported the South Vietnamese government but the local VC were forcing them to provide food and shelter to our enemy, for their own protection they had to deny that the VC were present. For the village, it was a lose-lose situation. No matter how the village elders handled things, they were going to lose. Such was the nature of the war in Vietnam.

With negotiations at a standoff, we withdrew from the village and set up a perimeter around it, and informed command via radio what was going on. About forty-five minutes later they called us back and instructed us to go into the village and speak to the elders one more time. If we still got the same answers, we were told to conduct a Zippo raid.

Zippo lighters were as ubiquitous in Vietnam as P-38s, the tiny can opener issued with C-rations. Often the Zippos were engraved with dates of arrival in country, with unit crests, or with lovable aphorisms such as: KILL 'EM ALL AND LET GOD SORT 'EM OUT. Zippos were incredibly reliable; they'd light time after time after time. They were used for lighting the variety of smoking materials found among military personnel; and they were used to light improvised cooking devices we created to heat a canteen cup of coffee or hot chocolate (take empty C-ration can and cut airholes in the sides near the bottom; fill can with dirt or sand; soak contents with gasoline; light with Zippo).

Zippos were also remarkably effective in burning down a village made up of thatched-roof houses. And when we got the same "No VC here" answer from the elders once again, that's what we did. We proceeded to burn the village to the ground.

At the time it didn't bother me. There were no moral pangs; no conflict between squad members about whether this was the right way to treat people; no philosophical discussion about whether this didn't just make more enemies for us. We got the order to Zippo the place, and that's what we did. Much later, when I remembered the mission, I remembered the anguished look on the villagers' faces as we burned their homes, homes they had lived in since God only knows when. But while we were doing it, no qualms.

We stayed in the area long enough to keep them from putting out the fires. Everything burned to the ground. Homes of young and old, bags of rice, everything we could get our hands on. And we ignored their pleas that they were not VC, that VC were "numbah ten," pointing rifles at them to prevent them from interfering with the process.

When the report went in, it was termed a successful operation, with quantities of enemy matériel and food stocks destroyed. The VC would later try for retribution by mortaring our base camp several nights in a row, but while it scared the crap out of us, the incoming rounds were mostly ineffective.

It was very early in the morning a few days after we burned the village that a messenger came by our tent to tell me that the old man wanted to see me. Once again I got that knot in the pit of my stomach. Had I screwed up? Was something wrong at home?

I reported to the captain in the bunker that served as company headquarters, and waited for the hammer to come down on my head. But all he said was "Mitchell, you did pretty good in the marksmanship training." That caught me off guard, because I expected something else.

I said, "Yes, sir, I guess I did." So he reaches behind his desk and picks up this hard rifle case. He opens it up, and there's an M-14 with a scope. He takes it out, hands it to me, and then gives me two loaded twenty-round magazines. I couldn't be sure if it was the same weapon I fired at the school.

He says, "We've got some people who want you to demonstrate how well you've learned. Go to the landing pad; there's a helicopter waiting on you. They'll take you out, where you'll be given the details on your target."

That was the moment when I realized what had happened. It was instantaneous. I couldn't believe how naive I had been, not figuring out what was going on. I took the rifle, but I just stood there looking at him like a fool. I can't even imagine what the look on my face was like, but he finally said, "Well, what're you waiting on?"

It never even entered my consciousness at that time that I wasn't going to get to zero this rifle—to take it to a range and fire at a fixed distance, adjusting the scope so that the bullet consistently went where I wanted it to go, not a few inches right or left, up or down. I've thought about that a lot, and the only thing that makes sense to me is that all the scopes were the same; all the rifles were the same. When I had turned my rifle in at the school, I knew that my personalized zero setting was three clicks right of center, two clicks south of level, and they had put that in the scope on the weapon the captain had just handed me. As long as I wasn't shooting more than a couple hundred meters, it wasn't critical.

Anyway, I went back to our tent, changed my helmet for a baseball cap, grabbed my web gear with a first-aid kit and canteen, and headed to the helicopter, carrying the rifle with one magazine loaded and the other in a cargo pocket of my fatigues. I was the only passenger on the Huey, a chopper that can easily carry eight combat troops in the back. We flew for maybe fifteen, twenty minutes, and then started circling. I could see we were at a crossroads, and nearby was an armored personnel carrier (APC). Did it make sense that there was a lone APC sitting out in the middle of nowhere? No. Next question.

We landed, and since there was nothing else in sight but the APC, it wasn't necessary for the crew chief to point me in that direction. But he did anyway. As I ducked low and headed toward the armored vehicle, a guy stuck his head out of the rear hatch, waved me in, and told me to sit on the side bench next to another kid from the 1st Cav carrying an M-16. The two men who were about to issue orders that could change our lives—or end them—were Americans. They wore standard jungle fatigues but had nothing on them identifying rank, unit, not even branch of service. Green fatigues, jungle boots. Period. They started talking, and you couldn't tell where they were from. No accent. No nothing. Two white guys with short haircuts, age thirty to forty.

"Okay, we're going to give you each a map. It's going to have two dots on it. One dot is where your target's going to be; the other is where your pickup point is going to be."

Then they handed me a photograph; I think it was a five-by-seven. "Here's your target. If you'll notice, there's a little scar above his eye." They let us study the photo for a minute, and then took it back. As we left the APC, the guy told us, "Don't talk about your units, and don't give full names. Just give your first name or a nickname. And pick up your brass."

They told us to wait outside, so after we exited the APC, I turned to the other kid and said, "My name's Mitch, and I've got seven and a half months left."

And he says, "Well, my name's Wayne, and I've got three months left."

We're standing there talking and smoking when the helicopter comes in. Wayne says, "I guess that's our transportation. I was hoping it wouldn't get here. I was on one of these things one time when we didn't have any transportation, and just waited for a while, and they got me a chopper ride back to my unit."

I said, "You've done this before?"

"Yeah," he says. And that was it. I didn't ask him anything else. I guess I was a perfect candidate for the job. I didn't ask a lot of questions. Got on the helicopter and had about half an hour to think about what was going on. And to be scared.

When we got off, Wayne checked his compass and we went into the wood line. The chopper left us, and there we were. He asked me if I could shoot well enough and run fast enough for us to get out of this alive, and I said, "God, I hope so!"

The two of us walked for about thirty minutes, till we came to a small open area, about a hundred meters long by a hundred meters wide. At the opposite side was a stream. Wayne was checking his map, and then looking at the clearing. We agreed that this must be the place. So I bent down and began looking through the scope. I got right beside one of the large trees, lay down, and could see everything in the clearing from there. And Wayne lay down next to me— not against me, but close enough that if either one of us had stretched our arm out about halfway, we could've touched the other.

About half an hour went by, and six North Vietnamese soldiers came into the open area, looking relaxed, just walking and talking. Then the main body of troops came in, about a dozen of them, and I remember whispering to Wayne, "Do you suppose a flank is going to walk over our asses?" We didn't know if they had a patrol out, protecting their flank.

I was still looking through the scope when I saw the troops talking to our target. I could only assume he was a high-ranking officer. I could distinguish his face, his eyes, and the scar we'd seen in the photo. This was very different from combat. This was hunting, but the target wasn't a deer or a rabbit; it was a man. Nothing in my training had prepared me for the moment when I realized that I had the power of life and death over another human being. If you can be shocked, angered, and in awe at the same time, I was. This was my John Wayne or Gary Cooper moment. They were the movie idols I grew up with. But the differences between being a Hollywood sniper and a real one were instantly clear to me, and I was terrified.

Wayne was looking through his spotter scope, and as soon as he saw the guy with a whole lot of rank on his shoulders and a scar over his eye, he said, "Have you got him?"

I said, "Yes."

And he said, "Okay, it's on you." That was like a line out of the movies. I could imagine the music dropping down till all you could hear was a drumroll. An insistent drumroll, building in volume and intensity, begging to be silenced by a single shot.

At the moment I saw the whole bunch of NVA it hit me that we were expendable, me and Wayne—just so much cannon fodder. Stop the movie scene. Enough of that drumroll. This was real. We'd never been taught sniper-craft. Just had to remember the stuff we learned on regular combat patrols and way back in advanced infantry training (AIT). Set up inside the wood line, well back from the edge. This was OJT—on-the-job training—and I realized that I was dead. I'm dead because there's a whole bunch of them and there's only two of us. I'm dead because I've got only forty rounds of ammunition, and I'm not sure how much Wayne is carrying for his M-16. No grenades; not even a .45. And contrary to what's been written by some military historians about sniper teams never being sent into the bush without a radio to call for reinforcements or for artillery or air support, we had no radio. Officially, I guess, we didn't exist. There wasn't going to be a notation in our 201 file that we'd been lent to the CIA or whoever those spooks were. We were on our own. And we were about to be dead.

I started to pick up a sight picture just as the target stopped at a stream and reached down to get a double handful of water to splash on his face. He had his back to me. He shook the water off his hands to the front, and then he stretched. He was in a crucifixion pose, and I took two breaths. On the second breath, I just let it half out. The reason is that at the shallowest part of your breath, when you've got nothing left in your lungs, there's a tremor. It's imperceptible, but it's there.

And at the top of your breath, when your lungs are full, there's a tremor just before you start exhaling. So you let about half of it out, which is the most stable part of your breathing cycle, and then you hold it.

In AIT they taught us to aim at the center of mass on the silhouette targets. On a man, it's the top of the breastbone. It's a perfect aiming point because if your rifle kicks up a little bit, you'll hit his head. If you drop the barrel a little bit, you're going to hit his heart. If you go left or right, you're going to get a lung. The target's back was to me, but it was still center of mass. He was less than two hundred meters away, so there wasn't going to be a lot of droppage of the round, and it wasn't a far enough distance to worry about the wind causing a deflection. It was just quick, down and dirty.

I held my breath and gently squeezed the trigger. The sound of the single shot in the relatively quiet forest seemed incredibly loud. He went headfirst into the stream, and Wayne said, "Clean." We slid backward; I grabbed the shell casing, and we took off. We'd run for a few minutes when we began hearing rounds whizzing through the underbrush. They sounded like a freight train coming through the air—nothing like the way it sounds on TV. It was a "pffft-*crack!*" So the round was passing before the sound of the shot got to us. And the bullets never stopped coming. They were still shooting at us as we got close to our pickup point.

Both of us could hear the helicopter sitting on the ground.

A brief digression for readers who are sticklers for proper procedure as set forth in various army training manuals: Was it bizarre that a chopper would wait on the ground out in the middle of nowhere, rather than orbit until we were spotted? Yes. The typical procedure for a pickup in a combat area was for the ground unit to pop colored smoke, radio the choppers to tell them what color they'd popped, listen for the pilot to acknowledge that he'd seen the smoke, and then have the Huey come in to make the pickup. There were a couple of reasons why that scenario was not going to work: We had no smoke grenades, and we had no radio. At some point in my sniper career, I recall being told that carrying that stuff would just add weight, it would slow us down, and it might get snagged as we ran through the bush, all of which was undeniably true. The fact that smoke and a radio might save our lives was also undeniable, but as I said earlier, I'd just figured out that we were expendable. I'll plead guilty to being a slow learner.

The briefers had told us that the chopper would sit for only ten minutes—maybe not even that long. If we weren't there, we were going to have to walk back from here, and we had no idea where *here* was. We hadn't been told where we were going to be. The map we'd been given was only about twelve inches by ten inches. It didn't have any border information, didn't have any of the legend. Nothing that really told us exactly where we were. So we had to get to that Huey. Otherwise we were just two more MIAs, and our families would never know that we'd been hung out to die.

Talk about surround sound. From behind us we're hearing automatic weapons fire; to our right and left, at our feet and over our heads, we're hearing the "pfft-*crack*" of rounds just missing; to our front we're hearing the RPMs on the chopper's rotor going up; we know the pilot's bringing the engine to flight idle. In seconds he'll pull pitch and that bird will be gone, leaving us to die.

When we heard the engines accelerating, we didn't say anything; we just looked at each other and started running harder, slamming branches and brush out of the way and tightening the grip we had on our rifles so we wouldn't accidentally drop them and have to stop. We'd given up any hope of camouflaging our movements. All that mattered was catching that helicopter.

Just as we came into the clearing, he lifted off and began to circle around to head back to wherever the hell he'd come from. We were shouting, "We're here, we're here!" We knew instinctively that there was no way he could hear us, but we kept shouting and waving. Desperate people do strange things. Luckily, the crew chief or door gunner must have seen us, because that bird circled back in and set down.

As it touched the ground, we dove in face-first, and we'd barely slammed onto the floor of the slick when the bird took off. We didn't get in the seats or strapped in or anything before we were up and gone. As we circled around, we took some fire—I could hear a "tik-tik-tik." The crew chief shouted at us, "Are you guys all right?"

As I acknowledged that we were, I realized that this was not the same crew that had dropped us off, and it dawned on me that we were part of something that had taken some fairly elaborate planning. What was going through my mind at that moment, however, was not the notion of congratulating the higher-ups on their logistical achievement. I was more wrapped up in practical considerations. *How do I get out of here alive? Am I ever going to see Texas again? What in God's holy name am I doing here?*

I looked at Wayne, and he looked at me, and we were both huffing and puffing. He reached into a pocket and pulled out a pack of cigarettes. They were Kools. I remember that because I didn't like Kools. He pulled out a Zippo and we sat there and smoked. I had no concept of time. All I remember is that we landed and dropped Wayne off, and then we flew back to my base camp—ten, fifteen, maybe twenty minutes. Touched down, I got off, and they were gone.

I took the rifle back to my commander, handed it to him, and left. He didn't ask me anything, and I was still too scared to talk. I returned to my tent and was sitting there when the squad leader stuck his head in. "Are you all right?"

"Yeah."

"Did everything go all right?"

"Yeah, I guess so." And he left. That was my debrief.

That was it. Later on I began to wonder how they knew that I didn't go out, lie in the woods, fire a round, and get on the helicopter. How did they know I'd actually made the kill?

Then I began to dwell on the nature of what I'd just done, examining it from several angles. It was absolutely unlike any combat experience I'd had to that point. In combat you're counting on your buddies and they're counting on you to do what has to be done to get everyone home alive. But getting assigned to kill a specific person? I began trying to figure out what got me through it. That's when I realized that up until the shot was fired, it was pretty mechanical. It was training kicking in. But once the rifle fires, the brain's response is all electrical and chemical. It's as though a little guy in a tux stands up between your ears and shouts, "Let's get ready to rumble," so loud that you're certain the enemy two or three hundred meters away can clearly him.

The instant result is nervous stimulation that causes the center of the adrenal glands that sit atop each of your kidneys to release two of the body's most powerful hormones directly into the bloodstream. The effects of this flood of adrenaline (epinephrine) and noradrenaline (norepinephrine) into the bloodstream are profound and almost instantaneous:

- There's an increase in the rate and strength of the heartbeat that results in increased blood pressure
- Blood is shunted from the skin and internal organs to the skeletal muscles, coronary arteries, liver, and brain
- Blood sugar levels rise
- Clotting time of the blood is reduced
- Metabolic rate increases
- Bronchial tubes dilate
- Pupils dilate
- Goose bumps develop and hairs stand on end

In terms of taking the body from find-and-shoot mode to get-me-the-hell-out-of-here mode, that all makes a lot of sense. Except for the goose bumps. As near as I can figure, the only useful function they perform is to help you confirm that at that precise moment you are so scared that if you had to think to breathe, you'd suffocate.

From that first shooting experience, I knew that getting real-time confirmation of that fact was not an issue. There was that momentary pause between the sound of the rifle firing and my spotter telling me it was a good hit. Then we instantly went into flight mode—I know it's usually called "flight or fight"—but trust me on this one; we weren't interested in any option other than *di-di*'ing out of there a lot faster than ASAP. We had to get up, get out, and survive the run to our helicopter. Someone once told me that adrenaline is the most powerful drug known to man. We were freakin' high on adrenaline, and we didn't really come down until we were safely out of the area. That's when I could begin rethinking what I'd just been through. And after that first shoot, all I could think was, *What have I gotten myself into? Can I do this? I don't have anybody to blame it on but myself.*

That night I cornered the squad leader. "Why didn't you tell me you were having me trained as a sniper?"

And his answer was "Oh, y'know, I've got all the confidence in the world that you can do whatever needs to be done, and that you've got the initiative and the know-how and the skills."

My response was a little hostile. "Well, thanks a lot, asshole. Why me?"

"We have our reasons," he said. And that was the only answer he'd ever give. I found out later that this was his second tour in Vietnam, and he'd been a sniper during his first tour. The guys who volunteer and are selected to go to sniper school in today's military are given batteries of psychological tests and examinations to see if they match a sniper profile that's been developed. Back in the Vietnam era, they didn't have me or any of the guys I trained with at marksmanship school examined by a shrink to determine our fitness for the job, so it seems to make sense that they would have turned to former snipers in the infantry and asked them to identify soldiers who had what it takes. But that's just supposition; since there's no paperwork, no notations in my records, I can only guess.

It sounds unbelievable that somebody could be as naive as I was and not ask questions before following orders to undertake an out-of-the-ordinary mission, but that was the army back then. You didn't ask a lot of questions. It was "do what you're told and do it well enough to get by, keep the sergeant off your ass, and survive." Later in my career it was a lot different. "I beg your pardon? Excuse me? Which one of us is crazy? One of us is on narcotics—I'll pee in a bottle right now, okay? What the hell do you mean, go off by our-selves, just the two of us?" But that was years later, after the country lost its innocence, after the revelations of the Pentagon Papers, after Nixon and Watergate, after Reagan, Ollie North, and Iran-Contra. Even those of us who had military careers learned that there were occasions when it was essential to question authority—although we never put the bumper sticker on our Hummers.

CHAPTER FIVE

The Woman Is Your Target

I'd been in Vietnam about three months and had knowingly killed two people. The first one had been in a combat situation, and even though it had obviously affected me, I didn't have to work too hard to rationalize it. We'd been ambushed, my buddies were under fire, and I could do something about it. So I did.

What happened to me on that operation is precisely what every sergeant I came in contact with in basic and AIT worked hard to achieve. When the right circumstances presented themselves, that fresh-faced kid from Granbury, Texas, who worried that his father would invoke capital punishment—or at least corporal punishment—if he got caught misbehaving, would kill.

In his Pulitzer Prize–nominated book, *On Killing: The Psychological Cost of Learning to Kill in War and Society,* former West Point psychologist Dave Grossman (who also happens to be a retired lieutenant colonel and Army Ranger) writes: "When faced with a living, breathing opponent, a significant majority of soldiers revert to a posturing mode in which they fire over their enemy's heads." He adds that soldiers must be trained intensively to overcome the natural reluctance to kill other people.

Based on my responses under fire, I can only guess that the reluctance threshold of some soldiers is lower than that of others. My first

sniper killing is a whole different ball game, and I still don't understand my response.

I accepted an assignment that had me hunting a man like I used to
hunt deer. Find a hide, lie in wait, confirm the target, kill him. What
was there about me that I could do it? What did the army know
about me that led them to choose me?

First, the squad leader says that I'm being sent to marksmanship
school because of all his guys, I'm the one who keeps his head in a
tough situation. He liked the way I handled myself. (When he said it
the first time, I didn't know he'd been a sniper on a previous tour in
Vietnam.) And I liked that he said it. I was flattered that he thought I
was exceptional.

Second, the instructors never let on that we were being taught to
operate in anything but a combat environment, with our unit. No one
ever asks why we'd have to knock off a target seven hundred meters
out during a unit operation in the jungles or mountains of Vietnam.
I'd been on infantry operations for a couple of months, and I was
never—not even once—in a situation where being able to hit a target
more than seven football fields away would have come in handy. Yet
it never dawned on me to raise my hand and ask the question.

Third, when the captain sent me out on the first mission, was he
that smooth that he had me on the chopper before it even crossed
my mind to ask what he was getting me into? I'm a nineteen-year-old
kid who enlisted to be a truck mechanic. I had been taught all my
life not just to trust authority, but also to obey it without question.
My parents. My teachers. The neighbors. The local cop. And then
my drill sergeants, who made it clear that if I paid attention to what
they could teach me, I might actually survive the war. And once I got
to Vietnam, my squad leader, platoon sergeant, first sergeant, and the
company commander. I thought they were all supposed to be interested in keeping me alive. No one sent up a flare and said, "Sorry,
Mitchell. New game plan."

Finally, there were the two spooks in the APC. The shit they laid on me was so slick I didn't even feel myself sliding down the slippery slope. I don't even know whether they knew it was my first time, but they certainly didn't leave any room in their spiel for me to say, "Uh, let's slow this thing down and talk about it. You want me to go where and do what?"

So what does it come down to with that first mission? I'll tell you. It's a five-word sentence that causes chills, because it has an ugly provenance: I was only following orders.

And now that they knew I'd done it once, they could pretty much count on the fact that I'd do it again.

If there is a joy to being with a combat unit in the military, it's found in the camaraderie you have with your buddies. While you may not be close with your entire squad, there are usually a couple of guys whom you enjoy hanging with, guys you feel comfortable talking to about anything. The problem I had was that after my first shoot, I didn't have anyone I could confide in.

I didn't want to discuss it in the squad because I didn't know how they'd react. I wasn't about to talk to my squad leader about it, because he was the one who got me into this mess in the first place, so he really wasn't high on my buddy list. All I could do was wonder when—or if—they'd be coming to get me again. Unfortunately, I had to wait only about a week.

The charge of quarters (CQ) woke me at about 2:30 in the morning and told me the company commander wanted to see me as soon as I could get there. Again, at that time, I thought that there were only two reasons the CO would want to see someone: Either you were in trouble or there was an emergency of some type at home. Since it was the middle of the night, which was not when discipline for minor infractions was meted out, I opted to believe something was wrong back in the States. What else could have gotten the CO out of his rack at that hour?

I dressed quickly, put on my web gear, and went to the bunker that served as the orderly room, hoping someone would be there to tell me what to expect before I saw the old man, but the CQ was the only one around. There was no opportunity for us to talk. He said the commander was waiting and I should report immediately. I knocked on the partition that separated his office from the rest of the bunker, and he called me in.

Sitting on his desk was a rifle case. The sight of it caused three things to occur instantaneously: complete relief at the realization that there was nothing wrong at home, understanding that I had again been selected for a shoot, and instant fear.

The last time had shown me that I really didn't want to be out in the jungle alongside only one other person, with the very strong possibility of someone chasing the two of us. Now it was apparent that it was going to happen again.

It seemed more than a bit odd to go through the formal "Specialist Mitchell reporting as ordered, sir" in the middle of the night, but I did it anyway. He told me there was a helicopter waiting for me at the airfield, so I'd better hurry. I saluted, took the rifle from the case, and left his office. I stepped out into the night and started for the airfield. I wanted to go back to my tent for a couple of things but thought better of it.

When I arrived at the airfield, the helicopter was sitting there running. The doors were open. I guess, since I was the only one who showed up with an M-14, they assumed that I was the guy they were waiting for. I climbed aboard and we lifted off into the pitch-black sky almost before I could get my seat belt fastened.

We flew north for a couple of hours. Just as dawn broke, we started down. Knowing that this was the most dangerous time of the day in Vietnam, I began to tense up somewhat. Once again, we landed near an armored personnel carrier. I grabbed my gear and started toward the APC when a guy stepped out and told me to take a smoke break in front of the vehicle. This was one of the same briefers whom I had met on the first mission.

I went around the track, sat down and lit a cigarette, making sure that I kept the cherry cupped in my hand. After what seemed ages, a second helicopter landed, and two GIs left the APC and got on the aircraft. One was carrying a rifle similar to mine. *This is going to be an interesting day,* I thought. At least two teams working simultaneously. I'd jumped to the conclusion on the first mission that only one of these operations was taking place at a time. Apparently I was wrong.

After about ten minutes another helicopter landed and dropped off a single passenger. Since I had the special rifle and he was carrying an M-16A1, it was a pretty good bet that he was my second. A few minutes later we were called inside the track and the briefing began much as before. Again, the briefers wore nothing to indicate rank, unit, or even branch of service. No preliminaries, no "good morning," just right down to business.

We quickly discovered that for us, this was to be an entirely different kind of shoot. We had barely sat down on one of the benches inside the APC when they handed us a piece of a map, and a photograph.

"Okay, there's two people in the picture. Look at the woman. Note the scar over one eyebrow. She's your target." Well, I looked at the guy who was with me, and I looked back at the picture. It was clear that we were stunned. The spook said, "Okay, we've noted your reaction. If you don't think you want to do this, let us know now so we can task somebody else." And then he moved right along so quickly that we didn't have a chance to say anything.

I was aware from the combat ops I'd been on that the VC actively recruited and used women, but to this point I'd not knowingly encountered one. It seemed as though that was about to change, in a very chilling way.

We were dismissed and stepped outside of the carrier. No helicopter was on the ground, and we didn't hear an inbound Huey, so we stepped over to the edge of the wood line and squatted down and lit a cigarette.

My spotter sighed. "A woman."

"Damn," I responded.

Clearly we were both taken aback by the mission, but there was no discussion between us. Finishing our smokes, we got up and strolled back over to the carrier and asked if they had any coffee left. They poured us some in, of all things, a paper cup. I hadn't seen a paper cup in quite a while. These guys knew how to live.

We stood in front of the carrier, drank our coffee, and smoked another cigarette. I should have been nervous about standing in the middle of nowhere, but somehow I was confident there was heavy security around the perimeter. I didn't think anyone with the authority that these folks seemed to have would be running around without it.

A few minutes later one of the spooks came out of the track and was looking around at nothing in particular, but you could tell he was seeing everything. I offered him a cigarette and he surprised me by accepting it. We all stood there just looking around, waiting.

Then I realized why he had come out. He was looking for our aircraft and at the same time checking on us, probably to evaluate our mental state. After about five minutes or so he stubbed out the cigarette and went back inside the carrier.

We just grinned at each other, and my spotter muttered something about the REMF (Rear Echelon Motherfucker) being a little jittery. We both laughed and smoked another cigarette. My partner wondered aloud if we should impose on them for another cup of coffee. "Why not?" I asked. But when we ambled over to the open rear hatch, one of the spooks said the coffee was gone and they were getting ready to depart.

For a second I wondered what they were going to do with us, but then, off in the distance, we could hear an inbound Huey. Problem solved. We took off on yet another green helicopter with no unit markings, manned by an American crew whose origins were equally mysterious, and flew south for about an hour and a half, which by my calculations put us only about a half hour north of Phuoc Vinh, near where this mission had begun in the middle of the night. It didn't make any sense. So what else was new?

The landing was more of a combat insertion than a passenger drop-off. No sooner had our boots hit the ground than the pilot pulled pitch and was out of there. Not a good sign, as far as I was concerned. We oriented our ground position with the map, located the two dots that told us how far we'd have to run once we'd taken out the target, and began what looked to be a six-hour mission on the ground.

We had been dropped about four kilometers from our scheduled firing position, and it took almost two hours to get there because the underbrush was so thick. When we arrived at the first dot, we found ourselves on the crest of a small hill overlooking the village. Now all we had to do was identify the target, which required that she show herself. We hadn't been instructed to go hooch to hooch trying to find her, which was a good thing, because it wasn't something I was interested in doing.

We lay there in hiding for about an hour, all the time regretting the coffee we had drunk earlier. There is an obvious and quite simple solution to that problem, but with memories of childhood unpleasantness in our heads, and not having had special operations training during which deliberately peeing in one's pants is taught as a sign of dedication to duty, honor, and mission, we opted to just lie there and suffer rather than wetting our pants.

Time began to get critical—for both the mission and our bladders. Our helo was due in three hours, and if we had no interference it was a two-hour walk to the pickup point on the map. Still, there was no movement at all around the village. Something was going to have to happen pretty quickly, or we would have to abort the shoot.

Our briefers had told us if something went wrong on any shoot, we could abort, but we had no idea what would happen if we did. In the military, there are always consequences—often bad ones—when lower-ranking soldiers start thinking for themselves. We were more worried about what our superiors would do to us if we called off the shoot than we were about whether we were going to miss our pickup. It's classic drama—we might have to choose not between a good solution and a bad one, but between two bad ones: potential punishment or being abandoned in Indian country by ourselves.

We really didn't know what to do, but sometimes the best choice is to do nothing, and that worked for us that day. Because about half an hour later, we began to hear noises to the east of the village. The villagers were returning from wherever they had been. We had no idea if they had been in their rice fields, visiting another village, or what. We were just extremely relieved that they had returned.

I eased into a comfortable shooting position, turned my baseball cap around backward, looked through the scope, and began to gently sweep across the village and villagers trying to find our target. I'd made a couple of passes when the second whispered, "Contact, two o'clock." Gently easing the rifle to the area he had pointed out, I saw two ladies standing talking to each other. The one on the right had the small scar on her forehead that we had been instructed to look for. She was the target!

The range was very short. It was about 250 meters, downhill. Not the best shooting angle. When you shoot downhill, you can misjudge distance easily. But it would have been worse if we had to also shoot over water. During my week at school, I'd learned that the movement of water causes some air turbulence, and that can affect the trajectory of the round.

I swept the area around her to see if anyone else was in my line of fire if the shot went astray, but the only other person who could be in danger was the woman the target was talking to. Glancing at my watch, I realized there was not a lot of time to wait and see if the second woman would leave, giving me a little more margin for error. Thinking like that was clearly nerves at work, because shooting with a scope at this range in bright sunlight, even downhill, did not require me to be Carlos Hathcock, the Marine Corps gunnery sergeant with ninety-three confirmed kills. If I could settle myself down, it would be an easy shot.

Out of the corner of my eye I saw my spotter looking over at me, nodding, and then looking back at the target. There was no point in putting it off any longer. I took a couple of deep breaths. On the second one I let half of the breath out and held, focusing intently on the sight picture. At 250 meters, the crosshairs were positioned right on the center of mass. I was perspiring profusely, but since it wasn't dripping into my eyes, it wasn't a real problem.

The object in this type of shooting is to actually surprise yourself when the weapon fires. That means the tip of your trigger finger moves imperceptively, first taking up the slack, then continuing to apply gentle pressure until the pad of tissue at the tip of the index finger is, itself, compressed. You keep squeezing until suddenly you feel the recoil, and as your entire body moves back with the rifle, then resettles, you see the gas from the round obscuring the sight picture for a second. With a muzzle velocity of about 855 meters per second, there's no question that by the time you comprehend that the weapon has fired, the bullet should have struck the target.

But even with a relatively close target like this one, there's still that moment of uncertainty when my view is obscured, when I don't really *know* whether or not I've hit the target, and if I have, whether it has been a killing shot. It seemed like an eternity, just lying there, neither of us moving. But it couldn't have been more than a second until my spotter simply whispered, "Target," so I knew even before the scope cleared that it had been a successful shoot.

Suddenly both of us realized that we were still lying in the same position. My memory here is a bit hazy, but I seem to recall hearing the phrase "Let's get the fuck out of here." I don't think I could have agreed more or phrased it more eloquently. As my partner began to scoot backward, I frantically looked to my right side, spotted the spent brass cartridge shell, and as I, too, scooted backward, grabbed it on the fly. When we had backed farther into the brush, we stood up, and, even though we couldn't see it, looked back toward the village as though we expected to see half the North Vietnamese Army coming after us.

The impulse, of course, is to run, but in a relatively quiet, forested area, two men running make more noise than a Texas twister tearing through a trailer park. We started off at a brisk walk, which seemed to get brisker by the moment because we had no idea if the village had a defense system in place or not. To tell the truth, I really didn't want to know. I just wanted to get out of there as fast as I could.

After about forty-five minutes, we stopped for a quick breather, and I wondered aloud if we were being followed, or if this was going to be an easy escape. My answer came in the form of a round zipping past us. We took off at a dead run, hoping that we were quick enough to outrun them, but knowing we couldn't outrun the rounds they were firing in our direction. After what seemed like forever we slowed to a fast walk, and I wondered aloud if they were still after us. As an afterthought, I asked my partner if we were still on course to our extraction site. Time was running short, and our margin for error was thin.

According to our calculations, we were about four hundred meters from a stream. If we were on course, there would be a bend just downstream from where we would cross. When we got to the stream it was flowing straight. The question was elementary: Were we above or below the bend we were looking for, and how far off were we? We had no success at all trying to find some sort of landmark we could orient with. We could see only about a hundred meters in any direction, so orienting to the map was pretty much out of the question.

We really had no choice other than to keep moving, hoping that we were not completely disoriented, and that we were still moving in the proper general direction. Hoping for that kind of good fortune in a combat zone is a recipe for disaster, but what choice did we have? Once again, we came face-to-face with the notion that we were expendable. With more than five hundred American GIs dying in combat each month in the summer of '69, who would notice two more? Who would even wonder what we were doing out by ourselves when they found our bodies—*if* they found our bodies?

Strangely, considering what the two of us had been conned into doing, we did spend some time talking about what would happen if we died. Not while we were trying to make sure it didn't happen, mind you, but while we were hanging out around the APC, waiting to go on this mission. It was important to me that my partner agree to try to carry my body to the helicopter. I didn't want to be abandoned in the jungle, left there to be picked over by the enemy, the animals, and the bugs. It just didn't seem right. It wasn't how I was brought up. A man should have a fitting burial, especially a man who dies for his country.

With luck, however, neither one of us was going to have to worry about bringing his buddy's body back. We apparently had managed to outrun our pursuers, but while there were no more bullets whizzing past us, we still didn't know where we were or which way we were supposed to head. Within minutes we came across a trail, but that did nothing to help orient us. Carefully examining our map fragment, neither one of us could see the trail. It meant that it either wasn't shown on the map, or we were going in the wrong direction. We were hoping for the former, but had no way of being certain until we finally came across a large stream that was on the map.

Turns out we had drifted about two kilometers off course, and were now about three klicks from our pickup point, with just over ninety minutes to get there. It doesn't sound like a problem—just over 1.8 miles to travel and an hour and a half to do it in. But we weren't running on a track; we were trying to race through heavy jungle carrying rifles, concerned that the enemy might be right behind us, and that our ride home could leave without us if we didn't make it.

We ignored almost everything we had ever been taught. We went in a straight line with no zigging or zagging. We went as directly and as fast as we could. When we were about a kilometer from the pickup point, we heard the aircraft approaching. We'd been told he would wait no longer than ten minutes for us once he was on the ground. What we had no way of knowing was how much longer till he landed and began counting down those ten minutes of ground time.

The sound of a helicopter is very indistinct in flight. You can hear it, but unless you can actually see it, you really can't make a decent guess at distance or speed. Our only choice was to run as though our lives depended on it, so we hit the trail that led to that magical dot on the map and ran like hell.

We were down to what we later calculated was about seven hundred meters when we heard the aircraft idle down. Time was running out, and we were both certainly running out of energy. I was hurting all over, scared I would hear the aircraft engine pitch change and trying not to start yelling. It wouldn't have done any good, because they wouldn't have been able to hear us anyway.

Suddenly we could see the bird. Again we strained to use any energy left in us to make it to the chopper. When we were about fifty meters away, but still in heavy jungle, we heard the pitch of the engine begin to change. Our lungs were about to burst, but that sound just about broke my heart. We were close to making it to safety, but close counts only in horseshoes, hand grenades, and nuclear weapons. Close wouldn't keep us alive. Just as we broke through the edge of the tree line, the Huey lifted off, pitched nose down, and began to turn and climb. We didn't know what to do. I was afraid because I knew that I was going to die right there at the crossing of two trails.

As the aircraft began to pick up altitude it circled back over the clearing, and the crew chief saw us waving desperately. For a second we couldn't be sure whether they were going to come down for us or not, but the pilot pulled his ship into a tight turn and dropped down. It didn't take more than three seconds for us to throw ourselves through the open door, grab hold of one of the seat stanchions, and find ourselves airborne.

Sitting on the cabin floor soaked with sweat that was quickly evaporating in the cooler air about fifteen hundred feet up, I had my first opportunity to reflect on what I'd just done. All my life I'd been raised to respect women. I had a difficult time putting a woman— even a Vietnamese woman—in the same category as a male enemy soldier. Yes, I knew that the Viet Cong were using not only women, but also children, to attack American troops. But that didn't mean I'd find it easy to kill them. Sure, if it were a heated moment, my unit under attack, a true us-or-them situation, I wouldn't have any qualms about doing what had to be done. But this—this planned, calculated shooting of a specific woman who was no immediate threat to me or my buddies—was something completely different. And I knew at that moment on the helicopter that I'd be dealing with this event in my young life for some time to come.

We flew for a while, those thoughts pounding in my head to the "whap-whap-whap" of the Huey's rotors, then landed in what seemed to be the middle of nowhere. Couldn't tell where we were, or if we'd been there before. The crew chief signaled for us to get off, which we did. They pulled pitch and left us standing in the middle of an open field—not a good place to be when you have no clue whether you're still in Indian country.

But before the sounds of our departing bird faded out, two Hueys circled in. We each got on a helicopter, and as we lifted off I could see my partner waving at me. I returned his wave and settled back in my uncomfortable seat for the trip to my base camp, and what I hoped would be a more normal combat assignment.

CHAPTER SIX

The Little Girl

Since my second sniper mission a few weeks earlier, I'd been out on some relatively routine patrols, but nothing out of the ordinary. Then we got tasked for something slightly different.

Our intelligence folks knew that the VC were collecting taxes from several villages within a few kilometers of our base camp near Phuoc Vinh, and the powers that be wanted us to do something about it.

Company B of the 2/7 got the assignment, and we worked in platoon sectors within the general area of the operation. There were a couple of small firefights, each lasting only a few minutes, but nothing significant. The VC would engage us briefly, and then withdraw.

On the last skirmish, one of our guys was hit, and from a blood trail that we found, we knew that at least one of the VC had taken a bullet. We lost time while waiting for a Dustoff to pull our wounded buddy out, and then we began tracking the enemy, knowing that we were at least fifteen minutes behind them.

The trail led to a village that was known to be loyal to the Saigon government. Our intel folks said that the village elders had provided sound intelligence for us on a couple of occasions, and that they'd denied support to the VC.

When we got into the village, we found that the enemy force we were trailing had, indeed, been there, and a little girl of three or four years had paid the price. The VC had asked for taxes and/or sanctuary from the elders, and when they were refused, they grabbed the girl and hacked off one leg about two inches above the knee with a machete. When we got to her she was in agony, and our medic said she could die soon from shock and loss of blood.

Our platoon sergeant put security around the village, notified command and called for a medical helicopter, then detailed me to help the medic. I would have rather gone out on the perimeter.

I'd seen dead bodies, both ours and theirs; I'd helped with our wounded; I'd watched guys die. It all comes along with being a grunt, and you learn how to handle it—or convince yourself that you've learned. That's what the GI mantra "It don't mean nothing" was all about—learning how to numb yourself to the horror that might confront you on a regular basis. But this was more than I wanted to be involved with.

I had to hold the little girl, who was writhing in pain, while the medic used a tourniquet to get the bleeding stopped and started an IV. We had to get her lower extremities higher than her head to try to keep as much blood flow as possible to her brain and major organs. Since her skin felt cold and clammy to the touch, we also had to try to keep her warm. She was in pain; she was scared—and now these strange-looking men were handling her in ways that her young mind couldn't comprehend.

All the while we were trying to treat her and keep her calmed down, her mother was screaming hysterically and trying to get her baby away from us. It took another guy from the platoon to restrain her. At the time we were doing it, the logic of keeping the mother away from her daughter made sense, but years later, rolling the incident around in my head, I found myself questioning what we did. As a parent, I know there's no way anyone could keep me from my child's side if he were critically hurt. How could we have done that to a poor Vietnamese mother who had no way of being sure that what we were doing to her daughter was an effort to help save her life? Frankly, I'm surprised she didn't try to kill us.

When the Dustoff arrived, we had another problem: There was no place for them to land. They had to lower a litter on a cable, and as it came down, the platoon sergeant warned everyone not to touch it. As soon as it was within reach, he whacked it with a steel rod that the medic carried to dissipate the static electricity that could knock you on your butt if you weren't careful.

While the Vietnamese trackers stood there shaking, with tears in their eyes, I placed the little girl in the basket as gently as I could. She had continued to cry, and occasionally scream, which made it that much more difficult for us American tough guys to deal with it. Once we had her strapped in, the aircrew lifted the basket and pulled it inside the aircraft.

As the Huey banked and started away, the mother suddenly realized that they were not going to wait for her. She became even more hysterical, attacking the medic and the platoon sergeant. Ultimately, the only way we could deal with her was to have the medic inject a sedative to calm her down.

After explaining to the village elders where the girl was being taken, and telling them that the mother would recover from the effects of the tranquilizer in a couple of hours, the classic tougher-than-nails platoon sergeant looked at the trackers and through tears in his eyes told them that we were not going to return to our base camp until we found the sons of bitches who did this.

By this time we were about an hour behind them, and the medic and I were covered in the little girl's blood. I was crying and felt sick to my stomach, and the doc, a guy who had a reputation for being calm and collected no matter what kind of hell was going on around him, had tears running down his cheeks.

It didn't take a genius to know what every guy in that platoon was thinking as we set out after the VC bastards who'd done this. The trackers were performing as they had never performed before, and they kept telling us that we were getting closer. I thought it was a miracle that they could follow the trail, because the jungle canopy was getting thicker, and even though it was only midafternoon, at ground level it was getting darker.

We continued to move, never stopping for a break. No one complained, not even the guys who were usually the first ones to ask when we were going back to base camp. I've never seen any group in my life that was more determined for revenge.

Right around nightfall one of the trackers lifted his arm in a signal for us to halt. We dropped to our knees and waited for the platoon sergeant to move up front to hear what the trackers had to say. It took just a second for him to turn around and give us the thumbs-up: We'd found them.

As quickly as possible, we deployed in squads to surround them. Once we were in position, one of the trackers shouted in Vietnamese that they were surrounded, and that we were going to take them prisoner.

It was clear that they had no idea we'd been on their trail, because when I was able to get in close I could see that they'd been sitting around a small fire, cooking rice. Their reaction to the tracker was unfortunate—for them. They made a couple of mistakes: First, they didn't immediately raise their hands in surrender, and second, they reached for their weapons.

Our platoon sergeant knew in an instant what was going to happen and tried to stop it. He really did want to take them alive, to haul them back to the village for interrogation. But his shout came a moment too late. Twenty rifles spoke as one.

Twenty riflemen of different marksmanship capabilities suddenly learned to aim true. Either that or the rifles were on fully automatic, in which case, you really don't need to be a good marksman. Just aim in the general direction and the recoil will give you a pretty good spread of your rounds.

Five VC all entered the hereafter simultaneously. The shooting lasted about three seconds. Personally, I emptied an eighteen-round magazine and wanted to shoot more, but it was over.

Since it was too dark to head back to the village with the bodies, we set up camp, put out security, and stayed for the night. The next morning we pulled, dragged, and carried the bodies back to the village and dropped them at the feet of the village elders.

When we arrived back at the base camp, we learned that the little girl would live. Her mother, along with a couple of the villagers, had walked roughly fifteen kilometers to the hospital, where the base commander had made arrangements for her to stay with her daughter.

Nowadays, when they talk about civilian casualties, they refer to it as "collateral damage." That makes it sound too clean and clinical. For my buddies and me that afternoon, it was about as ugly as war can get. That child had no control over whether her village paid taxes to the VC or supported the South Vietnamese government. She didn't have a say in whether her village furnished intelligence information to the U.S. military. She was innocent. And there wasn't one of us who made it through that mission who could toss off an "It don't mean nothing" with any degree of authority. All of us who'd been there for a while pretty much felt that our hearts had hardened to stone, that we'd seen so much awfulness that we couldn't feel any more.

That little girl proved that we were wrong. And you know something? That was probably a good thing.

CHAPTER SEVEN

Michelin Man

I was raised in a religious family. We attended the First Assembly of God Church in Granbury, Texas, went every Sunday morning, and also on Wednesday nights. I went because my family went, not because I was so religious. I really didn't have a lot of choice in the matter. If I wanted to get along with my parents, I'd go to church with them. I'm not even sure at what level I believed in God then, but how many eighteen-year-olds really do? You believe in your friends, you believe in girls, and you believe in cars. It was an *American Graffiti* life; even the news reports from Vietnam, the body counts, the assassinations of Martin Luther King and Bobby Kennedy, the antiwar demonstrations didn't make a significant impact.

Sitting in a hooch almost ten thousand miles from Granbury tends to give you a different perspective on what's important in life. With my second sniper assignment behind me, my life had radically changed. First, the two mystery men pop my cherry by having me kill an NVA officer. That must have been my test. Too bad I passed it. The next assignment they give me is to kill a woman. And I do it, no questions asked. That's gotta be as bad as it can get.

Mitchell, you dumb shit, you're wrong again.

We'd been out on patrol for forty-eight hours. Forty-eight miserable, stinking, wet, unproductive, monsoon rain–filled hours, and the entire squad was looking forward to a chance to get into some clean clothes, eat some hot chow, and just kick back. We were almost at the base camp when the radioman walked past me, up to the squad leader, and gave him the handset. He listened a bit, then came back to me, placed his hand on my shoulder, and said that the platoon sergeant wanted to see me when we got back in.

When you're living like we were in Vietnam, small pleasures can make your day, like using a three-holer instead of doing a squat-and-dump in the bush; showering with lukewarm water; putting on a pair of dry socks; or getting a cup of coffee out of a pot in the mess hall rather than having to make it yourself from the C-ration amenities packet. When it appears that for no good reason you have been singled out to be denied one or more of these pleasures, exasperation can set in.

I was irritated. I'd already jumped to the conclusion that the captain was going to hand me my special rifle and send me someplace where I would probably die. It was a good bet that helicopters weren't going to be flying in this weather, so I figured any travel would be by road, which meant I was going to be wet, uncomfortable, and extremely vulnerable. I asked the squad leader if I had time to change clothes and get a cup of coffee. He had no objections. In weather like this, he said, another thirty or forty minutes probably wouldn't make any difference.

I was sitting in the mess hall, enjoying a cigarette with my coffee, when the company clerk came in, sat down with me, and offhandedly mentioned, "The old man is not happy waiting for you." I may have been unhappy, but getting my company commander pissed off at me would definitely not have a positive impact on my situation, so I double-timed it over to the orderly room.

When I walked in, the captain handed me the rifle and told me there was a jeep waiting at the west gate. Great. I slogged through the deluge all the way across the compound, where I found the vehicle. In it were the same two smug anonymous guys who gave me my assignment on the last two missions. As we drove off, I felt a little confused. Was I the second? The spotter rather than the shooter? Where were we picking up the other guy? I was curious because it would give me a chance to see where he was based, even if I didn't know precisely what unit he was in. It's not that it mattered, just that I'd begun connecting the dots and trying to figure out what was going on, and I saw an opportunity here to gather some personal intel.

As we rolled down the road in the pouring rain, the guy behind the wheel started the briefing, and I noticed how nervous his partner seemed to be. Then the lightbulb went off and I understood: He was going to be the second on this mission. I tapped him on the shoulder and said, "Make sure you listen close." He just gave me a dirty look, and the driver laughed. I was right. The other guy was going with me on this one, and he wasn't happy about it.

Lighting a cigarette in the pouring rain was a trick and a half. Even though the canvas top was up, the jeep had no doors, and the poncho I had on was hardly keeping me dry. I kept waiting for the usual information about the target, but the driver just danced all around it, which did nothing to lower my anxiety level. I'd figured out after the first mission that these guys didn't care whether I lived or died. They weren't ugly about it; it's just that on their to-do list, making sure Gary Mitchell was upright when he went home to Texas was somewhat less than a high priority. The fact that one of them was going to put his ass on the line right next to mine was almost enough to make me smile.

We stopped at a compound to fill the jeep's gas tank, then got back on the road heading for the giant U.S. Army base at Long Binh, about twenty miles northeast of central Saigon, and just three or four miles from the U.S. Air Force base at Bien Hoa. I'd been on operations in the rubber plantations in this area, and wasn't thrilled about driving through them in a lone jeep. But after almost two hours on the road, we made it to the base without any problem, ending up at transient billeting. The briefer handed me a plastic bag and said

I had a bunk reserved. He'd keep the rifle and they'd pick me up the following morning. Before I could even get out of the rain, the two spooks had pulled away.

I was assigned a bunk, and after I found it I opened my plastic bag of goodies. A razor, shaving cream, deodorant, soap, and a towel, all new. I guess these guys wanted their snipers smelling springtime fresh. (I know, the notion of a sniper using any scented personal-hygiene product doesn't smell right. In today's army, they wouldn't allow it; they don't even accept smokers into sniper training now. But this is now and that was then, and I always had the feeling that they were making a lot of the rules up and ignoring all of the existing rules as they went along.) There were also ten dollars in military payment certificates (MPC) in the bag. This was the currency issued to our armed forces in order to keep greenbacks off the black market. I took my first really hot shower in a couple of months, dressed, and, since the rain had finally stopped, decided to look around.

The army in Vietnam served three types of rations. Cs were small cans packed in a cardboard box—one box was one full meal for one GI. Bs were essentially Cs, but in unit-sized containers, and mostly had to be reconstituted in a central kitchen. As were the meals we dreamed about. Fresh meat. Fresh vegetables. And wonder of wonders, fresh milk. This is what they were serving in the mess hall at Long Binh, and I wasn't shy about taking advantage of the opportunity. After downing at least half a steer and more fresh milk than I ever thought a guy could drink at one sitting, I decided to take in a movie.

Hard to believe that the guys stationed at Long Binh were in the same army I was. We called them REMFs, and in Vietnam there were roughly ten of them for every guy in the bush. That night, I joined the REMFs at the movies. They were showing a Western starring Gary Cooper; they had a popcorn machine. For almost two hours I was able to forget why I was in Long Binh and what I was going to be doing the next day.

When the movie ended, I went to the Enlisted Men's Club and was tempted to have a cold beer. You know those beer commercials that play on TV, the ones that show a close-up of an ice-cold, sweating bottle of beer, with drops of moisture dripping slowly down the side? That's how tempting the beer was at the club. But I didn't know what was in store for me in the morning, so I opted for a Coke. Didn't want anything cluttering up my thought processes. I was hoping to survive the next day and wanted to do what little I could to increase my odds. Yeah, I knew that Coke has caffeine in it, but by now you probably realize that I'm a heavy coffee drinker—definitely not decaf—so I wasn't concerned about the effect of a little more caffeine from the Coke.

Every so often I'd reflect back on what my life had been like just a little more than a year earlier, when I'd been a relatively carefree kid in Texas. That kid was gone, and I was no longer sure who I really was, what I'd become—and why, and what kind of future I might have.

They woke me at 0500 the next morning. I took another hot shower, shaved, and tried not to drown in the rainstorm as I walked to the mess hall for breakfast. I've always been blessed with a good appetite, and the mission ahead of me didn't change that. When I finished, I went back to the transient billeting area to wait for the people I had begun to call superspooks.

Shortly after noon they pulled up in the jeep and I climbed in. The rain that had started again during the night still hadn't let up, and we could barely see out the windshield. I knew we were heading south out of Long Binh, probably on the Vung Tau cutoff, past the village of Bear Cat. Three or four miles southeast is the town of Long Thanh, and between the two on the northeast side of the road is nothing but rubber plantations at least three miles deep.

When we reached the plantation area, the driver slowed to a crawl. He was obviously looking for something or someone. When he spotted a tiny road, he turned in. Now I was really unhappy. The rubber plantations were a living reminder of the French Colonial era—some of the largest still carried the Michelin name—and it was no secret that the Viet Cong had tunneled beneath many of them. My unit had fought battles in a number of the plantations, and in the end, the VC always managed to just disappear as though they'd evaporated. It was uncanny and never failed to unnerve us. Taking a slow jeep ride through one of these plantations without additional security was stupid—hell, I was the only one with a rifle, and even though the spooks were carrying sidearms, I had no confidence that they knew how to use them.

When we got about a quarter mile off the main highway, we came to a Buddhist monastery in the middle of a large clearing. "This is where you get off," said the briefer. He'd already given us a map, but it showed only one single dot. Missing was the second dot that on the two previous missions had designated the pickup point. The weather was so bad that helicopters probably weren't flying, so maybe there was no point in designating the extraction point. But its absence was definitely not a confidence builder.

I looked at the briefer and asked again about the target and the pickup. I'd already figured out that I was expendable, and I didn't think I could question the assignment, but if they were going to cut my head off, I had no intention of stretching my neck for them. I'd come to believe that the army owed me a chance to make it out alive. The driver pointed to an elderly, lone monk wearing a traditional saffron robe who was approaching us, and said that he would show us the target and where we would be picked up. "Trust him," the chief spook said. "He's loyal to the South. He and the others have been providing intelligence for years, and they've never been wrong. Just do what they say, when they say it."

With that the jeep drove off, and the monk beckoned my newbie second and me to follow him into an outlying building, where he pulled back a carpet and opened a well-concealed tunnel entrance in the wooden floor. I'd been down a tunnel before and could recall nothing pleasant about the experience. This assignment was getting worse by the moment.

The spook looked down, just sort of shrugged his shoulders, and jumped into the tunnel. There was a wooden ladder but we really didn't need it going down.

As I jumped in, I remember thinking, *Okay, we're all gonna die anyway.*

It was a large tunnel—much larger than the one I'd had to crawl through. There were probably still a couple inches of headroom when I stood straight up. We walked for about twenty yards and then the tunnel made a ninety-degree right turn, went another few yards, and made a left turn. There were two more turns and we entered a chamber about a third the size of a cheap motel room.

The room was lit by electric lights and stocked with C-rations, water, a couple of cots, and a civilian radio that the spook was able to tune to Armed Force Radio Vietnam (AFVN). It looked like the U.S. government had prepared the whole setup. I don't know where the air came from—I couldn't see any vents—but oxygen didn't seem to be a problem.

The monk said, "Wait here, and I'll come back and get you." That was a bad moment. We were in the rubber plantation, underground in a hostile area, and he was just going to go away and leave us? Now wouldn't that irritate the warts off of a toad's ass?

I finally drank some water, ate some Cs, and tried to pry information out of my second. "What's the deal with no target?" I asked. He didn't respond. What I'm thinking is that we're not coming back from this mission. I know it's beginning to sound like an obsession, but consider the circumstances and cut me some slack, okay? We've got one dot on the map where the kill is supposed to happen, and nothing to indicate transportation home. It says to me, "Mitchell, you're on a one-way ticket." But I didn't raise hell 'cause I was too scared and didn't want to rock the boat. Later in my career I'd have said, "It's my fucking boat; I'll turn this son of a bitch over if I want to. Let's get some answers." But most nineteen-year-olds don't mouth off like that, which is why they send nineteen-year-olds to war. So I did what GIs do under circumstances like this: I went to sleep. At least I could be well rested for my crossing of the River Jordan.

About four in the morning, the same monk came back. He told us that we must move very quietly so as not to disturb the sleep of the other monks, making it clear that not all of them were as loyal to the South as he was. He assured us that he and the other loyal monks knew which ones had to be watched, and they were very careful about it.

Great, I thought. *I'm underground in an area that's controlled by the VC, inside a monastery that may have VC posing as monks, or monks who are actually loyal to the cause of the VC, and now I'm supposed to go for a walk.*

Had I been more politically aware, I might have been able to figure out what was going on. But that would have required that I followed the politics of America's involvement in Vietnam, and even though my rifle and I were the physical embodiment of American foreign policy, like most kids my age I had no interest in international politics. I didn't pay attention to the changes of government in Saigon, and the active role the United States had played. And I didn't know anything about the Buddhists who were opposed to the war and our involvement in it. I just wanted to go home.

When a seventy-three-year-old monk named Thich Quang Duc assumed the lotus position in a busy Saigon intersection in 1963, had gasoline poured over his saffron robes, and then struck a match, immolating himself, I was still in grade school. The monk's very public suicide was the first of many demonstrations Vietnam's Buddhists held against the Catholic-run government and its principal backer, the United States. Six years after Quang Duc's death, Buddhist monks were still a thorn in the side of the Saigon government, and had I been paying attention, I could have figured out what I was doing there with my sniper rifle listening to one monk tell me there were others in this monastery who were not loyal to the South.

While I hadn't figured out the politics, I had concluded that this was my last mission, because there was no way to escape. The fact that I'd survived my first two killing assignments was no comfort. I had one rifle with two twenty-round magazines, but this time my second didn't have an M-16. Once again, we had no grenades, no radio, no signal flares. Was I scared? You couldn't have driven a straight pin up my ass with a ten-pound sledgehammer.

The three of us retraced our steps back to the trapdoor and climbed the ladder. The monk led us around the outside of the monastery and said we had to follow him in the darkness through the rubber plantation. Now this was not wise. I was sure of that. The VC moved at night; that was when army units set up ambushes. This monk might know what was going on inside his monastery, but he couldn't possibly know what VC units in the area were doing. Nevertheless, like a sheep going to slaughter, I followed him.

We walked in silence for about forty minutes until we reached the base of a huge rubber tree that concealed the opening to yet another tunnel. Down we went. We traveled underground for a pretty good distance before we came to the end of the tunnel and emerged next to another large tree. In the morning twilight I could make out that our position overlooked a relatively small, open area. Mercifully it wasn't raining, and we could see down a well-used trail on the other side. The monk told us to wait for him there. He said it might be a couple of hours, but we should wait patiently—and no smoking. The smell would attract any VC in the area and lead them right to us.

We sat down on the ground and waited for a very tense hour. I nearly launched into orbit when the monk suddenly spoke to us. He'd managed to return without making a sound. I have no idea where he came from; he was just there. He told us that in about another hour, five monks would be coming past our location. They would be wearing their bright orange robes with hoods over their heads.

"You must kill the other four," he told us.

"The other four?" I asked.

"Yes, we're all monks."

It took a second for it to sink in. This monk was going to be coming down the trail with four other monks; all dressed alike, all wearing hoods. I was to kill the other four.

"But what if I can't tell which one you are?" I asked.

"Shoot all of us. We will be coming down the trail."

At that moment it didn't register that this monk who was loyal to our government had just told me that, if it appeared that I had no other choice, I should kill him. Even if it had registered, I'm not sure that I would have argued with him. There was no time.

Then he calmly told us that after the shooting, we should go due west for about one and a half kilometers, to a clearing. We should wait there for a helicopter to pick us up. Checking our map, I could see that there was, indeed, a clearing precisely a klick and a half to the west. We would have to cross a stream to get there, but it should be a quick trip.

I was not very receptive to the idea of shooting monks. It would be like walking through the town where I now live and going to the Catholic church to get the priest. Then you go over to the Assembly of God church and you get the minister. And you go to the Episcopal church and you get their priest. And you go down the road to the synagogue and get the rabbi, and you take them all out and shoot them. I was having an even harder time dealing with the fact that the monk who had guided and protected us said that if we couldn't positively identify him, we should shoot them all. I flashed back to that engraved Zippo someone had shown me, the one that said SHOOT 'EM ALL AND LET GOD SORT 'EM OUT. At this moment, that seemed like a very bad joke.

My mind was reeling with all sorts of thoughts—most of them

ugly. Foremost was the notion that somebody in command, somewhere, didn't care whether or not I came back alive. A sniper's survival depends on his ability to fire one shot, make the kill, and move. While the people you're shooting at may be able to ascertain the general direction a single shot came from, they can't be sure where you are. Firing a second shot is tantamount to waving a red flag and yelling, "Hey, asshole, we're over here!" Firing four shots—maybe more if I missed on one of them—is suicidal. Then there was the matter of deliberately killing this man who was on our side. How could I do that? I panicked, my brain racing. I had to figure something out right this second. I looked at my spotter. Here's a guy who has to be making the big bucks. He's supposed to have the big picture. "You got any ideas?" It was not so much a question as a plea. He shook his head. No help there. I looked back at the monk, examining him from head to toe. Nothing. Not a single thing that would distinguish him from his brothers through my scope.

Then it dawned on me. Not a perfect solution, but one that increased his chances of living another day. "If my first shot isn't you, throw your hood off and run like hell and we'll try to pick you out." He smiled at us and walked back down the trail.

I turned to my second and said, "Did he just tell us that if we can't identify him, to kill all of them?"

And he said somberly, "I believe he did."

"I guess that proves that some people think that there are some things worth dying for," I responded. Still hoping that the spook had figured out something better, I asked, "Do you think you'll be able to spot our guy?"

My question was a waste of good breath. "We'll have to wait and see," he said.

It was beginning to dawn on me why the chief spook hadn't given me my target when he picked me up. If I'd had twelve hours to dwell on what I was being asked to do, maybe he thought I might refuse. But we were already in the middle of the rubber plantation, definitely Indian country, and I didn't have much of a choice. The trick now was to figure out how to accomplish the mission, and get out alive.

I checked my rifle for the thousandth time, popping out the magazine, clearing the round from the chamber, loading it back into the mag, then ramming the magazine back in, and listening as it stripped the round off the top and seated it back in the chamber. Still no rain, although the skies looked like they could open up at any moment. The shooting distance was relatively close, perhaps 150 meters. Concealment wasn't going to be an issue because we weren't going to di-di after just one round. My second was showing a lot more deference than he had when he'd been handing out the assignments on my first two missions. "What're you gonna do?" he asked.

"I'm gonna start with the guy in the back and hope it's not our guy."

"When are you gonna do it?"

"We'll wait until they get off the trail and out into the clearing."

I'd decided to start at the rear because when they fall, it's not as much of an alarm to the other people. Yeah, they'll all hear the shot, but it's like if you're hunting ducks. You shoot the one in the rear; the ones in the front don't necessarily know that the one in the rear is down. I also knew that I wanted them to take off running, not lie down or trip and fall over a body in front of them. On the ground they'd make a real small target to shoot at. An upright target—even one that's running—is easier to hit. While it may not sound like brilliant reasoning now, it made sense to this kid from Granbury who was hiding in the middle of a rubber plantation in Vietnam. The suddenly deferential spook certainly didn't have any better suggestions.

A few minutes later we began to hear faint chanting. They were coming. I lay down in a comfortable firing position. This was going to take either four or five shots, as quickly as I could get them off.

I was terrified. Scared that I wasn't up to the shoot. They were monks, after all. I was concerned we might not be able to spot the friendly monk. It was bad enough killing like this, but to kill someone who protected you, who helped you—how could I live with myself after that?

As they came into sight, I was watching through my scope, moving it from the face of the monk at the rear of the procession, quickly to number four, then three, two, and one. But the shadows thrown by the hoods prevented me from seeing their faces. Desperately I worked my way back to number five. No luck. I took my eye away from the scope and looked at my second. He had his scope up and was also scanning the monks.

"Yes?" I asked hopefully.

"No. They all look the same."

I couldn't wait a second longer. I leaned into the scope, put the crosshairs on the chest of number five, and squeezed the trigger. Feeling the recoil and sensing the spent cartridge automatically ejecting as the next round was seated, I moved the rifle slightly and saw that the rearmost monk was down. Out of the corner of my eye I saw number two throw his hood back. Even before he could break into a run, my second said, "Do you have him?"

I mumbled a yes as I swung the rifle to the right, putting the crosshairs on the chest of number one, and almost instantly pulled the trigger. He went down and our monk went running past him. By this time they were all running, squealing, yelling incomprehensibly. I picked up another target, number four, and shot again. A miss. The spook said nothing. I mumbled to myself, "Calm down, asshole! Just do it so we can get out of here!" Following number four through the scope, I led him just a bit and squeezed. He went down.

One more to go. I fired and as he went down our friend ran by us. He was crying. There were horrific sounds coming from the clearing. I looked back and saw that the second monk I'd shot—number one in the procession—was on the ground, twitching like a dog that had been hit by a car. It hadn't been a solid hit. It slammed him down, but he just lay there, shuddering and making an agonizing, hideous death rattle. For a second as I took in the scene, I imagined that I was seeing my pastor from Granbury lying there, writhing in pain, and the sick feeling that passed over me is indescribable.

The amazing thing was that in the heat of the moment, I could take it all in, all of it. See it and hear it. Even smell it. On some missions things went into extreme slow motion, and sometimes they went into warp speed. This whole shoot couldn't have taken five seconds, but it felt like an hour in slow-mo. We needed to give our guy a chance to get away so it wasn't just "bang-bang-bang-bang." It was "bang-bang, pause, bang-bang." And in the rubber plantations, sound seems to echo; it's magnified. Anyone within a couple of miles would have heard the shots. We had to hope that they'd have trouble figuring out what direction they were coming from.

Then there was the blood. It has its own smell. Some say it's like copper. It's distinctive, and we could smell it, almost taste it.

I should have been up and running, but for a small eternity everything just stopped. Then the second said, "Four for four," confirming that the wounded monk had died. I snapped out of my brief stupor and we took off running due west, wondering if our monk was waiting for us somewhere down the trail.

We had traveled about two hundred meters when we saw him. He was sitting with his knees drawn up and his arms wrapped around them, his head pressed to the left side of his knees, rocking back and forth with tears rolling down his cheeks. It was obvious that he was horrified at what he'd done. Everything that had just happened flew in the face of his Buddhist precepts. *Avoid killing any living thing. All tremble at violence. Life is dear to all. In times of war give rise in yourself to the mind of compassion, helping living beings abandon the will to fight.*

He looked up at us and gave a slight nod, and then stood and started down the trail. I had assumed he was elderly, but I had a hard time keeping up with him. He moved quickly, with long strides, and instinctively we found ourselves stepping in his footprints. For one thing, the maneuver conceals the number of people in a group.

For another, if he stepped there and didn't set off a mine or booby trap, it must be safe.

I'd barely noticed that rain was now coming down with a vengeance. It was so heavy we could hardly see ahead of us, which was why we suddenly broke out into the clearing where our ride was supposed to be waiting. Despite the weather, a Huey was there. The monk turned around and sort of bowed to us, and he was gone.

I'd learned during my relatively short time in country that you're not out of the woods till you're out of the woods. One look at the pilots told me that getting off the ground and safely back to base in this weather was not going to be a slam dunk. They looked as frightened as we were, and if they were scared, I just knew I should be terrified. Conditions were absolutely below acceptable minimums for flying, visibility was zero, and clouds were down to the ground. As they cranked the engines up and lifted off, it was a certainty that they were flying blind. How the aviators navigated back to Long Binh is something I don't even want to know. When we landed, the senior spook met us at the airfield. He took the rifle and gave me another plastic bag, and then the two of them drove me back to the transient billets. The last thing he said to me was, "I'll pick you up tomorrow morning." That was it. No questions, no comments.

I dropped my stuff on a bunk and went over to the EM Club, where I sat alone and drank several beers. Didn't talk to anyone. Just drank and thought about what I'd done. I knew right then that I'd remember, until I drew my last breath, the cries of anguish from the monk who had guided us. The four that I killed had different political opinions, but they were still his brethren. And I guess it would've been like taking four members of my own squad and setting them up to be killed. What kind of person can do that? You've got to be dedicated to a cause. That cause has to mean more to you than your very life. It's still amazing to me.

But just as I question how the monk could do what he did, I know there are people who will question how I could do what I did. And it all goes back to the standard answer: "Training, training, training." A psychologist might call it: "Conditioning, conditioning, conditioning." You're taught from the first day you're in the military to respond, and respond immediately, especially in a combat situation, because you don't have time to ask questions and get answers. It's got to be an instantaneous, automatic response without question. So that's what I did. They said, "Do it," and I did it. True, this wasn't the kind of killing that they prepare you for in a pitched battle, where you don't have any time to think about it. This was a preplanned assassination, and in comparison to combat I had plenty of time to think about it, to decide whether it was something I was willing to do. But that same conditioning took over. I'd been given an assignment; I had to carry it out.

I didn't even think about why I would do something so horrendous. And no one cautioned me that decades later I'd be paying a price for that decision, that I'd be second-guessing my actions.

I'm certain that everyone in the military who gets assigned as a sniper hates the thought that people might think you're an executioner. I'm a shooter. A sniper. Not an executioner. But sometimes, I confess, the certainty that was my best defense mechanism thirty-five years ago evaporates. It happens when I make that turn and wind up in a mental cul-de-sac, going in circles. It happens when I relive shooting four Buddhist monks in the middle of a rubber plantation, watching the blood seep onto their saffron robes, hearing the death cries of the one who I didn't kill cleanly. That's when I have to deal with the knowledge that if I were the fly on the wall, watching what I had done, I would say, "You're an executioner." But the fly isn't here—he's in my head. I can't allow myself to call myself an executioner, however irrational that may sound. It may not even make sense to anyone but me, but that's the way it is. I just did what I had to do, and it changed my life forever.

CHAPTER EIGHT

Recovery from the A Shau

Talk about contrasts. I'd spent a little over three months in an infantry platoon, humping through the jungle on search-and-destroy missions, vulnerable to everything and anything the enemy could throw at me, with only a helmet, flak jacket, my buddies, and my M-16 for protection.

Then they transferred me to Phu Bai, promoted me to spec 5, and made me the commander of an M-88 armored recovery vehicle. Now when I go outside the wire I'm surrounded by about fifty-six tons of cast and rolled armor in a twenty-eight-foot-long tracked vehicle powered by a 980-horsepower, 1790-cubic-inch, twelve-cylinder, air-cooled gasoline engine. I wouldn't be so bold as to say the thing was indestructible but . . . it sure was a contrast to the way I had been fighting the war.

Our unit at Phu Bai was responsible for direct support of a variety of units—medical, transport, signal, and supply to mention a few—and, of course, a number of artillery fire support bases (FSB) strung out from the South China Sea almost all the way to Vietnam's western border with Laos.

Without the front lines common to the large unit warfare of WWII and Korea, the American military needed to find a way to have artillery support constantly out in the field to protect infantry units that could be inserted quickly, anywhere, under the somewhat newly developed airmobile concept. The accepted solution to this problem was to secure fire support bases—sometimes just called firebases—in strategic positions throughout the country.

In I Corps, the northernmost sector of South Vietnam, there were many of these, most often secured after significant battles with entrenched North Vietnamese Army units. The 101st Airborne Division headquartered at Camp Eagle, nine kilometers west of Phu Bai, had various units, among them the 1/83rd Artillery, more or less permanently based at FSBs Birmingham, Bastogne, and Blaze.

In July 1969, a few months before I was transferred to Phu Bai, Blaze was turned into a forward supply point for the 3rd Brigade of the 101st. Our maintenance unit was designated as the backup repair facility for armor and tracked artillery vehicles at Blaze, which was roughly twenty-seven kilometers—about seventeen miles from Phu Bai as the Huey flies. I don't remember what the road mileage was; suffice it to say it was longer, slower, and more dangerous than hopping a helo at the Phu Bai–Hue Airfield.

The firebases we supported were in territory that included the dreaded A Shau Valley, well-known as an entry point for North Vietnamese units, troops, and supplies being infiltrated from the north. Each firebase usually had several artillery batteries, firing cannons ranging from the small 105mm Howitzers, which could fire close to the base, to the much-longer-range guns, such as the 155mms and 175mms responsible for supporting ground units operating in its area of responsibility, which might be up to twenty-two miles out. To provide perimeter defense for the artillery, each firebase had a platoon of at least five tanks, as well as an infantry company that was part of a full battalion working the area nearby. The infantry unit, most often from the 101st Airborne, would rotate the companies between the field and the FSB. In addition, each firebase had at least a squad of combat engineers whose sole mission was to keep the jungle a reasonable distance from the perimeter, which was without question a full-time task. The good news for me was that my unit wasn't required to stay out on one of the fire support bases—we went in and out as required.

That's why I was less than thrilled, shortly after being made the commander of one of our M-88s, to be given the assignment of hauling out to Firebase Blaze and bringing back a disabled M-60 tank with a blown engine.

The whole thing about being in charge made me uncomfortable. Not because I didn't think I could do the job, but because I realized that if I made a mistake, made a bad decision, one of my men, one of my friends, could be injured or killed, and what bothered me even more was that I knew a couple of them were married and had children. I was haunted by the notion that my decisions, often made in split seconds, had a direct effect, for good or for bad, on people that I had never met up to that time, and still haven't met some thirty-five years later. For an old man of twenty, this was an awesome responsibility, one that would keep me awake at night.

Departure preparation from Phu Bai was the standard procedure. We made sure we had fuel—the beast was always refueled after returning from a mission, but we double-checked anyway. We made certain that all ammunition had been replenished, oil levels were at the correct levels, and extra oil was stored on the vehicle, and we did a full radio check from each position—commander, driver, mechanic, and rigger. Two of us tended to the .50-caliber heavy machine gun that I'd likely be manning if we got hit, making sure that the head space and timing were properly set. The consequences of improper settings are not pleasant: The gun can be damaged, the gunner can be damaged, or the thing won't fire on full automatic when it's needed the most. We've learned that it pays to take the time to do it right.

Finally, everyone went to the latrine, because pit stops on the road to any of the firebases were not recommended, although given the nature of gastrointestinal systems under extreme stress, sometimes they couldn't be avoided.

We rolled out of the Phu Bai cantonment area by ourselves, no other vehicles, no accompanying escort. Just a long trip on a dirt road that offered numerous opportunities for the enemy to pay us a visit. I guess the theory was that if we got in trouble, air support would be available. At least, I like to think that someone in charge had given some thought to the matter.

As we passed out of the gate, I inserted the ammunition belt into the .50-caliber gun and half cocked it. In order to fire the first round, a .50 has to have the charging handle pulled twice. We rode with it pulled once. If something happened, we had to pull only one more time, which could be done in the blink of an eye.

The M-88 has a maximum speed of roughly twenty-five miles per hour, so if a mission is uneventful—and we always hoped it would be—there's lots of time for one's mind to wander. In my case, as we drove out to Blaze I found myself thinking about life in Granbury, which, from the perspective of being in the middle of a war zone, more and more resembled Mayberry. At one point I found myself almost laughing out loud as I recalled the terror that had torn through my guts when the local Barney Fife pulled me over and made me think that life as I knew it was about to come to a complete halt because I was underage and had a case of Pearl beer in a cooler on the backseat. The perspective check that confronted most of us every day was the surgeon general's warning on the side of every package of cigarettes we smoked. There wasn't one of us chain-smokers who didn't wish that we'd be given the opportunity to live long enough to die of lung cancer.

When we arrived at FSB Blaze, I told the crew that we wanted this to be a quick turnaround. There shouldn't have been any problem getting back home to Phu Bai before dark, but there was no point in lollygagging and tempting fate. I'm a firm believer that Murphy never rests. If it can go wrong, it will, at the worst possible time, and towing a broken-down tank for hours down a dirt road offers lots of opportunities for Murphy to ply his craft.

In less than an hour, my crew had refueled the M-88, prepared the tank for towing, and hooked everything up. The maintenance sergeant signed off on the paperwork, took my receipt for his tank, and we were out of there. With luck, we'd be back in Phu Bai by 1300 hours, in plenty of time to hit the mess hall before it closed. We had a final cup of coffee, and started the trip back.

Everything went fine until we got to the first of a series of hills we had to climb in order to get out of the A Shau Valley. That's when the notion of being back in time for lunch began to diminish. The problem was simple: It had rained the night before, the road was slippery red clay, and with a combined weight of 116 tons (56 for the loaded M-88 and 60 for the Patton tank), our recovery vehicle was running at full RPM and getting no traction. The tracks were simply spinning, which is not a good thing when you're on a narrow road with jungle on both sides. Actually, it wouldn't even be a good thing if we were on Interstate 5 climbing the Grapevine on the highway from Los Angeles to Bakersfield, near where I now live, because once those tracks start spinning, steering and braking control are minimal, and in some cases nonexistent. It tends to get really uncomfortable for the guy who is supposed to be in charge and keep these things from happening.

What I opted to do was back ourselves down to the bottom of the incline, where we took a break in order to try to figure out how to proceed. I called the firebase on the radio and told them we were having problems, and the maintenance sergeant said they'd be right out to help.

I was so focused on the spinning tracks that I hadn't given much thought to security and, just as on the outbound leg of this mission, we had no escort vehicles, no infantry on the ground looking out for us. I knew there was a reason the guys with lots of stripes on their sleeves got the big bucks, because when the sergeant from the firebase arrived, he'd brought a full squad of infantrymen to provide security for us while we worked.

What we decided to do was disconnect the tank from the M-88, drive my vehicle to the top of the incline, and then try to winch the tank up the hill. Setting up for an operation like this sounds simple, but keep in mind that the main winch cable on an M-88 is 1.25 inches in diameter and not that easy for guys on slippery ground to move around. We got the cable on the tank, but before we could back the M-88 up the hill, paying cable out the front, the tow truck from AAA arrived. Okay, so it wasn't from AAA. Just checking to see if you're paying attention. It was a dozer from the combat engineers based at Blaze. After some discussion they maneuvered around and hooked the front of their vehicle to the back of ours.

When we were ready to try it, I had everyone in my crew drop down inside and close the armored hatches over our heads—just in case the cable snapped. The dozer pulled forward, and my driver applied power in reverse, putting tension on the cable. Our combined weight at this point was 138 tons, roughly the takeoff weight of a Boeing 757-200, if you're into meaningless comparisons.

As the dozer accelerated, so did we, and our little-engine-that-could began to pull the tank up the hill. I was quite nervous, especially since we were barely moving and both towing vehicles were putting out as much torque as they safely could. The engineers had the dozer at full acceleration; my driver was giving the M-88 as much gas as possible without losing traction.

We began creeping up the hill, the steel cables fore and aft singing from the stress of the pull. We were moving so slowly that the grunts could leisurely stroll along beside us, perhaps unaware that they were in the danger zone should one of the cables snap.

At some point during this little parade it struck me that we were at the edge of the dreaded A Shau Valley, violating the number one rule for convoys: No matter what happens, keep moving. The top speed we could achieve towing the tank and safely maintaining control was eighteen to twenty miles per hour, reasonably fast for our combined weight, but not so fast that we wouldn't be an easy target if Charlie or the NVA wanted to cause trouble.

My crew was buttoned up inside a vehicle with armor plating that was supposed to stop everything from bullets to rocket-propelled grenades (RPGs). Unfortunately, I was standing in the commander's hatch with the ring mount of the .50-caliber machine gun loosened, so I could spin 360 degrees if necessary, but unlike with the newer M-88s, and even the old M-113 armored personnel carriers, I didn't have any sort of armor-plated cupola to protect me.

While I wasn't exactly comfortable with my own exposure, I realized that if we were attacked, the option was there for me to drop down and button up the hatch. The dozer driver, on the other hand, was sitting out in the open with only a steel cage to protect him from a broken cable.

All this anxiety over the possibility of being ambushed appeared to be wasted, however, when we got to the top of the hill unscathed. My rigger hopped down to help unhook us from the dozer, then jumped back up on the M-88 and dropped into his hatch. As soon as the dozer cleared the road, my driver put the pedal to the metal and we were off. ETA back at Phu Bai had slipped to 1500. So we miss lunch, but we're first in line for dinner.

Or so we thought. Fifteen miles farther down the road, we began having problems again. The tank was not trailing properly and my driver was having a hard time keeping us on the road. He had a very small, oblong steering wheel that controls the treads. Trying to keep us on the road towing the wayward tank is similar to driving a pickup truck on a freeway while towing a trailer that's got a flat tire. Except, of course, we were on a dirt road in Vietnam, not on a freeway, we weighed about fifty times more than the pickup-trailer combination, and, generally speaking, it's unlikely bad guys with guns would be stalking the pickup truck on the Golden State Freeway. Or maybe not.

I asked my driver if he thought we could make it another couple of miles, which would put us near Firebase Bastogne. I told him it would make me feel a whole lot better about dismounting and checking things out if we had a few hundred guys keeping an eye on us, rather than doing it by our lonesome out on the road. He said he'd try, and to his credit, he got us there.

That was when we discovered that one of the final drive shafts on the tank had slipped a bit, making one track drag slightly. As is often the case with sixty-ton tanks or the family car, the diagnosis took longer than the repair, but once we figured it out, we fixed it and got back on our way.

But just as we began climbing the last little hill out of the A Shau, our visions of an early dinner were shattered when we were ambushed from both sides of the road. As the sound of pinging rounds striking the sides of the M-88 and the tank echoed, and richochets were flying in every direction, my driver and crew mechanic dropped down, buttoned up, and, using the periscopes to watch the road, jammed on the gas. While our top speed dragging a tank is twenty miles per hour, you don't get that going uphill. You crawl, and at that moment we were crawling through the kill zone of a well-prepared NVA or VC ambush at a narrowing of the road, where the jungle closed in on both sides.

I was firing to one side with the .50-caliber, and my rigger was firing to the other with the light machine gun. Both of us were doing everything within our power to burn up the barrels when a hand grenade landed on the top deck of the M-88, rolling around between the mounts and various attachments. You might think that with all the gunfire, there'd be no way to hear the grenade, but trust me on this one—you hear it. It's a sickening, metal-on-metal clunk that instantly gets your attention. And when it starts rolling around, you can't help but keep your eyes on it.

Both my rigger and I saw it and yelled, "Grenade!" simultaneously. He dropped inside the crew compartment. I took a fraction of a second to decide that I had to try to get the grenade off the vehicle. It was a foolish decision that someone with the experience I'd had in combat shouldn't have made. But experience just improves the chances that you'll make the right choice under duress; it doesn't guarantee it. It's realistic, not cynical, to say that bad decisions that turn out well often make heroes. The ones that don't turn out well make widows.

I should have done the same thing my rigger did when we saw the grenade: dropped down inside the armored vehicle. The grenade would have exploded within seconds, doing no damage of any consequence, and I could have just popped back up and resumed firing the machine gun. But I didn't.

Arming a grenade is usually a two-step process. The grenade has a spoonlike device that is held in place by the pin. Generally, if you're going to throw one, you'll hold the spoon against the grenade while pulling the pin with your other hand. (Only movie stars are allowed—and are able—to pull a pin using their teeth. Ordinary mortals have to pull it by hand.) Once you pull the pin, you have two choices: You can just throw the thing at the enemy, which, given that the fuse on a U.S. grenade is supposed to burn for eight seconds, might allow time for him to throw it back at you before it blows up; or you can let the spoon fly off into space and count to three before tossing it. This gives the enemy a lot less time to try to toss it back to you.

In this instance, however, I lost the coin toss, and the opposition had decided that I would receive. I had no idea what the NVA or VC field manual for grenades taught them to do, or whether the guy who threw it at us was following the rules, or whether this was a factory-made Chinese Communist version or a homemade job that might have a fuse of arbitrary length. As a result, I had no way of calculating how much time I had before the thing blew up. I can tell you that it was long enough for my life to flash in front of my eyes, but at age twenty, that doesn't take very long.

As I started to reach for it, I could see that the grenade had hung up between the deck of the M-88 and the A-frame lifting boom. There was no way I could get to it with enough time left to get rid of it, so I changed plans, turned, and had started to drop into the hatch when it detonated.

The sound of the explosion was nothing compared to the hot, searing pain I felt on the back of my right shoulder. My first reaction was that I was going to die. I'm not sure whether or not I actually said the words out loud, but the words my mind composed were *Dear God, I'm going to die!*

Very quickly I realized that I'd survived the blast, and the logical part of my brain that had started to function again was telling me that my three crew members were safe, protected from the blast by the heavy armor of our vehicle. I could feel blood running down my back and right arm, but there was no time to stop and evaluate the extent of my wounds. Since I could still move my arms and head, I figured I'd be able to shoot, so the rigger and I popped back up, grabbed the machine guns, and began firing. The only good news at that moment was that the driver was still doing his best to get us out of there. I could tell from the sound of the engine that he had not released the accelerator in the slightest—not even when the grenade went off.

We finally made it to the top of the hill and out of the kill zone, and began to pick up speed. I could hear the difference in the pitch of the engine. That was when the rigger told my crew that I'd been hit. He and the mechanic pulled me down inside the crew compartment to check me out. The rigger ripped my shirt off, and the mechanic climbed up into my hatch to man the .50-caliber gun.

As soon as the mechanic got my shirt off, he could see that my shoulder had taken a lot of shrapnel from the grenade. I could hear the mechanic—who was second in command just for eventualities like this—calling for a medical helicopter. He gave them our position, and told them we were going to keep moving toward Phu Bai.

Since they'd be coming from that direction, we might cut a couple of minutes off the time it would take to get me off the track and on the way to a hospital.

It seemed like hours but was probably only minutes before I sensed more than felt the driver backing off the accelerator and beginning to brake. The instant we stopped, the driver and rigger jumped off the M-88 with their M-3 grease guns to provide what little security they could for the chopper.

The mechanic stayed with me, all the while maintaining radio contact with the incoming aircraft. Once it landed, he crawled around inside the vehicle and popped open the side door, calling for the medic. As soon as he got to us, I crawled out of the vehicle and began walking to the chopper. Given all the blood that was pouring out of my back, I was justified in thinking that the wounds were more severe than they actually were. The medic had given me a cursory check, and when he saw that I could walk, he decided that I was one patient who was going to make it to the hospital alive and repairable. He, of course, was trained to make those judgments. I wasn't—and I was the guy oozing blood. The distinction clearly affected my outlook on life at that moment.

By the time they got me on the Dustoff, the pain had subsided some—or maybe I was a little numb—and the bleeding had pretty much stopped. In circumstances like this, most people tend to fear what they don't know or haven't previously experienced. I'd survived the head wound on the convoy earlier in my tour, and had actually kept driving. But this was completely different. I was sure that I was going to die, and if that didn't happen, then I would never be able to use my arm again. Or they might just take it off. Optimism has never been my strong suit, so for the duration of the entire fifteen-minute ride to the 85th Evacuation Hospital in Phu Bai, I assumed the worst.

My fears were unfounded and luck was with me, because when the medic got me inside the hospital, I had the entire emergency staff to myself: a couple of nurses, one doctor, and several medics. They washed me, put me facedown on a gurney, and wheeled me over to X-ray.

While we were waiting for the film to be developed, the doctor did his best to make me feel better by telling me that he was pretty sure this was not a "million-dollar wound." That's one that's serious enough to get you evacuated to a hospital outside Vietnam, most likely in Japan, and from there back to a military hospital in the States. When the X-rays arrived, they confirmed his judgment. My back might look like raw meat, and I might be in a lot of pain, but it wasn't enough to send me home. If my sense of humor had been intact, I would have said, "Doc, you call that good news?"

What I didn't realize was that the fun hadn't even begun. The doc had to get the little tiny pieces of shrapnel out of my shoulder, and I'm not sure what medical school he went to, but what they taught him was the Braille method of fragment removal. The first step is to send the guy who usually administers anesthetic to do his laundry or see a movie. Then, when there's no chance that someone is going to be available to put me under for the procedure, the doc tells me that he's going to start sticking a probe into the holes in my back, and it's my job to tell him when he's found a chunk of metal. As the doc soon discovered, I speak Texan, broken English, and fluent profanity.

For the next couple of hours I was demonstrating my multilingual proficiency, occasionally at very high decibels, often indicating a familiarity with the doctor's mother and his parents' marital status. When it was all over, there were thirty-two tiny pieces of shrapnel in a basin. Then, in an imitation of every bad TV commercial he'd ever seen, the doc said, "But wait, there's more." Actually, that's not what he said. He just quietly told me that as time passed, more shrapnel would move around in my back, and he'd have to go in and get it.

So on subsequent days, the doc and I had a ritual we'd go through. He'd come in and ask how I was feeling. I'd say, "Fine," and he'd say something along the lines of "Let's see if we can change that." Even though he was proud of his bedside manner, comedy was definitely not his strong suit. Then the doc and his torture team would start the process all over again: X-rays, followed by probing, and then pulling shrapnel out of my back.

At the end of each session, the doctor would tell me that everything was going to be fine. Then the nurses or medics would bandage me, and after they left I'd walk down the hall to the latrine, go into a stall, shut the door, and cry. I became convinced that these painful sessions would end only when the doc felt I couldn't take any more.

Finally, the shrapnel count was up to eighty-one, and my doc made the surprising announcement that he was done with me. "The rest," he said, "will have to work their way out by themselves." Upon hearing this statement, I embarrassed myself by breaking down and crying in front of everyone. The pain in my back was still intense, but the knowledge that they weren't going to put me through the extraction procedure again was just more than I could emotionally handle.

One of the nurses—I wish I could remember her name to thank her properly—walked me back to my bed, put her arms around me, and let me cry on her shoulder. She didn't have to do it; she just did it. That hug did me more good than she will ever know. Or maybe she did know.

About a week later they released me from the hospital, telling me to return every couple of days for physical therapy. The movement in my right shoulder was slow to come back. I healed, but I never did get my entire range of motion back. The holes were so small that there wasn't much scarring, and by now most of them have gone away completely. The doc later told me that if he'd knocked me out and taken me into surgery to remove the shrapnel, it would have left scars that would have never gone away and would have caused additional damage to the tissue. After about two months, I was back to full duty, once again riding the M-88.

CHAPTER NINE

Faces I've Seen

Talk about shitty duty.

Until one has had the pleasure of spending several hours of a beautiful blue-sky morning pouring diesel fuel into the half barrels that serve as collection devices beneath our two- and three-holers, stirring with a paddle until it's thoroughly mixed with an abundance of organically reprocessed B- and C-rations, igniting the concoction, and then tending to its purification by fire, one has not had the shittiest job in this man's army.

Even when I attempt to speed up the procedure by using jet fuel instead of diesel, the nature of the job doesn't improve. Actually, it just turns potentially lethal. I'm not going to go into great detail here, but I ignored the Vietnamese local who'd been hired by our unit and who'd become a pro at the job, and despite his warning shouts of "GI, you dinky-dau, beaucoup dinky-dau" (loose translation: "You're freakin' nuts"), I torched the mixture with my ever-faithful Zippo. He ran fast enough; I didn't. Moments later, as the two of us were extinguishing globs of burning crap that had spread across the landscape, I had a vision of the headline in my home-town newspaper:

LOCAL MAN KILLED IN VIETNAM
BY EXPLODING SHITCAN

How, I wondered, would my parents live that down?

Yes, that had to be the worst job in the United States Army. At least, that's how I thought at the time. That all changed when my section chief at the service and evacuation platoon in the direct support maintenance company to which I'd been transferred at Phu Bai told me that I'd been selected for a special detail. "Report to the company commander," he said. I wasn't happy about this. I had thought that when I moved from the infantry to driving an M-88 recovery vehicle, there'd be no more special assignments from my CO.

I reported to the captain, expecting him to hand me the rifle and tell me that I was to go to the airfield. Instead, he told me that due to heavy combat activity in the area, the Graves Registration section in Da Nang was overworked and underpaid, and I was among a select few from our unit who had volunteered (strange—I failed to recall having volunteered—obviously I was confused) to give them a little help.

Later that morning, three of us boarded a truck, each lugging a duffel bag with enough clothing for a week, and we were off on a two-hour drive to Da Nang. Shortly after lunch we arrived at Graves Registration HQ, and were welcomed by the first sergeant, who had his clerk help us draw linens and get bunks assigned. For a brief moment this TDY was looking good: The beds at Da Nang were larger and more comfortable than the cots we had at Phu Bai.

We were turned over to an E-7, who actually thanked us for coming and said we were really needed. The three of us piled into his jeep and took off on the fifteen-minute ride to the morgue. One of my buddies asked him what we'd be doing there. He just grinned and said, "Anything that's needed."

We pulled up in front of a group of semipermanent buildings that were painted a sterile white. There was a single large sign with one word printed in large black letters:

MORGUE

What the hell am I doing here? I wondered. *Send me back to the infantry. I've got no business or desire to be messing with any dead people.* But here I was, and I was scheduled to be here for an entire week. My mom had always taught me to make the best out of any opportunity I was presented with. Somehow I'm sure she had no concept of this particular possibility.

We were led into the administration area, which didn't look that unusual, just an office space with desks, phones, files, and the like. Why was everyone looking at us and grinning?

Probably because they could see that that the three of us were terrified, and had absolutely no idea what to expect or what might be expected of us. It pissed me off that they were enjoying our discomfort. Then I remembered how we used to treat FNGs about to go out on their first patrol with us. Payback is a bitch.

The E-7 ordered a spec 4 to give us a tour. He didn't seem particularly happy about playing tour guide. He explained that in the office, all the data on each corpse was collected from the various sections and merged into a single file: insurance forms, next-of-kin notification, mortician's report, death certificate, finance and personnel records, shipping instructions, escort requirements, receiving funeral home info if available—everything that it took to receive, prepare, and ship remains to Hawaii, where final preparations would be completed before the shipment to the soldier's or marine's hometown.

From there he took us to supply. I had been in supply areas before, but nothing like this. Body bags, shipping containers, embalming supplies, and shelf after shelf of United States flags.

Next came the personal-effects area. I don't know whether our guide was taking the shortest route through the entire facility, or was deliberately postponing the inevitable, but the longer we could avoid seeing bodies, the happier we would all be. Personal effects is where everything that was on the body at the time of death or hospitalization was collected. The items were inspected to ensure that nothing was government property, nothing was classified, and nothing was pornographic. The remaining effects would go to Hawaii, where they would be packaged with the effects that the deceased's unit sent directly there, and one shipment would then be sent to the next of kin.

We continued on to the Receiving and Identification Branch, where we got our first glimpse of death on a wholesale scale. Here the remains were received from the hospitals, from battalion aid stations, from anywhere that had a dead body to be sent home. There was a helipad to receive bodies being flown in, and loading docks for those being brought by ambulance or truck. This was where unit identification took place. A squad leader, platoon sergeant, or someone else from the guy's unit would physically look at the remains and verify the identification. Fingerprints were also taken and forwarded somewhere to be matched with official records to confirm the ID. Everything possible was done to ensure that a death notification was not sent in error.

My first impression was that there must have been twenty tables in the receiving area, and they were all occupied, with more bodies lying on gurneys outside, waiting their turn. One of my buddies became very ill at this point, ran out the door, and lost his lunch. I was just shocked by the whole scene, but did what I usually do under grossly unpleasant circumstances in which I'm forced to participate—just held it inside.

I'd been on patrols where guys had been killed, but I had never considered the clinical manner in which these things had to be taken care of. There were so many details, major and minor, before a body was sent home. At age twenty, I was getting one more lesson I never wanted in the facts of war.

Next we went to the preparation rooms, where embalming was taking place on a massive scale. I'd never seen anything like it before, but managed to survive the visit without embarrassing myself. In retrospect, that was probably a mistake.

In the shipping area, each prepared body was placed in a body bag, and then into one of the shipping containers. Each body had a tag with ID information that was also entered on a shipping document attached to the outside of the container. Then the container was placed in a cooler to await shipment. Once flight arrangements to Hawaii were made, the container would be removed from the cooler and respectfully covered with one of the flags we'd seen earlier in supply.

Our guide told us that in Hawaii, another ID process would take place; the body would be dressed in the appropriate uniform and placed in a military casket. It, in turn, would be draped with the flag, and the honor escort would then accompany the remains home, while the shipping container would be sanitized and recycled back to Vietnam for further use.

At the conclusion of our tour we went back to the sergeant's office. He looked at the spec 4 and asked him what he thought. That's when I realized that the purpose of the tour was twofold: to show us what went on in the morgue, while assessing our ability to cope with it. His judgment was quick and ruthless. Send my buddy who puked his guts out back to his unit. Send my other buddy who demonstrated serious discomfort in the prep room to work in admin, supply, or shipping.

Then he looked at me, and said I could handle receiving or prep because I didn't get sick and didn't need a babysitter. Had I only figured out their scheme before the tour ended, I could have deliberately lost my lunch, been put on a truck, and been back at Phu Bai in time for dinner.

We were told that new guys started on the night shift, working from six in the evening until four in the morning, with a break for lunch at midnight. To give us a decent shot at adjusting to the overnight work, we were allowed that first night off, and told to stay up as late as possible so we'd be able to sleep the next day in preparation for our first shift in the morgue.

How do you kill time when you're deliberately trying to stay awake? We're Americans. We go to the movies. And what do Americans in a combat zone watch? A comedy? Don't be silly. That night's flick was *The Alamo,* starring celluloid war hero John Wayne. After the movie we shot pool, and then took a ten-minute walk to a club on the base. By one in the morning I couldn't take it anymore. It had been too much of a day, and I was as exhausted as I'd ever been after a forty-eight-hour patrol.

I was up at noon the next day, woke my buddy, had lunch, killed time comparing notes on life and love (he had a girlfriend; I had barely lost my virginity before I enlisted). Then we forced ourselves to eat dinner before reporting to the morgue at 1800 hours.

A spec 5 from Receiving and Identification collected me, and off we went. All of the tables were still full, and I wondered aloud if they were the same bodies I had seen the day before. He sort of laughed, and then told me that bodies were only there for four hours each. "Figure it out," he said. "There are eighteen tables, and there've been two full ten-hour shifts since you were here yesterday. Twenty hours, five bodies per table. Eighteen tables, ninety bodies."

"Ninety bodies?" I repeated incredulously.

"Well, actually things slowed down and there were only about fifty," he acknowledged. My TDY (temporary duty) at the morgue was taking place right around the Vietnamese Tet holiday celebrating the lunar new year, and while fighting in the area had been heavy, it was nothing like the battles throughout South Vietnam during Tet 1968.

I recall being stunned. Fifty is still a lot of dead GIs. But he didn't give me time to worry about it. My assignment that first night, he told me, would be "the easy job. Help unload bodies from vehicles or aircraft and get them on gurneys. Then move bodies from the table to prep, and from the holding area into R and I."

He took me to supply, where they gave me a pair of knee-high rubber boots, a long wraparound rubber apron, and a pair of thick rubber gloves that reached to my elbows. Strangely, I hadn't really noticed what the workers were wearing during my tour of the place, so I wasn't prepared for it.

I spent that entire night moving bodies; we received more than twenty before midnight, another ten before my shift ended at 0400.

On my second night in the morgue they sent me to the prep room. There I was taught how to give each body two baths—one before preparation, and one afterward. Rather than being repulsed by the whole process, I found myself intrigued by what the embalming technicians were able to do. There were guys who were burned, maimed, with large and small holes and every other condition of bodily destruction and deterioration that I might imagine in my worst nightmare. When the bodies came into the morgue, they were often in shocking condition. But the embalmers were able to make them look more like they were asleep than in pain or distress. When all was said and done, in many cases the remains that left the Da Nang morgue were viewable by family and friends. I suppose that's one of the things that made working at the morgue tolerable—the thought that you weren't just mechanically preparing a body to go from point A to point B, where it would be buried, but making it possible for a family to conduct what was considered to be the standard American funeral, complete with open casket, and take what comfort they could in the experience.

By the end of that second night, I had developed an interest in how it was done, and for the next three nights I worked in the prep room, learning more and more. But I also learned something about what man was capable of doing to man, realizing that I'd been trained in, and was successful at, doing some of these very things; now I was seeing the hideous results of someone else's training.

At the end of the week I was more than ready to go back to my unit and drive a recovery vehicle, back to the infantry and ambush patrols in the jungle, or anywhere else in the country that didn't require me to handle dead bodies. I went by the orderly room on the afternoon prior to my final shift and asked how I was going to get back to Phu Bai in the morning. That was when I received the bad news: I'd done such a good job I wouldn't be going back for a while. My assistance in the morgue had been requested for another two weeks. You'd think I would have learned a lesson from what happened following my success at sniper training. But it never crossed my mind to deliberately screw up, even though it would have saved me a lot of agony. This work ethic is a character flaw that I should probably work on.

By the end of my second week, I was handling the less difficult cases under the watchful eye of one of the embalmers. They'd seen that I had both an interest and a talent for the work, and were happy to have the help. A week later I was doing a large number of all but the most difficult cases alone. You guessed it. They wanted me to stay, but I managed to convince them that my company commander and first sergeant were getting annoyed that I hadn't been returned to regular duty at my unit, so they let me go.

During my three weeks in the Da Nang morgue, I learned more about war than I learned from everything I'd done before and after in the military. I can still see the faces, some young, others older, all of them frozen in death. I don't know their names, where they were from, whether they were single or married, with or without kids, but I can still see each one of them when I shut my eyes. Their injuries, the grotesque positions in which some breathed their last breath, even the color and smell of death. Yes, the smell was sometimes almost more than I could stand, and the odors of the prep room are embedded in my sense memory. For years after my morgue experience

I couldn't eat ham. There was something about the smell that triggered a flashback to my TDY in Da Nang.

I found myself thinking the same kinds of thoughts about the men I helped prepare that I had after each of my sniper missions. But I could relate to these men more, because they were like me: They wore the same uniform I did, spoke the same language I did. None of them would ever again walk down a street in the sunshine, never have children or grandchildren. They'd never kiss a girl, laugh with a friend, drive a car, or see a movie. They'd never be any more than they were on the day they died. It didn't matter whether they had died quickly or slowly, in the field or in a hospital, feeling horrific pain or not. For them it was over. They were just dead.

In my mind's eye I can still see the faces of more than a hundred men, all races, probably all religions. Some died as heroes; some were just in the wrong place at the wrong time, but they were all equal in death. I believed they were all mourned by those they left behind: mothers and fathers, wives, sons and daughters, brothers and sisters, friends and colleagues, who deep down—outward appearances and patriotic statements notwithstanding—would wonder if their loved one's death had real meaning. Because without it, I wondered, can there be any solace?

CHAPTER TEN

My Decision

It was another hot day when my M-88 crew drew the assignment to head out to Firebase Blaze and bring in a self-propelled artillery piece that needed a new gun tube and a new engine. The artillery boys at Blaze had actually blown the engine on the 155 a couple of days earlier, but since the gun tube still had some rounds remaining before it had to be changed, the decision was made to finish the tube off and then send it in to have all the work done at one time.

I'd been working with the same crew since I arrived at Phu Bai. There was our driver, Bill, from New York, married with one child. We were about the same age, but he weighed a lot more than the 135 pounds I carried soaking wet.

The mechanic on our M-88 was also named Bill. He was tall and slender with blond hair, also married. Our rigger was Dave, from either Kentucky or Tennessee. He was strong as a bull ox, but quiet, with a great sense of humor.

My platoon leader's plan for our day was an ambitious one. We were supposed to get an early start, get out to FB Blaze, rig the gun for towing, drag it back to Phu Bai, where mechanics would change the engine and the gun tube, and then we were to tow it back to the firebase before dark. It's not that they needed to use it that night—it's just that no one with good sense would want to be ambling down the road outside of an American base perimeter after dark.

Murphy must have been off duty when we were driving out to Blaze, because nothing at all went wrong: The M-88 drove the way it was supposed to; the enemy didn't have any en route surprises for us; even the weather cooperated. We made excellent time getting out there, and when we arrived they had the gun ready for us to tow. All we had to do was refuel, hook up, grab some coffee, and start back. We typically never had any security escort for these missions. There might be a tow truck or even an M-578 light recovery vehicle with us, but nothing with any real firepower. Everybody was equipped with radios and guns, so I guess the theory was that we could call for help and fight off the bad guys while waiting for it to arrive.

We were about halfway back to Phu Bai when the scariest thing in the world happened. We hit a land mine!

For a split second I couldn't breathe. I don't know whether the explosion just sort of instantly sucked up all the air, leaving us in this vacuum, or whether I was so scared that I just forgot to breathe. The explosion was deafening. For a few moments—I couldn't honestly say whether it was seconds or a couple of minutes—I know I was deaf, and it took a while for my hearing to return to normal. I remember it ramping up slowly, as though someone were turning up the volume on a radio. (Actually, my hearing never did return to the way it was before the explosion; it's a problem that I'm dealing with decades after Vietnam.)

It seemed as though my vehicle and crew were in a huge bubble—or maybe it was just the dust cloud from the blast. We were wearing dust goggles that somehow managed to stay on when the mine went off. If they hadn't, who knows what would have happened to us? I was suddenly struck with the realization that we'd been blown up by a command-detonated mine. That might not have been the case, but since we were immediately attacked after the explosion, it seemed to be a reasonable conclusion to draw. Sure, it could have been your basic pressure-detonated mine that they had planted and just waited for a piece of equipment to run right over it, but at the time that didn't make as much sense as thinking that someone had waited for just the right moment to hit the switch and try to blow us to kingdom come. In any event, a fraction of a second after I'd decided it was a command-detonated mine, we were being raked with rifle and machine gun fire. There we were, in the kill zone of a single-side ambush.

The first thing that happens is panic. It feels like the world is coming to an end. At age twenty, I was experiencing fear that can be understood only by a person who has experienced combat. All kinds of things go through your mind. Am I going to die? Am I going to be wounded? Am I going to screw up? What do I do now? All of that is instantaneous—then, out of reflex/training, you begin to do all of the things you need to do without even thinking, because consciously you don't know whether to shit or go blind, or maybe both.

Sometimes things go into superspeed, and other times they slow down in a slow motion that is so precise that you can see each and every movement. While Dave and I were returning fire, the other two guys had dropped into the vehicle, with our driver trying to do what he could to make the beast move. If it's possible to pray and curse at the same time, I did. Or maybe I alternated between the two. I'm sure God could figure out which words were intended for him and which for the bastards who were trying to kill us at that moment, so I wasn't going to worry about it.

Once I had the panic under control, I tried to figure out where the enemy was, while at the same time screaming into the open hatch for Bill to get us out of there. Talk about multitasking. Even as I was shouting at him, another part of my brain was processing the fact that one of the sounds I heard was our own engine at full acceleration. But there was another, really ugly sound of links from our right track slapping the metal hull. The mine had broken the track, and we weren't going anywhere under our own power.

I had automatically grabbed the butterfly handles on the .50-caliber machine gun, spun around in the cupola, and begun firing into the wood line where our attackers were hiding. A quick glance to my right and I could see that Dave was manning the light machine gun, and it dawned on me that neither of us had been hit. I yelled at the guys inside to get us more ammunition, not realizing that our mechanic was already breaking open the metal ammunition boxes. As the last rounds in the belt were fired, he was already handing up the lead end of a new belt for the .50, and then doing the same for Dave's M-60 machine gun.

Describing it makes it seem as though everything were neat, ordered, and sequential, but that's not the way it is. It's all happening at once. Every single one of my senses was firing on full automatic. I could see it, hear it, touch it, taste it, and smell it simultaneously, and my brain was on overload. I knew for sure from my time with the cav that there were no atheists in foxholes. At that moment I wasn't sure if prayer would help, but I also knew that I had to chance that it did. Praying in a circumstance like that wasn't something I *decided* to do; I just did it while I was firing the .50. Must've been that religious upbringing that my folks gave me as I was growing up. Truth be told, I was a terrified kid who, until that moment, had convinced himself that he was a man.

It took an event like this one for me to understand the song lyric that goes "Praise the Lord and pass the ammunition," because I think we were all doing both.

Dave and I were burning through ammunition as fast as the two Bills could hand it to us. What you hope is that you're knocking them dead, but you can't see anything because the wood line comes almost right up to the edge of the dirt road. Unfortunately, there must have been a lot more of them than our two guns could handle, because they began advancing toward us. They had intermittent cover and were advancing to our side. I kept looking to see if any of the attackers would break cover and run onto the road in front of or behind us, but they didn't.

When we could catch a glimpse of them, we saw they were wearing traditional Vietnamese peasant clothing, not uniforms. Some had rifles and one or two had AK-47s. While we felt as though an entire division were there, intent on shooting us to pieces, there were probably only ten or twelve of them. Some of the time they would shoot as they advanced, and other times they would shoot from behind a tree or in a depression. I saw at least one go down, but I couldn't tell if it was Dave or me who hit him, not that it matters under those circumstances. What I can tell you is that someone figured out that the American military in Vietnam fired fifty thousand bullets for every enemy soldier killed. On that day we did nothing to help lower the ratio. We fired continuously, reloading as fast as humanly possible and burning our way through another belt of ammo. As I moved the gun onto the deck of the M-88, the brass was dropping all around, down through the hatch, sometimes hitting me as it sprayed from the gun and bounced around. I didn't have time to worry about whether I was getting burned, because that would have been the least of my problems.

We were clearly outnumbered. The enemy had at least a dozen guys firing weapons, we had two, and I felt a sense of panic rising in me like acid roiling out of my stomach and up into my throat. Despite the fire Dave and I were pouring at them, one of the enemy popped up right at the side of the M-88 and began firing right at us with his AK-47.

Dave was hit in the chest by a couple of rounds and dropped down into the rigger's compartment. The mechanic who had been passing ammunition jumped up and grabbed the M-60, while Bill, the driver, took over the task of both opening ammunition cans and passing the belts up to the two of us.

We just needed to end this thing in order to be able to try to keep Dave alive, and the enemy was definitely not cooperating. I could see more of them moving toward us through the wood line, and I spun the .50 around and cut loose. When a .50-caliber bullet hits a human, it is devastating. Not only do you see the hole punched into living flesh; you see the target fly backward from the impact. A .50-cal is a half inch in diameter; it's a huge round. If it doesn't kill you, it will certainly make you wish you were dead. At some time during the skirmish, I'm sure I thought about the fact that I was killing or wounding someone, but I can't be positive—maybe this is just another little demon that plays with me in my older years.

My heart was beating so hard I swear I could hear it over the spitting of the machine gun. I used to wonder how soldiers could function in the middle of a battle like this. Now I realize that it's not a choice. Not a real one, anyway, because the self-preservation instinct is impossible to overcome. You can keep fighting, or give up and die. Remember what General Patton said to his troops—a line made famous, coincidentally, in the movie that was released in February 1970, somewhere around the time I found myself under attack in the M-88: "No bastard ever won a war by dying for his country. He won it by making the other poor dumb bastard die for his country."

I didn't think about winning the Vietnam War while I was hanging on to that .50-caliber, but I sure hoped and prayed that I was going to make a bunch of Charlies die for their country; and I guess that at some point they decided that the cost of killing Gary and friends was going to be too high on this day, or they knew that they had screwed with us enough, so they fell back.

The instant that happened, we checked our ammunition, and both Bills dragged Dave up onto the deck, where they could better administer first aid. While they were doing what they could for him, I grabbed the radio and desperately tried to contact Phu Bai Dustoff. If Dave was going to make it we needed a medevac, and we needed it now. Fortunately, the intensity of my message got through, and if they didn't already have a chopper in the air, it must have been sitting on the pad at the 85th Evac with rotors turning, because the guy at the other end gave me an ETA of no more than ten minutes—we were only about fourteen kilometers away.

After I made the radio call, I had our driver come up and man the .50-caliber so I could help with Dave. He had a classic sucking chest wound, and we were using every trick we'd been taught to try to seal the entrance and exit wounds, stop the bleeding, and encourage him to hang on—all at the same time. Even while I was putting pressure on the foil that I hoped would stop air from bubbling out of the wound, I was able to maintain radio contact with the Dustoff. While the radio itself is inside the vehicle, it can be keyed by a switch on the right side of the combat vehicle crewman's (CVC) helmet we all wore. Earphones inside the helmet and a boom microphone attached to the right side make its operation almost hands-free.

When they told me they were only two minutes out, I yelled for Bill to switch places with me, and I went back to the machine gun, grabbing a smoke grenade from just inside the vehicle. I told the pilot that the best landing area was on the road behind the artillery piece we were towing, and then I popped a purple smoke grenade and asked if he could identify it.

"Identify Goofy Grape," he responded.

"Goofy Grape is beautiful," I replied, and he started his descent.

We continued to work on Dave, preparing to move him off the deck of the vehicle as soon as the bird landed, and the medic got to us with a stretcher. I could see Dave looking at me and everyone else with panic in his eyes. You can't keep a guy who's been shot in the chest from knowing how serious his wound is.

Then, just as the Dustoff flared for a landing on the road behind us, the enemy began shooting at us again. I jumped over to the machine gun, swung it around, and began firing, but as I did so, I hit the transmit key on my radio.

"Pull out. Pull out. We're taking heavy fire again."

I had no other choice. When Dave heard the change of pitch in the aircraft rotors, he knew what I'd done. He looked at me with confusion and fear. I don't think I saw anger in his face—but saying that doesn't necessarily make it so. It's one of those things you say to make yourself feel better under impossible circumstances like this.

We finally managed to suppress the enemy fire—I'm not even sure whether it took more than two minutes. The helo landed and they ended up taking Dave away in a body bag. He died before we could get help for him.

Not that it matters to Dave, but I know I made the right decision in telling the pilot to pull out. Intellectually I know that it was the right thing to do, the only responsible thing to do. Do you sacrifice the lives of four men on the Dustoff to save one guy whose chances of making it are iffy, at best? But that doesn't keep me from seeing the look on Dave's face when he heard the aircraft start to lift. The look was almost more than I could bear, and I still see it today, thirty-five years later. He was my buddy, and he was confused, hurt, and scared. He knew he didn't have much time. And I'm the one who made the decision that sealed his fate. As I said, intellectually I know I made the right decision, but emotionally—now that's a completely different side of the story.

"Sorry 'bout that" doesn't cut it. The Vietnam GI's declaration of numbness in battle—"It don't mean nothing"—is a lie. Maybe it just takes a few years away from the war for the anesthetic of combat to wear off and for you to figure out that it means a lot to lose a buddy, and that unless you're sometimes less than a complete human being, the loss is going to be with you for a lifetime.

By the time the Dustoff landed and we got Dave on the stretcher, he was gone. All we could do at that point was help carry him to the helicopter, put him aboard, and go back and see if we could repair the track enough to make the few miles back to Phu Bai.

The three of us worked in silence for about an hour. We took the spare track off the storage rack, and while one person manned the gun, the other two changed it out. It meant removing two damaged track blocks and replacing them, then putting the track back on.

When we were nearly finished, a truck came by and the guys offered to help us out, but by then the heavy lifting was done. We routed the track over the idler wheel at the front and reconnected things. Then we tightened the track just enough to get us out of there, driving back to Phu Bai on our own power. It seemed like a million miles and many hours away, but the trip was actually fairly quick and, fortunately, uneventful.

I'd been dreading being asked to go in and make the formal identification of Dave's body, but another guy in the unit volunteered. I sat down that night to write a letter home to the folks back in Granbury, and told them—nothing.

CHAPTER ELEVEN

Phu Bai Sniper

If you do something often enough, you'd expect it would become routine. But that didn't hold true in Vietnam. Your last ambush could be more exciting than your first, today's combat assault more electrifying than yesterday's.

It was the same with my sniping assignments. No matter how many times I got called to go see the old man, got handed my special rifle, and headed out, it never got to be ordinary. Just the anticipation was enough to make my palms sweat and my pulse rate increase. I've read about some snipers with extremely high kill counts for whom it was all in a day's work; apparently it was work they enjoyed, and they never broke a sweat. Maybe they never even thought about it again.

But that wasn't me. Hell, that *isn't* me. I found myself dwelling on the fact that the people I shot would never see their families again; never know the joy of holding a child, of taking a spouse, of making love. Of course, it's a lot easier to pull the trigger if you can dehumanize what you're seeing through the scope, and that's the way the army has taught killing for decades. "Just another gook" is a much easier kill than Major Truong, Mrs. Nguyen, or a monk named Thich An Danh.

Pretty much anyone who's known the joy of military life in Vietnam, which was long before air-conditioned tents were more common than armored Hummers, is familiar with waking up in the early morning already coated with a sheen of perspiration from the absolute humidity coupled with unbearable heat. If you wake up in all but the cooler mountainous regions of the country and your sheets aren't soaked with sweat, odds are it's not yet time to roll out of the sack.

And that's exactly what happened in the small hours of the night early in 1970 at Phu Bai. We had no assigned missions for our M-88, and I'd expected to spend the day in the motor pool, doing preventive maintenance on the beast one of my crew had given the unwieldy name *I'm a Stranger Here, Lord.* A runner rolled me out of the rack and said the commander wanted to see me. It sparked the usual surge of adrenaline, the natural concern that something bad had happened at home, to the point that when I walked into the orderly room and saw the rifle, I was almost relieved.

The instructions were the customary ones, and when I got to the airfield there was only one Huey sitting there with rotors turning. It had to be my ride and, as usual on the outbound flight, I was the solo passenger.

When we arrived at the armored personnel carrier where the two mysterious men were waiting to brief me, I took a close look to see if there were any identifying marks—we called them "USA numbers," like 4J13283 as an example. But there were none.

I've since learned from other Vietnam vets that it wasn't all that unusual to occasionally see army-looking helicopters with no numbers carrying a strange collection of people on board and being given priority access to facilities and supplies at the bases where they turned up. Bottom line on this: There was no shortage of spooks or spook-driven activity in the war zone.

When I was out there with the briefers in the APC, I also never saw any security, but could only guess that anyone with the kind of authority the two briefers exercised must have had some sort of protection. I mean, APCs are APCs, but they're not impenetrable. They're just made of aircraft-quality aluminum—hell, they can float—so if Charlie had the right weapon, he could easily obliterate it. The only way to avoid that was to keep Charlie out of firing range. As a footnote, I would add that the APC was never fired on, at least when I was around.

On this mission, as in the past, the briefers—the same two guys who had sent me out several times before—wore sterile jungle fatigues, no insignia, no rank, no markings of any kind. By the time I arrived my spotter was already there. We got our briefing, took a look at a photograph of the intended target, were handed our map, and were told that on the way to the site we'd ride in one Huey, but on the way back there'd be two choppers waiting. Mine would be the one in front. The assumption was that if we didn't screw up and get on the wrong helicopter, the pilots would deliver us to our proper homes. It was a strange change in the way we'd been operating that didn't seem to make sense because it just made the coordination of the mission that much more difficult. But I didn't ask about it. Even if I had, the sense I got was that the briefers held nothing but disdain for the troops they were sending out to do the wet work and that they wouldn't have responded anyway.

After a relatively short flight, we were dropped off in a clearing. We had six hours to find and eliminate the target and get back to our pickup point. It was a much longer time than I'd ever been allotted before, and the only reason for that, as near as I could figure, was that our handlers weren't certain exactly what time the target would arrive. What that meant from a practical standpoint was that we were either going to have to wait an excessive amount of time before the shoot, or hide for an equally long time afterward. Neither was near the top of my hit parade of ways I wanted to while away the hours in the Vietnamese countryside.

The area we had to move through was characterized by low hills and valleys. The mission planners—whoever they were—determined that we could be dropped off just a couple of klicks from the village where we'd find our target, because the terrain would prevent anyone there from hearing or seeing our Huey land and then take off. The result was that we had a lot of time to move a relatively short distance through the woods.

Thinking back on missions like this, trying to remember every aspect of them, I realize there are some things that just aren't in the memory bank. It would be nice to be able to describe the sounds in the woods or jungle, the birdcalls or the buzzing of insects, or even the noise that rain makes falling through the canopy. But here's the truth: Early in my tour I learned to completely tune that stuff out and focus only on sounds that served to warn us of danger, things like the rustling of leaves in a way that you know it's not the wind, or sudden cries of alarm from birds, rather than ordinary chirping and calling.

I do remember that the instant we hit the wood line, the bugs began feasting on their daily dose of GI blood. There were times I'd swear that the little plastic squeeze bottles of jungle juice that most guys carried on their helmets just attracted insects, because even though I used the stuff religiously, it didn't take long in country to have bites on your bites.

I had hoped when I moved from down south and the cav up to Phu Bai that my sniper days were over. When I learned that they weren't, I began hoping that we might be sent out on those missions better equipped, especially for communications. Never happen, GI. We still had no radio, no smoke grenades, and no firepower beyond a couple of magazines each for my M-14 and my spotter's M-16. We weren't even supposed to take rations to the field, but occasionally I'd manage to stuff a few cans in my cargo pockets.

We still wore a boonie hat or baseball cap, because a helmet in the woods looks like . . . a helmet in the woods. No flak jackets—they'd just heat us up and slow us down. The truth is that we were the sacrificial lambs of someone else's mission, and we never knew whose mission it really was. We were out there feeling very much alone and very, very scared. It's difficult to explain the level or intensity of fear that you experience when you are so alone in the woods or jungle, no radio, no way of communicating with any person or group that could assist you in any way. Not even a way to talk with the aviators who were assigned to pick us up. If we had met with an unfortunate end, the pilots wouldn't have known. They would have just reported that their scheduled passengers didn't show. It's more than thirty-five years later, and I still want to know who I can curse out for putting me in that position. But I digress. . . .

We made our way through the woods until we reached an embankment across a small creek from the village where our target was supposed to be. As villages go, it was a small one, with probably six or seven thatch-roofed hooches in a semicircle. We could see a path that went down to the stream, so it was a good guess that it, rather than a well, was their source of water.

If there's anything more difficult than running from a shoot, it's waiting before one. In this case, we were there for at least two, maybe three hours, waiting for the target to arrive. We just lay there without moving. Obviously we couldn't smoke or talk. Didn't eat, didn't move around. It was almost like we were set up in an ambush point, waiting for the enemy to wander by.

Finally we saw three people coming into the village, and both of us were able to identify our target as one of the three. I looked around the village a bit, and then picked up a sight picture with the scope. My spotter whispered to me, "You got 'im?"

I mouthed more than said yes, then took in a breath, let it halfway out and held it, took up the slack in the trigger, and continued pulling with my fingertip. It always surprised me when the rifle went off, but that's the way it's supposed to be. The spotter said something to indicate it was a clean hit, and as soon as the scope cleared I could see that the target had flown backward before sinking to the ground. The two guys who were with him had dropped and were now low-crawling to a house sitting just beside the stream.

That was enough sightseeing for us. We crawled back a bit, and I picked up the expended cartridge; then we went down the hill and headed back to the same field we'd been dropped off in hours earlier. It was the only time I could remember that drop-off and pickup were in pretty much the same location.

Our wait for the helicopter seemed to take forever. We just lay on the ground next to a tree and willed ourselves to become invisible and not to emit a smell that was detectable. No water, no smoking, no movement of any kind that might draw attention to us. You think about the little things that can get you killed. Did the GI-issue insect repellent serve as a warning to any VC approaching? I couldn't tell if they could smell it, because I couldn't smell it myself—but that didn't mean I didn't reek of it. Think about wearing aftershave. Once you've had it on for a few minutes, no matter how much you slapped on your face, you don't really smell it anymore, right? Same problem with the jungle juice. So that problem builds and builds and builds inside your mind. And you can't turn to your buddy and ask him, because he's wearing it, too. Even if he weren't, you couldn't ask him, because neither one of you dares to breathe a word.

It's very strange, because you're really alone, even though you're with another person and he's within reach. You begin rethinking everything that has happened in the past few hours and dwelling on everything that could happen in the next few. The introspection becomes simplified in the extreme. *I could have died today, but I didn't. Oh, wait. The day's not over. There's still time.*

Introspection is not something that nineteen- or twenty-year-olds in Vietnam are terribly good at unless fortified by copious quantities of something like the pride of Singapore, Tiger Beer, which had almost twice the alcoholic content of the Schlitz or Budweiser sold at the club. Inside my head I relived the day's mission in stark terms. *The shoot was successful; it was actually a pretty good shot; can we get out of here alive?* At this stage in my life I still wasn't questioning what I'd done. There was no regret, no remorse, no concern that in my head I'd still be going on these missions decades from now. I certainly didn't feel sorrow for having taken a life in the coldest, most calculating way possible.

Despite our having two or three hours to wait, there was no time for deep thinking, because reality would always intrude. Was the helicopter we could hear the one we were waiting for? Not possible; it was still too early. Was my heart beating as loudly as I thought it was? Because if it was, I was dead meat. Charlie had to be able to hear it, and if he could, I'd never hear him coming, because the sound of my heart would drown him out. I didn't say the thoughts were rational, but I was in the middle of a year's worth of irrational.

I've often said that I was scared only one time while I was in Vietnam—that would be from the time I got there till the time I left. Of course, the level of that fear could, and did, vary significantly, depending upon what events were taking place at the moment. And since at the moment I was in the prone position, concealed near the edge of an open field, not knowing if I'd live long enough to board the helicopter that we hoped would be coming for us, the fear level was higher than the audience at a Grateful Dead concert.

Fear makes you wonder if the men who were with our target are right behind us or running away from us. It makes you wonder how many bad guys heard the report of the rifle, and what action they're taking.

Anything and everything goes through your mind. You think about the guys back at the base and how they'll react if you don't come back. You think about how you'll look on one of those tables at the Da Nang morgue, and whether they'll be able to make you look good enough for an open-casket funeral. That, of course, forces you to imagine what you'd look like lying there in your class-A greens, your face waxy with the stuff embalmers use to fool the next of kin into thinking that you died a peaceful, pleasant death. You think about home, the letter you should have written, but didn't, telling your parents how much you love and appreciate them. You wonder if you'll ever get back to Texas again, alive. For a few seconds you think of the girls back home, of some good times you had in your pickup truck at the drive-in, and you wonder if you'll ever see them again.

The fact that you haven't had anything to eat or drink for hours begins to play in your mind, and you wonder if you'll ever again sit in a restaurant or café and have a Coke poured from a bottle, a cup of coffee, or a burger. And that leads you to begin listing the food you miss the most, the dishes Mom made every week, not just for the holidays. *Will I ever again have a chicken-fried steak with cream gravy?*

Before I could come to any conclusions about the likelihood of ever again eating meals that could result in the Heart Association's picketing Mom's kitchen, we heard our helicopter coming in. We knew the approach would be low and fast, especially since we had no way of warning the pilots if the LZ was hot.

They bounced the Huey down, and I don't think it sat on the ground for ten seconds before we dove in. The pilot pulled pitch, put her in a nose-down attitude, and di-di'ed out of there. The flight was short; within minutes they brought the ship down at the intersection of two roads, and the crew chief motioned my spotter and me to jump off.

We did, that helo left, and a short time later two other aircraft came into sight and landed. Per the instructions we'd been given that morning, I jumped in the first one and my buddy climbed into the second. Less than half an hour later I was on the ground at Phu Bai, walking back to my unit.

There was no way I could recognize how much I'd changed in the months I'd been in Vietnam. When everyone around you stinks, you don't know how bad you smell. One thing is certain: I never thought about whether I'd fit in back home in Granbury; all I knew was that I wanted to get there. Would it happen? It probably depended on how many more assignments like this one I'd get, because I knew that the longer I kept rolling the dice, the better the odds were that I'd crap out.

CHAPTER TWELVE

Free-Fire Zone

I t was February or March of 1970, and I had three or four months remaining on my one-year tour when, early one morning just as I was about ready to start pulling maintenance on my recovery vehicle, I was summoned to the company commander's office. My body's response was both unpleasant and predictable. My heart raced, and my mind went through the usual list of potential reasons for the call, ranging from an emergency at home to another damned mission with the rifle.

When I entered his office and saw the rifle, it was a classic good news–bad news situation. The good news was that nothing untoward had occurred with my family; the bad news was that someone wanted me to put my life on the line and go kill someone—again.

I was instructed to go across the base at Phu Bai to the XXIV Corps Artillery headquarters. Next to the headquarters was a temporary office building that almost looked like a small mobile home or mobile office from the outside. Parked outside were two unmarked jeeps.

I went inside and found the two anonymous briefers sitting there, waiting. The other half of my team hadn't yet arrived, so we all sat around in silence. There were a lot of questions I would have liked to ask the spooks, starting off with an admittedly selfish one: Why me? When they'd satisfactorily answered that one, my fantasy had me inquiring whether or not it bothered them that the conditions they sent us out under were not necessarily conducive to our getting out alive, for we had no radio, no backup, and no alternative for evacuation if trouble arose and we missed our pickup.

Why didn't that bother them? And I suppose if I really got belligerent, I could suggest that since they were getting the big bucks, they might want to explain why they weren't taking the chances, but passing the hazardous work on to a couple of low-ranking enlisted men who hadn't joined the army to be shooters. Much later I learned that the infantry troops had a nickname for snipers—all of them, not just the ones doing the wet work for anonymous spooks. They called us "Murder, Incorporated," and to say that I resented it is an understatement. In all of my nightmares since Vietnam, I've never considered myself a murderer!

But instead of getting into it with them, I just sat there quietly and waited. After about fifteen minutes my second arrived. He introduced himself as Smitty; I told him I was Mitch, and without any preface the briefing began.

We were given the usual information about transportation, schedule, and extraction location, but for only the second time since I began this orchestrated killing, I wasn't given a specific target. Since the other time this had happened was when I was ordered to kill four Buddhist monks, the omission of the target details seriously concerned me.

When I questioned the two spooks, they somewhat reluctantly told us that there would not be a specific target. After we were inserted, our job was to find someone, anyone, and kill them. The impression we were given was, the more, the merrier. We both realized at that point that we were being sent to a free-fire zone.

A free-fire zone is somewhat unnatural. Its boundaries are limited by both geography and time, according to the rules established by the powers that be—and for reasons you're about to hear, I have to assume that those powers were at least as high as the commanding general of the Military Assistance Command Vietnam (MACV), but possibly much higher and residing in an office not on the banks of the Mekong River, but the Potomac. Why? Because the concept of a free-fire zone most likely violates international law, and when that occurs as a matter of policy, it's a good bet that someone a lot higher than a battalion commander came up with the idea.

In a free-fire zone, anyone that moves between a specific start time and a specific end time within the physical boundaries is considered to be the enemy, and is therefore both an acceptable and viable target. Translation: Shoot anyone that moves. Military or civilian. In uniform or out. Male or female. Old or young. If they're there, you can and should kill them.

I didn't know it at the time—and even if I had, I'm not sure what I would have done differently—but just the concept of a free-fire zone violates the letter and the spirit of the Geneva Conventions, because they prohibit indiscriminate attacks on civilians.

According to Protocol I, Article 51, Section 4, "Indiscriminate attacks are those which are not directed at a specific military objective or those which use a method of attack that cannot be directed at or limited to a specific military objective." I'm not an international human rights lawyer, but that makes it pretty clear that whacking a peasant who happens to wander through the area with his water buffalo is somewhat verboten. So is firing an artillery barrage into an area without making certain that any humans who happen to be in the impact zone are bona fide enemy combatants. That's covered under Section 5a, which says that "area bombardment, where a number of clearly separated military objectives are treated as a single military objective, and where there is a similar concentration of civilians or civilian objects" is proscribed. Finally, with respect to what the American forces called free-fire zones, there's Article 57, which says, "If it becomes apparent that an objective in an attack is not a military one, or if that attack could cause incidental loss of civilian life or damage to civilian objects, then the attack must be called off."

On my other shoots where the assigned targets were apparently civilians, I suppose it's possible that whoever picked the people I was to kill had evidence that they were not innocent civilians, but were agents of the Viet Cong or the North Vietnamese Army. I would have no way of knowing if that were the case, but it is one possibility. However, when I'm told to set up in an area at a specific time and blast away indiscriminately at anyone who happens to come by, not even Johnnie Cochran could have made that one look righteous.

But no matter how much I disliked the assignment or felt I was being misused, I wasn't inclined to object, or to take that step into the abyss of military justice and refuse what some judge advocate general—the military version of a prosecutor—could and most certainly would construe as a lawful order. Truth be told, I'd rather do the killing than have Leavenworth, Kansas, 66048, become my mailing address for the foreseeable future.

So my second took the map and I shouldered my rifle and we climbed into one of the unmarked jeeps for a short ride to the airfield. En route, the spook picked a flashlight with a red lens off the floorboard and handed it to the second, saying, "When the aircraft lands to pick you up, flash it twice so the crew will know it's you. After all, you don't want one of the crewmen shooting at you, now, do you?" Clearly we were dealing with a first-class prick whose concern for our well-being was somewhat less than sincere. Looking back, it was almost as if he wanted the aircrewmen to make the mistake.

Had I known one little fact then that I know now, I would have been more than a bit alarmed at his comment about getting shot by the gunners on the helo coming in to get us. In documents made public long after the Vietnam War ended, it was noted that at one point, orders had been given to eliminate some of the U.S. military personnel involved in the CIA's campaign of murder and assassination of civilians.

My second and I boarded the Huey, which immediately took off and headed west, flying us past Camp Eagle, firebases Bastogne and Birmingham, and finally set us down just inside the infamous A Shau Valley. The A Shau, dubbed the A Shit Valley by the Americans sent there to fight, is located near the Laotian border in the Thua Thien province of I Corps, the northernmost of the four corps areas into which the military had divided South Vietnam. Actually composed of several valleys and mountains, the A Shau was one of the principal entry points of the Ho Chi Minh Trail, down which the North Vietnamese Army sent supplies and additional troops.

The area we were being dropped into was critical to the North Vietnamese Army and Viet Cong units operating in I Corps. That's why it had been the target of several major operations, many of which were conducted by the 101st Airborne Division, the most infamous of these having taken place in May and June of 1969, approximately eight or nine months earlier. Officially, it was Operation Apache Snow, but it quickly became known as the battle of Hamburger Hill.

The purpose of the operation was to cut off the North Vietnamese and prevent them from mounting an attack on the coastal provinces. A year earlier the NVA had launched its Tet attack on the city of Hue from the A Shau. After an eleven-day battle that involved ten infantry assaults by elements of the 101st Airborne Division and the 9th Marine Regiment, Ap Bia Mountain was taken. But the cost was horrific. The U.S. reported 56 killed and 420 wounded. North Vietnamese dead were put at 597, but it was always assumed, since it was their standard practice, that the retreating NVA forces took many additional dead along with their wounded across the border into Laos. Because the operation was not intended to hold territory but rather to keep the North Vietnamese Army off balance, the mountain was abandoned soon after the battle and occupied by the North Vietnamese a month later.

American public outrage over what appeared to be a senseless loss of American lives was exacerbated by the publication in *LIFE* magazine of the pictures of the 241 U.S. soldiers killed the week of the Hamburger Hill battle. It was reported that shortly after Hamburger Hill, MACV commander Gen. Creighton Abrams was ordered by the White House to avoid major battles that would produce heavy casualties. That apparently began the shift to Vietnamization of the war, a policy designed to hand responsibility for the fighting over to the South Vietnamese.

That policy didn't have any bearing on the mission my second and I were now embarked upon, because there we were, alone, in the A Shau. Exiting the aircraft at a run, we dashed into the wood line and waited for the helicopter to take off. We sat there for a couple of moments to catch our breath—or was it to get up our nerve?—and then walked about halfway down the hill to where we could see down a trail.

Our briefers told us we could shoot after 1400 hours (two p.m.), so we had about an hour before we could begin firing. Since our ride home was scheduled to meet us at 2000 hours (eight p.m.) in the same location where we were dropped off, we would have about six hours to locate, engage, and eliminate as many targets as possible, and still get to the pickup point, alive and hopefully unwounded.

We moved uphill another hundred meters along the trail we'd found, staying within the wood line in order to minimize the likelihood of our being seen. We elected to go up the trail so that on our way out, when we had to move quickly, we would be going downhill.

The shooting location we found gave us a view both ways up and down the trail, but we could see only about forty meters up and another twenty-five or thirty meters down. The good thing was that we would be shooting from a small rise and could drop back behind it and be quickly out of sight once I'd fired a shot.

The shooting on this mission was going to be different from on previous occasions. There would be no time for hesitation, because the targets would be on the move. The scope really wasn't necessary, because either one of us could have thrown a rock and hit anyone on the trail. I would have to shoot from the sitting position, rather than the prone. Sitting allows a greater opportunity to make a last-minute adjustment in the direction you're shooting. This was important, because we didn't know from which direction any potential target would come.

We were all set and ready to begin at 1330 hours (one thirty p.m.), which gave us half an hour to relax. When the start time came and went with no one on the trail, we were surprised. I really don't know what we expected. I suppose we thought that at the start time, people would just begin moving up or down the trail for our convenience, but it didn't happen.

Finally, after we'd been in position for nearly two hours, we heard someone coming up the trail. It was clearly a woman's voice, and she was speaking to someone. I pulled the rifle into my shoulder and assumed a firing position, thinking that if I were quick enough, I could get at least two. Besides, the second had an M-16, so if necessary he could take out one or two also.

For a second I flashed back on the second sniper killing I'd done. Months earlier, I'd felt twinges of something—maybe guilt, maybe not—when I shot and killed a woman. Now I was about to do it again. This time, I don't recall even thinking about it as something special. It was like they said, "It don't mean nothin'." Had I become one of those soulless killers with the thousand-yard stare? That's way too much introspection for a hot, sticky day in Vietnam—or so I thought.

I settled into position and began to stabilize my breathing. As soon as she rounded the little crook in the trail, I almost fired, because she came right into the sight picture. Then I saw movement to her left side and realized that she was leading a small child. Slowly I lowered the rifle. Both my second and I passed on the hit—not in front of her child. And even though I'd seen what the VC would deliberately do to a youngster, even though I'd already done things for my spook handlers that I wouldn't ever have thought I'd do, there was no way I'd consider shooting the child. Vietnam may have torn my soul, but I refused to allow it to be ripped from my body.

After a period of time we saw a lone man coming down the trail. He was dressed in the usual Vietnamese garb, so I had to assume he was a civilian, or possibly a guerrilla, but not NVA. I quickly pulled the rifle into my shoulder again and fired. I don't think he ever knew we were there, and if he did we gave him no time to react. One moment he was walking down the path, and the next moment his body had been knocked completely off the other side of the trail.

We quickly grabbed the empty casing and slid off the small rise out of sight, and then sat for a moment intently listening to see if we could hear anyone else moving. Hearing nothing, we moved down the trail to the bottom of the hill, where another trail intersected the one we were on. We watched all four directions to ensure that no one else was in the area and then crossed, continuing on the same trail we'd come down.

Eventually it took us up the relatively steep side of another hill, and after we'd traveled a total of about 450 meters from the first firing position, we located another position that we could shoot from. From this vantage point we could see about eighty meters down the hill, but only about ten or fifteen meters up the hill. It meant I'd be forced to shoot downhill, irrespective of which direction the target was walking.

Around 1700 (five p.m.) we heard someone coming down the trail. I snugged the rifle into the pocket of my shoulder and waited. It was another man dressed similarly to our first target, walking down the hill with a bundle balanced on his left shoulder.

Wondering what was in the bundle, I hesitated a second or two and then feathered the trigger. He flew forward, tumbling farther down the hill, his bundle rolling after him, spilling its cargo of some kind of rather large green leaves.

We quickly moved back into the wood line and sat for a moment. I can't say for sure what my second was doing, but I was trying to control my breathing, and I was probably doing a little praying, too. It wasn't that this shoot was more difficult than the first, or that I suddenly felt more threatened by where we were and what we were doing. It's just that while I may have lost my naïveté in Vietnam, I hadn't yet lost my conscience. For me, taking another human life was never an easy thing to do, and to do it methodically, even mechanically, twice in a few hours and still have time left to do it again made me think about what I'd become—and the thoughts were not especially attractive.

The two of us scampered down the hill, staying off the trail. The foliage was somewhat light, definitely not thick enough to make it difficult to walk, but we were probably making enough noise to lead anyone directly to us. When we came to the trail that we had crossed earlier, we turned to our right, still staying near, but not on the trail.

After what seemed like an eternity, we stopped and sat down, just looking at each other. Both of us were wet with sweat and breathing heavily. We drank from our canteens, and probably violated recommended procedure by not emptying them. We knew that water sloshing around inside a half-full canteen could give us away, but I guess we figured that considering what we were doing out there, it wasn't a big deal.

Within a short time we had regained control of our breathing, so we stood up and started walking. We carefully crossed the trail and found a position, settled in, and waited. We estimated that this position was only about five hundred meters from our scheduled pickup point.

For the rest of the afternoon and as dusk began to fall, we waited. Finally, about 1900 hours, the second said, "I've had all the fun I can stand. Let's get the hell out of here." He got no objections from me. A half hour later we were in position, watching the pickup point and listening for an aircraft. We were at the same LZ we'd dropped into earlier in the day. It was a relatively small natural clearing. Neither one of us questioned the logic of drop-off and pickup being in the same location. How about that for being malleable? It was pretty much, *You know, whatever, I'm gonna die anyway, so what difference does it make?*

After what seemed like a lifetime and a half, we finally heard an inbound Huey. As it settled onto the ground the second flashed the red light twice in the direction of the aircraft. Without waiting for any confirmation—because we hadn't been told to expect any—we started toward the aircraft at a run.

Obviously the aircrew was as unhappy about being in the A Shau Valley as we were, because as soon as we dove through the door they lifted off again and headed east, low and fast. Every once in a while during the flight, my second and I would look at each other, but of course, we couldn't talk without yelling. Anyway, we probably didn't need words to communicate what we were feeling and thinking. *We're alive! We're not wounded! Did you see that gook tumble when the round hit? What the fuck am I doing here? I'll sure be glad to get back home!* After flying for about thirty or forty-five minutes, we landed at the Phu Bai airfield, where the two briefers were waiting for us, one in each unmarked jeep. I climbed into one, the second mounted the other, and with a small wave toward each other, we were on our way back to our respective units. We'd never see each other again.

A postscript: The area we were sent into remained an NVA stronghold for the remainder of the war. A few months after our mission, another element of the 101st Airborne (B/1/327th) was combat-assaulted to Hill 882 on a search-and-destroy operation and ran into a sapper base camp. What they didn't know at the time is that they were facing a full North Vietnamese Army division that was preparing to attack Fire Support Base Ripcord in a plan to keep forces away from the A Shau for much of the summer of 1970.

CHAPTER THIRTEEN

Getting Short

Everyone in Vietnam had a short-timer's calendar. If not an actual physical device—a paper calendar or a stick into which you carved notches—it was a mental countdown clock, so that you always knew how many days you had left on your tour. Unlike our current war in Iraq, where a sequence of morale-dumping surprise extensions of time in the war zone have rendered short-timer calendars essentially meaningless, the promise that army troops would spend no more than a year in the war zone and marines no more than thirteen months was inviolate. The war was unpopular enough at home; the politicians running it certainly didn't want to do the one thing guaranteed to bring the wrath of military families down on their heads. Therefore, the only way a person stayed more than the standard tour of duty was if they voluntarily extended. There were no extensions, no "stop loss."

From the day I arrived in country, I knew that I could count on boarding a Freedom Bird home no later than June 12, 1970. Of course, newbies didn't talk about their rotation date home—way too depressing. That was left for the guys who were truly short to do. And the shorter they were, the more they relished making those of us who were still looking at more than half our tour to go miserable. The rules of short-timer calendars were simple: You didn't count today, and you didn't count your departure day, which was the "wake-up," as in, "I have twelve days and a wake-up to go."

We all hoped to live long enough to inflict that delicious misery on anyone who wasn't as short as we were. And make no mistake about it, the infliction of misery was absolutely intentional, in part because it even allowed us to stick it to those who outranked us—the senior NCOs and officers.

"Hey, Mitch, how short are you?"

"I'm so short I have to look up to see a snake's belly."

"I'm so short I can't see over the toes of my boots."

"I'm so short I can sit on a dime and swing my legs."

"I'm so short I have to reach up to tie my boots."

"I'm so short I can do backflips under my cot."

"I'm so short I can limbo under the door."

"I'm so short I have to cuff my underwear."

"I'm so short I can work as a teller at a piggy bank."

"I'm so short, the only way I can piss is up."

Eventually, "I'm so short . . ." morphed into "I'm too short . . ." as in "I'm too short to do laundry" or "I'm too short to give a shit" or "I'm too short to worry."

But the truth of the matter was that until you were safely out of Vietnamese airspace, you weren't too short to die, which is why the shorter we got, the more careful we got, sometimes to the point of what in the real world might be considered paranoia, but in Vietnam was just the exercise of common sense. All we were really doing was taking to an extreme the notion that anything you do in a combat zone can get you killed, including nothing.

That's why it was common practice in many units to give short-timers the privilege of hanging out in the base camp rather than con-tinuing to go on operations where, if one played the odds, the chances of getting hurt—or worse—were considerably greater. At Phu Bai, the deal I had with the platoon sergeant was that when I got down to thirty days, he'd take me off recovery missions. That would allow me to spend my last weeks in Vietnam in relative safety, while leisurely going through the convoluted paperwork involved in out-processing. I knew some guys who were so psycho during their last month that they refused to go anywhere in the base camp without a helmet and flak jacket. And some guys were so frightened of the possibility of a relatively routine mortar attack that they decided where they'd go—and where they wouldn't go—based on how far the route took them from a bunker. A friend of mine decided that he would be way too exposed going from his hooch to the mess hall, so for his last two weeks in country he never went to eat. We brought food back to the hooch for him, or he lived on C-rations or care packages from home, just so he could stay close to a bunker. I'd have to agree that his theory was sound: There wasn't anything they served in the mess hall that was worth dying for.

By April 12, 1970, I was getting short. I still had another thirty days on the road to survive before I'd get to kick back and enjoy life in the office for my last month in country, but I was feeling cautiously optimistic about surviving Vietnam. That was until my platoon sergeant, Hook Soo Yung, came by my hooch and said, "Mitchell, the first sergeant wants to see you. What the hell have you done?"

Even though I'd made spec 5, the equivalent in pay grade of a three-stripe buck sergeant, there was still no more feared man in uniform than my first sergeant. It's almost impossible to explain if you haven't been in the service, but try imagining if the dean of discipline at your high school possessed the power of life or death over you, and you begin to approach the authority of a first sergeant. This was clearly a man who could make your life miserable in ways you were unable even to imagine. First sergeants had the capacity to be offended by anything. Early in my military career I had a first sergeant who took a dislike to me because I gave him "a case of the ass." To this day, I still don't know what "a case of the ass" is, but I know that whatever it is, it was bad enough to cost me several weekends of freedom.

So when I was told to report to the first sergeant, I went through a mental checklist of the reasons I might be in trouble. I'd pulled all the duty I was supposed to, so it wasn't that. There was still the rifle, which I'd last used two weeks earlier, but when I'd been called to pick it up it was always the company commander who gave me the assignment. That left the possibility that always came to mind: Something was wrong at home.

I began to move out, but SFC Yung said, "Wait, I gotta go with you." Well, that made it even more serious. Having to see the first sergeant is bad, but if your platoon sergeant has to go with you, you've got a real problem on your hands.

We walked into the top's office and he looked up and said, "Well, it took you long enough to get here." He paused long enough to allow my life to flash before my eyes, then added, "Mitchell, what in the hell did you do?" I didn't know what to say because I didn't know what I'd done. Then he went into a real rant. "I got a damned company to run here, and here I am escorting pantywaist bird sergeants around. Now I've gotta take you to battalion headquarters, as if I don't have *important* shit to do."

Suddenly I found myself being marched to battalion HQ by both my platoon sergeant and my first sergeant, and, suffice it to say, I was freaking out. They marched me into the Personnel Services NCO's office, and the guy was expecting me. "Well, my, my, my, Specialist Mitchell. I haven't seen you since you made E-5." I didn't know where this was going, but I was certain it wasn't anywhere good.

"When do you leave?" he asked me, but before I could tell him, he said, "Anybody want coffee?" The two senior sergeants declined, but I jumped on the opportunity to delay whatever bad shit was about to rain down on my sorry ass. I got some coffee, adding milk and sugar to the paper cup.

When I was back in front of his desk, he asked me again, "How long do you have left in country?"

"Fifty-eight and a wake-up, Sergeant."

"Are you sure?" he asked me. Now there were a lot of things that happened to me in Vietnam that I wasn't sure about, but the one thing I was positive about was how many days I had left in this vacation paradise. But he was an E-7, a sergeant first class, so it wasn't going to be in my best interests to say, "Well, you asshole, if I know anything, it's how short I am."

So I just began to mumble, "Yes, Sergeant, that's—"

But he interrupts me like he's not interested in anything I have to say, and while he's digging through papers on his desk, he says, "Well, I don't think that's right. Let me check here." He picks up some papers and looks at them real close, then looks up at my first sergeant and at Sergeant Yung, and, dead seriously, says, "I thought you guys told me this was a good troop. That he's honest. That you could always depend on him."

At this point, I remembered that when shit hits the fan, it *never* spreads evenly. Clearly, before this session was over, I was likely to be the only one in the office neck-deep in crap. I'm ready to crawl in a hole, even a VC tunnel, just to get out of there, but there is no escape. The first sergeant, Rudy Bureau, said, "Well, he's never given us cause to question him before now. Of course, he's pulled some bullshit stunts, but nothing serious." My platoon sergeant just shrugs. It becomes very apparent that there is no way he's going to save my sorry ass.

Then the PSNCO says, "Mitchell, you're lying to me." I turn five shades of white. The tan I've developed over the past ten months just up and disappears.

He waves the papers in front of my face and says, "Specialist, you certainly do not have fifty-eight and a wake-up; you have three days—I don't know why or how, but you got a fifty-six-day drop!"

By that time I'm shaking so bad, when he says "drop," I do just that with the cup of coffee. All I can say is "Holy shit!"

All three of the senior NCOs break up laughing, and as the PSNCO hands me my orders, he says, "It looks like you're going to Fort Hood."

I say, "Fort Hood, I'm going to Fort Hood. I live close to there," still not believing what's happening to me.

The first sergeant says, "You'd better get over to my orderly room and see the clerk to get your clearing papers. If you've only got three days left, you don't have time to waste."

I took off like I'd been shot from a gun, ran all the way to the company orderly room, and ran inside, only to find Captain Gluth standing there. "Mitchell, what the hell are you doing running in my orderly room?" he asked. Had I looked closely, I probably would have noticed that he was fighting hard to conceal a grin. But I was in "don't know whether to shit or go blind" mode, and not exactly absorbing the subtleties of the moment.

Besides, I was puffing so hard that I could barely catch my breath. All I could manage to blurt out was "I got a drop. I'm going home."

The captain then broke out into a smile, handed me a fistful of papers, and said, "Well, I think everybody ought to do that once in a while. Here's your clearing papers." These were the orders that were going to get me from Phu Bai to Da Nang, from Da Nang to Cam Ranh Bay, then onto a Freedom Bird heading to the Continental United States, and on to my new assignment at Fort Hood. Before I could get on my way to start packing, Captain Gluth said, "We have one little detail that we need taken care of before you leave. Come with me."

We went into his office, where I saw the rifle sitting on his desk in the case. He shut the door and said, "You need to clean that." It was the quickest cleaning job I'd ever done on a weapon. Then he had me wrap it in Cosmoline paper, which is what you package a rifle in that's going to be stored for a period of time. When I finished, I put it back in the case and closed it. He gave me a little metal seal—I still remember the number. It was 06652. And I put the seal on—it had a ball on one part and you pushed the wire back into the ball and it latched. He checked to make sure it was secured, then said, "Now get out of here. Take my jeep and get your clearing done."

It didn't cross my mind at that moment to wonder whether the fifty-six-day drop and the off-the-books sniper assignments were linked. When I looked at the paperwork, I saw that the clerk had already gotten most of the signatures needed before I could leave. I had to turn in some gear at supply, sign an authorization for the supply sergeant to ship my nonaccompanying baggage home in my footlocker, pick up my medical, dental, finance, and personnel records, and stop at the mailroom to give them a copy of my orders so they could forward mail to me stateside. Then I had to go to the repair shop, where they had me inventory the weapons on the M-88. Finally, I packed the bag that I was going to carry with me. All you're allowed on the plane is sixty-six pounds, and it doesn't take much to reach that limit. A couple sets of jungle fatigues, some underwear, an extra pair of boots, my shaving kit, and I was good to go. All the photographs I had I put in the footlocker that would be shipped to me.

The rushed process left me no more than fifteen minutes to say my farewells to guys I'd served with for many months. I ran through the section and said, "I'm gone, bye, have a good one, take care of yourself, I'll see you back in the world." I wasn't leaving Vietnam for three days, but I had to be out of Phu Bai in fifteen minutes. Someone ran me down to the airfield in the jeep, where I hooked up with another guy from my unit, Stanley Coutu from Chicago, who was also going home. We caught a ride on a C-130 that would take us to Da Nang.

Years later I'd reflect on the fact that there were guys I should have said good-bye to, but didn't have the chance. There were guys whose home addresses I should have gotten, but never did. There were people I had grown closer to than my own family, but I would never write to them, never see them again. Unlike veterans from World War II, who went home as a unit on board troop ships where they could decompress together, who stayed in touch, who joined VFW and Legion posts to keep the connection, Vietnam vets rarely did, and we were the worse for it. Maybe we thought that when our war was over, we really wanted it to be over, with all ties to it severed. Or if we didn't consciously think it, we acted as though we did. What I had no way of knowing as I rushed to get the chopper for the first leg of the journey home was that while I may have been finished with the war, it wasn't finished with me. By the time I realized that it might help if I could find the guys who lived through it with me, they weren't there to be found, and I had no idea how to find them.

Stan and I spent an uneventful night in the transient tents in Da Nang, if you don't count sirens going off because there was supposedly an enemy probe of the perimeter. The FNGs who were in the tent with us were so green they were still peeing stateside water. When the permanent party NCOs began screaming for everyone to hit the bunkers, the newbies ran as though their lives depended on it. Outwardly, I took a more blasé approach to the situation, which pissed off the NCOs who would be the ones to write up the paperwork if something happened to us while we were in their tents. Truth be told, if a medic had put a blood pressure cuff on me just then, he would have slammed me in the hospital right quick. All I could think was *This close to home, and I'm gonna die.*

When the all-clear sounded a few minutes later, I got back in bed, but wasn't able to sleep. It's like I always said: You're not out of the woods till you're out of the woods, and I still had another twenty-four hours in country before I'd be on that outbound Freedom Bird.

Early the next morning Stan and I got on another C-130 and flew to Cam Ranh Bay, where we reported to the holding area and turned in a copy of our orders. After a while, they ordered everyone into a formation so they could explain the procedure. Calling it a "formation" is giving it much more dignity than it's entitled to. Imagine a couple of hundred guys who are so short, they've already had their last wake-up. Motivating us to do anything other than board the plane was nearly impossible.

"Okay, we got an airplane leaving here this afternoon, so we're going to call your name off. When you hear your name, get your bag; take it over there. You have to go through customs to make sure you're not taking back any bombs, bullets, hand grenades, or other toys." The MPs were set up to go through it all, and they had dogs sniffing everything and everybody to make sure we weren't taking any drugs on the plane.

When they called, "Mitchell, Gary D.," I answered loud enough to wake up the dead. I wanted to make sure there was no doubt that I was there, present and accounted for, and ready to board. After we cleared customs and threw our tagged bags on a truck, I had my last and final strange Vietnam experience.

They put us on a bus with only two ways out: an emergency door in the back that's locked, and the entrance door in the front. The windows were down, but there was wire mesh over the openings so Charlie couldn't toss in a grenade as a parting gift. None of us had weapons, but we were going on a ride that took us past a lot of Vietnamese civilians. It was the longest fifteen-minute ride of my life, and it was absolutely uneventful.

Once we got close to the ramp area we could see a United Airlines stretch DC-8 waiting for us. This was our Freedom Bird. Once again they called the roll, and I think I must've run up those boarding steps two at a time. Within minutes the pilot came on the intercom and said, "Welcome aboard. We're number four in the takeoff sequence. Got a cargo plane, a sortie of two fighters that's our escort out of here, another cargo plane, and then it's our turn."

We began to taxi, and minutes later the pilot said, "Stewardesses"— don't forget, this is ancient history and that's what they were called back then—"we've been cleared for takeoff," and those girls went running for their seats. I guess they'd done this a few times, because the pilot didn't stop, lock the brakes, and wind the engines up. He just turned the corner onto the active runway, throttled up, and we were gone. It was the most wonderful feeling in the world to feel that surge of power push you back into the seat.

When he rotated, gained a bit of altitude, and raised the landing gear, everybody clapped and cheered. If we hadn't been strapped in, we would have jumped up and down. It was a very steep climb out, and after about ten minutes or so, he said, "If you look out the window you can wave good-bye to our escorts." We all watched the fighters waggle their wings and turn back to Vietnam, while we continued on our way back home.

After hopscotching across the Pacific, with one stop in Hawaii, where they let us off the plane while it was serviced, we finally arrived back in the world, the land of the big PX. To the cheers of everyone on board, the plane touched down at McCord Air Force Base adjacent to the army's Fort Lewis in Washington, south of Seattle.

We were bused to an in-processing center, where we got fitted for dress green uniforms, got paid in cash, and were fed unlimited quantities of steak, mashed potatoes, ice cream, pie, and—miracle of miracles—real whole milk. Then it was a bus ride to the Seattle-Tacoma International Airport, where we swarmed the airline counters. Since I was going to Dallas Love Field, I targeted Braniff, and managed to buy a seat on a plane leaving later that evening.

With time to kill, I went into the airport restaurant and ordered a cup of coffee. While I was sitting there, a young man walked up and started staring at me. I hadn't been warned what to expect, or if I had, in my euphoria at getting back home I wasn't paying attention. I looked up and said, "Hi, how're you doing?"

"Well, well, well," he said. "The conquering hero returns."

I didn't understand.

"How many babies did you have to kill to get here?" And then he spit on my brand-spanking-new uniform.

Believe it or not, it still didn't compute that I had just taken center stage in an anti–Vietnam War protest, but it sure made an impression on three older guys sitting at a nearby table. As it turned out, two of them were World War II vets, and the third had served in Korea. They sort of invited the guy and all his friends to leave the coffee shop. In fact, one of them suggested less than politely, "If you come back in here again, I'll whip your ass and pay the fine with a smile." All the while that confrontation was playing out, the waitress was wiping the spittle off my uniform, and I was wondering what the hell had just happened.

Bottom line—the protester left, and the three vets informed the waitress that my money was no good. They would pay for whatever I wanted. So I had a piece of pie and another cup of coffee, and as I was getting ready to go, and the waitress was wiping my uniform off again, I found out that her husband was in Vietnam with about ninety days left.

The red-eye flight home to Texas was as unexciting as you'd want it to be. We landed at about 5:30 in the morning. I came down the ramp and didn't see my mother and sister there to meet me until they slammed me into a wall. I was the baby of the family, and I'm sure that I never realized how much of a strain it was on the whole family, and my mother in particular, to have me in Vietnam. My mom was crying her eyes out, and my sister was saying, "Thank God, thank God he made it." They had no idea.

We got in the car and drove to the filling station that my folks owned. As we pulled in, I remember seeing my dad putting gas in a car, and he just stopped and ran and grabbed me and wrapped his arms around me and wouldn't let go. I think that was when I really began to understand what it meant to my folks to have a child in the service. Between 1943, when one of my brothers joined the army, until 1992, when I retired, my mother always had at least one son on active duty. That's just shy of fifty years of having a family member in uniform. And what none of us knew that morning in Dallas was that even once you were out of uniform, it wasn't over when it was over.

CHAPTER FOURTEEN

Maybe You Can't Go Home Again

I hadn't been home forty-eight hours when I had my first nightmare. The pillow and sheets were soaked with sweat; I'd tossed the blankets onto the floor, and had probably been screaming. I say "probably," because no one came and woke me up. But it was clear that my parents knew something was wrong.

My mother, rest her soul, said that I went to Vietnam her little boy, and I came back somebody she didn't recognize. She always said she loved me, loved me dearly, but moms have a way of knowing the truth, even if they don't speak it. I could tell by the way she looked at me that she knew I wasn't the same sweet, innocent, naive boy that she watched enter the army and go off to war.

No one warned me before I enlisted that the army would change me. Hell, I'd just graduated from high school, the future was tomorrow, and the distant future was next week. I'm not even sure that I consciously realized that by joining the army in 1968, the odds were that I'd be going to Vietnam.

And while I was in Vietnam, following orders and doing what I had to do to stay alive, I certainly didn't contemplate the fact that though I had within me the capacity to kill, to do so would haunt me for the rest of my life. Every bullet I fired that took a life hit me as well. My wounds may not bleed, but they are at least as painful as, and sometimes more so than, the ones that do. For a normal person—and by that I mean someone like me who takes no pleasure in killing—pain and guilt are the legacy of success in war.

My first month home after Vietnam I did my best to pick up with life in Granbury where I had left it. But it was clear pretty quickly that I no longer fit in. I went over a nineteen-year-old kid and came back a twenty-year-old who needed geriatric care. I was an old man. My outlook on life had changed.

Even though I was home in Texas, I still felt responsible for my crew and my friends that were still in Vietnam. Was it survivor's guilt? I'm not sure, but I suppose it could have been. The last person on my M-88 crew was due to rotate in September 1970. Even though I didn't have contact with them—something I regret now—I was concerned about them. On more than one occasion I tossed and turned thinking about what they might still be going through, trying to figure out if I'd trained them well enough to survive.

During that thirty-day home leave, I got together with a bunch of kids I had gone to school with. It was a Saturday night and we were talking about going to the movies. I remember them debating what we were going to see like it was so important. I said, "C'mon, guys, be realistic. This is Granbury, Texas. It's summer. We've got one drive-in with one screen. We can either watch the early picture, or wait and go to the late movie. Unless we drive to Fort Worth, that's the choice."

The truth was, I couldn't even believe I was in the middle of this discussion, and I told them so. "It's just not important, y'know? It doesn't mean anything; it just doesn't mean anything." Clearly they didn't get it. Or possibly I was the one who didn't get it.

I was thinking, *We're going to a movie, or we're not. We're going on a date with a girl, or we're not. She's going to give it up or she's not. C'mon, folks; nobody's dying over this. It doesn't make any difference. If you don't go tonight, you go tomorrow night. If she doesn't give it up tonight, she'll give it up tomorrow night. Or maybe she won't give it up at all. Who cares?* I just knew that nothing that mattered to my friends made any difference to me anymore. Coming home after surviving Vietnam didn't make me a hero; it made me a stranger, and no one I knew was prepared to deal with me on those terms.

My brother-in-law Denver nearly paid the ultimate price for not paying attention to my little mental souvenirs of the war. While I was home on leave he kept insisting that I go out hunting with him. When I was growing up, and especially while I was in high school, we'd gone hunting together quite a bit. Deer, rabbits, varmints—everything that kids growing up in rural or small-town Texas got their marksmanship training on. But Denver didn't sense the change that had taken place in me during my time in Vietnam, and he kept giving me these verbal pokes in the shoulder, the way brothers can do to each other, to get me to relive the good old days.

Finally I relented, and we took our .22 rifles—mine was a semiautomatic—and drove out of town, parked the car along the road, and began hiking in the brush looking for rabbits or squirrels. I'd warned him several times during the drive out of town, and again when we began walking, that he couldn't fire a shot without first letting me know that he was going to shoot. I don't know whether he thought I was kidding, whether he thought he'd have some fun with me, or whether he just plain forgot when he flushed the rabbit or bird or whatever out of the underbrush. Fortunately for him, he was only about thirty feet away from me, because he didn't bother shouting before he shouldered the rifle and fired, and I didn't bother shouting before I dropped to the ground and pumped out several shots in his general direction before I got a grip on myself and stopped squeezing the trigger. He started yelling, skipping and jumping, and even cursing a little bit. He looked like he wanted to cry but he sort of laughed instead. His only comment was "Damn, son, let's go home. I've had enough hunting for one day."

I slowly got up and just looked at him, realizing, more so than he, how close I had come to killing him. That was also the last time I ever went hunting.

We didn't talk about the incident when we returned home; in fact, we never discussed it then or at any of the family gatherings in years to come. The way I felt or reacted was something I could never have explained to my family. I just knew it would be futile to try. Maybe that was one of the reasons I would opt to stay in the army. In the service I knew there were a lot of guys just like me, guys who had done things in Vietnam that they couldn't—or wouldn't—tell anybody about at home. If we had so much to be proud about, why were we afraid to talk about our feelings? Why were we carrying all this guilt?

A month after I got back to Granbury, I packed my bags and reported to Fort Hood, sixty miles north of Austin, Texas, and a three-hour drive from home. I signed in at the replacement company, turned in my records, did the usual in-processing, and spent the next two or three days making sure that lawns were mowed to regulation height and that the grounds, as well as areas under the old WWII-vintage barracks, were free of offending cigarette butts.

Most of the guys coming through were just back from Vietnam, and since we were assigned to the replacement depot and couldn't wander off, we tended to sort ourselves out based on what we'd done in the war—the grunts hung around over here, the cannon cockers over there. So we'd sit on the steps outside these old WWII barracks and smoke and talk, or we'd wander off to the dayroom and shoot pool. Right across the street from the reception center was a little snack bar, which, of course, was off-limits to us for reasons that must have made sense to someone who had nothing better to do than think up ways to annoy people, but that didn't stop us from sneaking over there every so often to buy some of the 3.2 beer they sold.

After a couple of days of this Mickey Mouse, I was assigned as a recovery specialist in E Company, 123rd Maintenance Battalion of the First Armored Division. I got settled into life at a stateside army post, and got married.

Her name was Alinda Francis. I'd gone to high school with her, and we'd been on a couple of dates before I went to Vietnam, but it was nothing serious. When I returned to Granbury I began seeing her again. She was seventeen and I was twenty, and I guess we were in love. She had already left school when we got married, and we moved into a three-bedroom house off post that cost me $90 a month—furnished.

Shortly after that I reenlisted, but it wasn't because I liked the food. What I actually enjoyed was the regimentation. There were very few decisions that I had to make. They told me what to wear, what to eat, where to be, and how to get there, and even though I'd had some horrible experiences in Vietnam, I still thought the army was a great place for this kid from Granbury.

Okay, so the reenlistment bonus helped. What they'd come up with was a variable reenlistment bonus based on how critical your MOS (military occupational specialty) was. I had a reasonably high variable, so when I signed up for six years, I got about ten thousand dollars. That's in 1970 dollars. We bought a new car, a mobile home; we thought we had money to throw in the wind. Of course, we were also pregnant with twins, but we didn't know that until the first one was born and the doctor surprised us. The boys were born just ten months after we got married.

My first few months back in the world were a whirlwind. I returned from Vietnam in April of '70 and reenlisted less than ninety days later, in June, right around the time I got married. Then came a real kick in the head: A month later I came down on a levy to go back to Vietnam.

I'm not one to piss and moan about the unfairness of life, but if ever there was a time to see the chaplain and get my TS (tough shit) card punched, this was it. Instead, I took a shot with the divisional personnel center, where I whimpered and cried, "Oh, wait, guys, I've only been back ninety days. It's not my turn."

Fortunately, the captain I spoke with agreed. "Well, y'know, Mitchell, I guess you're right. It's probably not your turn. There are too many other guys here who haven't been."

Assuming my problem had been fixed, I said, "Good!" Should've remembered what my drill sergeant in basic taught us about "assuming makes an ass of U and me." In August I came down on the Vietnam levy again.

I went back and saw the same captain again. "Y'know, I'm only back a hundred and twenty days, and I'm married, she's pregnant, and, like I said, I've only been back a hundred and twenty days. Seems like we oughta share the wealth of these tours!"

He looked up. "She's pregnant?" He took care of me again.

In 1971 the 1st Armored Division was moved to Germany, and the 1st Cavalry Division was rotated back to the United States from Vietnam for the first time since the Korean conflict. So now, here I was back in the 1st Cavalry Division, but this time I wasn't an infantryman. The unit structure changed, and as part of that realignment I was assigned to B Company, 315th Composite Support Battalion (provisional), and I was still a recovery specialist. Things were actually going pretty well, when fourteen months after my last Vietnam scare, the phone rang again.

They called me and said, "You're on a levy. Go to the orderly room." I was thinking, "Oh, man, I've been back over a year. There's nothing that's going to keep them from shipping me back to the war." I was thinking about Alinda and imagining her trying to deal with the two babies by herself. I was thinking that it was only by the grace of God that I survived the first tour over there; the likelihood of making it through another tour when the North Vietnamese had a much stronger foothold in the country was not good. A lot of things go through your mind, including whether I could give up Budweiser in favor of Molson or Labatt's. I knew it wasn't just draft dodgers who'd gone to Canada; there'd been lots of newspaper stories about deserters being welcomed up there, and even in Sweden. Surprisingly, it turned out the levy wasn't for the war. They were sending me to Germany, which had the reputation of being really good duty for Americans in uniform.

Despite the positive things that had been happening in my life to this point, the demons remained with me, paying regular but un-scheduled visits. I still had nightmares, still woke up with cold sweats that drenched the linens. There was no way to hide it from Alinda, because she could see and hear what was going on, but even though she asked questions, I was not inclined to give any kind of detailed answers. I'd just tell her not to touch me. At the risk of sounding like I'm putting words in her mouth, I think she was hoping that if she ignored it, it would go away. She probably thought, *He hasn't been back long; the war is still fresh in his mind.* Her dad was a World War II vet, a Seabee in the Pacific. I never knew whether he came home with any problems. Somehow, although I never asked Alinda, I have the feeling that she may have talked to her mother about it—but I don't really know.

Then there were the other PTSD symptoms I had—even though my condition had yet to be labeled. I had a startle response that was second to none, and when you consider all the armor and artillery units that were assigned, trained, and maneuvered at Fort Hood, I recall spending a lot of time trying to hide my jumpiness so no one would know. After all, I was a man, right? The Fourth of July was no treat for me, especially in Texas, where any fool could buy fireworks from a roadside stand. It took a while for the people I worked with to learn not to come from behind and touch me without first speaking to me. I needed to know they were there before I heard them. After a while I just told 'em flat out, "Don't do that, because it might not be a pleasant experience for you, and it's certainly not going to be a pleasant experience for me when it's over, because I'm going to be saying, 'Oh, shit, what have I done?' "

I wasn't like a lot of vets who got out of the army; the sound of helicopters didn't bother me that much. Fort Hood was home to a corps headquarters and two combat divisions, so there were chop-pers flying night and day. When we went to the field and they'd come in flying nap-of-the-earth, you could tell which aviators had been to Vietnam and which hadn't just by watching them fly. A low pass over my head did tend to get my attention, however.

One time Alinda and I had gone to a department store in Killeen, and she was trying on a dress while I wandered between the racks, looking for something I thought she might like. Everything was just fine until two women walked behind me and started conversing in Vietnamese. Talk about a chill down your spine. I didn't say anything, and I consciously had to keep myself from an overt physical reaction—like diving under the clothes racks. Because just like that—boom!—I was somewhere else. This happened at a time when I wasn't sleeping well, anyhow, and the sudden mental trip back to the war didn't help.

But then we were off to Erlangen, Germany, where I became a recovery NCO with 3/37th Armor of the 1st Armored Division, and in less than a year that assignment morphed into my becoming the assistant motor sergeant of the newly redesignated 3/37—it became the 2/81st Armor of the 1st Armored Division.

Three years after the twins, Doug and Don, were born, our youngest son, Kevin, came along. Having three young children at home was difficult, and the fact that I was given to mood swings and awful displays of temper didn't help my relationship with Alinda. The nightmares were still with me, and there were times I literally thought that my Vietnam demons were sitting on my shoulder, talking to me.

There were several that paid me regular visits: the woman whom I killed on my second sniper assignment; the four Buddhist monks on my third; my buddy Dave, who died after I waved off the medevac helicopter coming to get him; and my rigger, Bill, whose brain was splattered all over me when an enemy sniper picked him off the back of our M-88.

Bill's death was one of those dumb things that happen in war. Who knew a guy could die because he drank too much coffee? We were on the road to one of the fire bases to pull a gun back to Phu

Bai for repair, when Bill told me we needed to stop so he could take a leak. So at the top of the next rise, we stopped. He got down, took care of business, and climbed back up, taking the mechanic's position in the right front hatch.

Just as we started to move, a single shot range out, hitting Bill in the head, spraying gore everywhere. Frantically, we tried to locate the shooter, but my sniper experience taught me that if you only fire one shot, the odds of being spotted are slim.

I remember calling for a Dustoff to evacuate his body, and then reaching inside the track to find a towel so I could wipe myself off. Strange what you remember years later. When I got back to Phu Bai, I recall that I was almost hysterical trying to get the organic splatter that had been part of my buddy off of me. I couldn't get it done fast enough.

I was not given to a lot of daytime flashbacks. Most of the time I had nightmares. I knew some people who had only flashbacks, and some had both nightmares and flashbacks. In my case the little demons would share my pillow and whisper in my ear. I would wake up in a cold sweat, breathing very fast, and sometimes crying. It always seemed to take place within the first half hour of sleep. I would start tossing and turning, talking in my sleep. Your heart races, you break out into a sweat, your respiration rate is really high, like you have just run three or four races back-to-back without a rest period. You are confused about where you are and what you are doing. It takes a few minutes for you to settle down enough to cry.

Alinda and I made it through another year in Germany, but it was clear to her that our future together was destined to be rocky. She was unhappy living with a person who was obviously miserable. After a period of time she took the kids and left Germany. It was a real blow to my pride, an "I can't hold on to my woman" kind of thing.

Just before Christmas 1974, my dad was hospitalized and I was given emergency leave to go home, and then four months later, when Dad died, I got a compassionate reassignment back to Fort Hood as a recovery NCO with the 1/7th Armored Cavalry of the 1st Cav. Somehow Alinda and I got back together. A year and a half later we found ourselves living in air force housing at Vance Air Force Base when I was assigned to a two-man recruiting station in Enid, Oklahoma.

It marked the beginning of the end of our marriage. I'd begun drinking heavily, and I was still unable to control my temper. I believe the appropriate description of me at the time was "flaming asshole." You know the kind. If assholes were jets, I would have outrun the shuttle.

In June 1978, I was reassigned as motor sergeant of C Battery, 1/333rd Field Artillery, a Lance missile outfit, stationed in Wiesbaden, Germany. It was supposed to be a two-year tour, and we'd decided that Alinda and the boys would remain in the United States. I hadn't been there two months when I got a long brown envelope.

Getting served with divorce papers was devastating, but looking back, I'm not sure if it was because I was in love with her, or because it was an affront to my male ego. I was hurt and angry at the same time. The impact on me was something that I would not wish on my worst enemy. In addition to the PTSD, now I had a "failure as a man" kind of thing going on. The loss of my sons, who were eight and five years old, was devastating, but I really didn't go out of my way to avoid terminal damage to my relationship with the three boys.

I stayed in Germany another three and a half years, seeing the boys only once or twice each year. I don't know which is the chicken and which is the egg here, but they felt I had deserted them and we grew apart.

I now have a relationship with one son, and would like to reestablish a relationship with the other two, but to this point—and it's probably my fault—that has not happened.

CHAPTER FIFTEEN

I Can't Dance; Don't Ask Me

I was truly shitfaced.

It was a Friday evening in June 1980, and my unit at Camp Pieri near the big air force base at Wiesbaden, Germany, had just come through an IG inspection with a rating of 97 percent. We had our outbrief in midafternoon, and by three thirty we all headed to the club for country night. By eight o'clock I was feeling no pain. In fact, I wasn't feeling much of anything when a friend of mine, also a Vietnam vet, named Michael Shively came over and said, "C'mon over; I've got this girl I want you to meet."

I said, "Okay, but let me finish my drink first." I was drinking pretty heavily then, but I don't think it was because of the marriage breakup. I'd been self-medicating before my marriage to Alinda fell apart, and it had continued. I'd figured out that after a night of binge drinking, when I went to sleep I didn't have the dreams—or at least I didn't wake up and remember them. While it wasn't a long-term solution to the problem, it worked for a while.

When Shively invited me to meet this girl, I was already half in the bag. Or maybe farther. I guess I finished the drink; I don't know. I don't remember. But I went across the club to where Shively was sitting and he introduced me to Ellen, who had the biggest blue eyes

I'd ever seen in my life. She had a big smile and was wearing a green blouse and green pants with heels.

Ellen remembers the event that ultimately led to our marriage in a bit more detail. "I saw a fairly drunk, very happy, pretty good-looking guy about my age come staggering over to meet me. He was, y'know, kind of 'real glad to meetcha' kind of thing. He had a real nice Texas accent, and it was clear that he was trying to really maintain. He could still walk, but even that was getting a little iffy."

She's telling the truth—sort of. The fact is that I was just struck dumb by her. I sat down at the table and looked at her. I'm not sure how long it took me to speak, but the first thing I said was "I'm sorry, what was your name again?"

Actually, I must have asked for her name at least five times. Based on my performance at the club that night, I'm surprised that she wanted to see me again. But Ellen says there was just something about me that hooked her. "He was sweet and kind and polite. If I went to stand up, even as inebriated as he was, he'd stand up, clumsily, and pull my chair out for me. Guys just don't do that that often. He just made me feel good."

The other thing that was going on is that my buddy Shively had set me up by telling Ellen that I really like to dance. Truth? I can't dance; don't ask me. But when I came back from the bathroom and once more said, "I'm sorry. What was your name again?" she told me, but added, "I hear you really love to dance."

Even if sober, I would have been just as confused. "You did? I do?"

"Yeah," she said, "that's what Mike tells me. So do you want to dance?"

I did what any red-blooded American male would do under these circumstances. I said, "Uh, sure. But it has to be a slow one."

When the band started playing "Blue Eyes Cryin' in the Rain," Willie Nelson's number one hit and Grammy winner from a few years earlier, we got up, and it was like we had been dancing together all of our lives, her head on my shoulder, my arms holding her close, and the lyrics of a sad song about lost love.

If I hadn't known better, I'd swear it was a setup. Here I am, drunk out of my mind, but on the dance floor holding on to a woman with blue eyes to rival Bo Derek's, and I still couldn't remember her name. I don't even remember leaving the club. I woke up the next morning, opened my eyes and looked around, and thought, *This is not my room.* I raised my head up, looked around some more, and realized that I was in somebody's government quarters, and I said, "My God, what have I done?" followed immediately by "More important, who have I done it with?"

It turned out I was sleeping on a couch covered by a sheet. I lifted it up, took a look, and figured that I must have been good, because I still had my clothes on. My car keys were on the coffee table and my shoes were sitting there. Amazingly, awake now, I did remember Ellen's name. I got up, crept over to the window, and looked out. My car was sitting there. Okay, that was a good sign. So I slipped on my shoes, opened the door, and left. To this day I cannot tell you whose quarters I was in, how I got there, what I did, if anything, after I got there, or who it might have been with. I went back to my own room and went to sleep. The odd thing is, no one ever mentioned it, which was totally out of character for my friends, who must have known.

Once I recovered from the evening's excesses, I began questioning Shively about Ellen. He didn't know all that much. She was a private, just arrived in Germany from Lance missile training school at Fort Sill, Oklahoma. She'd gotten married when she was nineteen, separated five years later, and finally divorced at twenty-seven, just before she enlisted.

I wanted to see her again, but thought I may have killed that possibility with my liquor-induced behavior at the club. Since I had no recollection of our parting that night, I didn't know whether she'd left the possibility open for a second encounter. But I decided to take a shot. A group of us were going to Luxembourg for the Fourth of July, and I asked her to go with us.

Sometimes I think a good case could be made that men and women are actually representatives of different species. I thought that by inviting her on the trip, I was including her in what should be a fun outing. She didn't quite see it that way.

"I wasn't impressed at all. I mean, really—one girl, Gary, and a bunch of other guys? I told him, 'No, thank you very much.' And I didn't speak to him again for about three weeks. Then he asked me out again."

I tried to have a simple date with her at the Eagle's Nest, the little club on post. But she lived in a coed barracks, and one of the guys decided she needed his company wherever she went, including on what I had hoped would be our first date. For whatever reason, Ellen couldn't keep him from coming along. It wasn't a good sign. There we were, the three of us together. Not quite what I'd hoped for. I knew I had to do something, or Miss Blue Eyes and I would have no future worth speaking of.

At long last, the third wheel got up to go to the bathroom, and I leaned over and said, "Y'know, if you can get rid of your bodyguard, why don't we do this again tomorrow night?" She agreed, and the next night Ellen literally had to sneak out of the barracks. We went to the same club and just sat there and talked about all sorts of things.

She says, "I learned that he was a Vietnam veteran and was waiting to be promoted to E-7, sergeant first class. I found out our ages were really close—he was thirty and I was twenty-seven. It made him a little nervous that I was an E-nothing, and he was soon to be promoted to E-7, which would make him a senior NCO. Talk about the appearance of fraternization. The good thing was that he was the motor pool sergeant and not in my Lance missile battery. I learned that he was the youngest of fourteen children, and was a Texas boy through and through—grits, greens, and fried green tomatoes, while I was from Southern California."

It was fairly obvious that I was attracted to her, and I was quite nervous about dealing with some of the heavy stuff in my life. I'd been divorced for two years and had three kids whom I didn't have much contact with. I had no idea how she'd deal with that. But she said it wasn't a problem; she was also divorced. Truth is, it took a while before I was comfortable enough to share the details of why my marriage had fallen apart, and by the time I did, we were engaged.

Actually, I proposed to Ellen on the second date we had without the bodyguard. I walked her back to her barracks and said, "Let's just sit here on the steps." We were about halfway down the stairway to the arms room, just sitting there and talking, when I proposed to her. Actually, I think I made a statement that we were going to get married rather than asking her. It was probably a bigger shock to me than it was to her. I'd told my mother after the divorce that I'd never get married again, and she'd said to me, "Now, son, one of these days a woman's going to come along and sweep you right off your feet, and you will get married again."

I remember saying to her, "She'd better have a damned big broom."

And that was what I said to Ellen—that she had a damned big broom. I wanted her to say yes, but had no idea what her response would be. She thought for a moment, and then said, "I'm flattered. But I don't think I'm going to say yes or no at this point. Let's give it a year and we'll see how things work out."

It wasn't a week later that Ellen got to see a sample of what I'd been living with since I came back from Vietnam. She was spending the night in my room and witnessed me having nightmares firsthand.

Ellen describes it like this. "Gary would wake up every night, three and four times a night, screaming. He'd wake me up, first calling out call signs, and then telling somebody to be careful. And then he started yelling, 'You gotta move! You gotta move now!' It was just awful.

"And then he would wake up; it would be like a springboard action. He'd spring forward and be stiff as a board in a cold sweat.

I couldn't bend an arm or anything. The sweat would pour off of him, and he didn't know where he was. In his mind he'd woken up in Vietnam, so I had to be real careful around him. He never hit me, but I knew that was a possibility.

"I would start talking to him immediately, telling him, 'Honey, it's okay, you're here, you're not in Vietnam. I'm sitting right here beside you,' and I'd take his hand and start to rub it a little bit. And his breathing would go from being labored to shallow and panting. It was terrible. It would take a good five minutes for him to come back around."

Ellen asked me what I was dreaming, but there was no way I could tell her. There was no way she could understand. So all I'd say was "I can't tell you that. It's awful and I can't tell you."

At the same time she was seeing me have the nightmares, Ellen was also getting the sense that I had a drinking problem. I had my own stool at the club. If I came in and somebody else was sitting there, the bartender would make him move. And by the time I got from the door to the bar, my first drink would be sitting there waiting for me. Coupled with the drinking, I also had anger-management issues. Anything could trigger a tirade; it didn't matter whether it was a family issue at home or a job-related situation on the base. When you add up the nightmares, the drinking, and the anger problems, it should have been clear that something wasn't quite right with me and I needed help. But this was 1980. The army wasn't all that supportive of troops with emotional or mental issues, so walking into the docs and asking for help would not have been a good career move.

Even for Vietnam vets who were no longer in the service, getting help with post-traumatic stress disorder was problematic. The first vet center (more formally, the Veterans Readjustment Counseling Center) wasn't established until late in 1979 after a full ten years of political debate about the need for the services they would provide. And when Public Law 96-22 was finally passed, it still didn't deal with the situation realistically. The VA opened ninety-one centers nationwide in 1980, but the law that funded them mandated one year of buildup, one year of operation, and one year of wind-down. The assumption was that the need for services would be met in those three years. What it said to vets was that the government really didn't take our condition seriously, because there's no other explanation for such a wham-bam-thank-you-ma'am approach to mental health care. And if you want to put this all in the context of the times, the nation's first acknowledgment that Vietnam veterans deserved national recognition, the dedication of the Vietnam Memorial on the Mall in Washington, didn't take place until 1982.

Anyway, there I was in Germany, a package of raw nerve endings wrapped up in an army uniform, trying to be loving and lovable while drunk, angry, and, at times, terrified. I knew that my problems had already cost me one marriage, and the loss of the marriage eventually cost me a relationship with my three sons. The problems were exacerbated by the fact that I was halfway around the world, and seldom got to see them. Now that I'd found someone who thought that I was, if not wonderful, at least redeemable, I feared losing her if she found out the source of my problems. So every time Ellen asked me about my nightmares, I declined to tell her.

About the sixth or seventh time it happened and I refused to answer her questions, she'd had enough. She asked me directly, "What were you dreaming?"

I said, "I can't tell you that. It's awful, and I just can't tell you."

"Nope," she said to me, "that's not going to work anymore. Obviously there's something really wrong here. Have you ever talked to anyone about your experiences in Vietnam?"

I said, "No."

And she said, "Well, you're going to tonight, and we're going to start right now, and I don't care how long it takes. I don't care what you tell me. I just want you to start from the beginning and go to the end and just tell me."

So the two of us sat there on my little single bed in the small barracks room, and I told her about Vietnam. What she didn't know was that I didn't tell her all of it. There was no way I felt she was prepared to hear some of the things I'd done.

Ellen remembers the night precisely. "He starts telling me different stories from Vietnam, and some of them were horrendous. Some of them were funny—but most were horrendous. And as I learned years later, he wasn't telling me the sniper stories. He was holding back.

"I think Gary saw a chance to be able to tell somebody something, but he was so convinced that if anybody knew what he had done in the military, he'd be a pariah. But he did tell me about his best friend being hit—that was Dave. And about another buddy being hit and his brain matter splattering all over him. That was one of the most horrific experiences that he had."

That conversation went on for more than three hours. We talked, and I cried, and we talked some more, and I cried some more. She never interrupted, never asked for clarification. She just let me talk. But I was holding back on the stuff that I thought would make her hate me and cause her to leave, and it hurt because I couldn't let her know that there was more to tell. Even so, over the course of time I felt different. The nightmares didn't stop immediately, but their frequency diminished. Instead of five and six a night, I'd have maybe three a night, and then two, and then one, until it got down to one a week. That was a huge improvement.

Three months later things seemed to be working out between us, and she said, "Okay, we can consider ourselves engaged. I accept your proposal." We went right down to the PX at Wiesbaden and picked out an engagement ring together.

When word got around, I got called into my commander's office and received a lecture about fraternization. I'd been promoted to E-7 and Ellen was still a private. Technically we weren't violating any regs, because I wasn't her supervisor. But my CO advised me to not make things look so obvious on post—not to go around kissing and holding hands. Camp Pieri was small—very small. So we had to be more than a little circumspect.

In the meantime, of course, Ellen was getting the word on me from my so-called friends. The highlight, or maybe lowlight, was their description of me jumping from windows when husbands were coming home. It's just the sort of thing you want your fiancée to hear.

It was about three months after we got engaged that we revisited my Vietnam experiences. I'd sewn on my E-7 stripes and moved into the place they called Amelia Earhart, a military hotel that had three floors dedicated as the senior NCO billeting facility. I was transferred to a combat aviation helicopter unit at Lindsey Air Station, and the sergeant major from that outfit was retiring. The timing was bad for me to go to a party and get loaded, because Ellen was going through a cancer scare. She'd had a bad Pap smear, and the doctors were talking about uterine cancer. She got the results—thankfully negative—the day of the party.

Instead of being with her waiting for the results, I went to the retirement dinner and came back late at night, commode hugging, nonwalking drunk, without even remembering that she was supposed to get the results of the tests that day. When I walked into the room after having vomited all over myself, I found a very angry woman waiting for me. Realizing that I was in no condition to discuss my shortcomings as a concerned fiancé, she told me to sleep it off, and left.

When Ellen returned to confront me, she was still very angry, but she saw that I was distraught. Ellen recalls having read: "A lot of people go to war and do what they have to do, and they're able to compartmentalize everything. 'This was war, so therefore it was okay, and it doesn't need to interfere when you return to a normal life.' But it turns out that like many people, Gary wasn't able to do that. In his case, I think it was his religious upbringing: It's a sin to kill, period. And there's no compartmentalization there. You're doing it because you're told to do it, and you're in the army, so it has to happen. But there's nowhere to put it to make it okay. It just floats around and bings around in their brain, somewhat like a Ping-Pong ball with no real place to settle, and it does horrible things.

"One of the things Gary would do when he was very angry at himself—he didn't even know why he'd do some of these things— he would hit himself, hard, in the face, in the chest, on the arms, on the legs, in the stomach, with a clenched fist.

"When I confronted him with his behavior—coming back drunk as he was, and not being there for me on a very scary day—this was his way of dealing with it. Punching himself everywhere he could. And that was scary. But I just knew that a lot of this had to be tied somehow to Vietnam. Nobody had ever mentioned PTSD; that was not anything that was even discussed. But his bizarre behavior just seemed to pop out in heavily stress-laden circumstances. There was nothing normal about it, and he knew it.

"So once he got through that particular episode, I said to him, 'Okay, there have to be other things that you didn't tell me. Let's do it now. Just sit down and start telling me.'"

Without saying it, Ellen was offering me a choice between calling off the engagement or spilling my guts about Vietnam. Not much of a choice when I'd already lost one wife and my kids over it. I didn't know how to explain to her that I was so angry that I had to hit something—and I didn't want it to be her. So I hit myself, sometimes until there were some very ugly bruises.

So while I wasn't ready to tell her everything, I had to share some of what I'd done in Vietnam. I told her that I'd been in country for a short time when they sent me to a sniper training school and taught me how to shoot under every condition imaginable. Then I told her that I went back to my unit, and from there I was sent on quite a few sniper missions where I killed people. I never got specific, but made it clear that killing unsuspecting people on assignment is different from killing in combat, where it's kill or be killed.

I remember Ellen sitting there and listening, and not acting as though what I'd told her was shocking. Years later she let me know that she had been shocked, but she said, "It wasn't like you'd done something horrible. You had no choice. You couldn't go to your company commander and say, 'Excuse me, I don't think so.'"

Ellen would go through a conversation like that with me, telling me that I did what I was told and that was my only course of action at the time, and I'd sit there nodding my head in agreement. If it made her feel better to think she was making me feel better by saying that stuff, what the hell? I had to keep in mind where she was coming from. She was relatively new to the army and was still showing the effects of the indoctrination a recruit receives in basic and advanced training. She also didn't have any rank on her sleeve that would allow her to attempt to even negotiate what she felt was a bad order. As for me, I knew that had I been an E-7 in Vietnam instead of an E-4 when I got assignments that were problematic, I might have had some tools to better deal with the situation.

Ellen was right when she said that back in Vietnam, the thought that I could say no didn't cross my mind. I never thought I had a freakin' choice to turn down any order I received there. The people giving the orders weren't concerned with my future mental health or how the assignments they were giving me were colliding head-on with my moral compass. Hell, I'm certain that some of those people, especially the anonymous ones who handed out orders from an unmarked armored personnel carrier, really weren't concerned with my future at all—or whether I had one beyond the next few hours.

We were trained to follow orders immediately, without question, because actions or lack of actions could have cost someone his life, or at the very least, been responsible for setting him up for a life of agony.

On November 6, 1981, Ellen and I got married in Mission Hills, California, a suburb in the San Fernando Valley. We'd flown from Germany to Texas to see my family, then on to California for the wedding. My mom and my one surviving brother, Howard, attended. Out of my thirteen brothers and sisters, I had only the one brother and two sisters left at that point, and there's only one sister still with us now.

We had three days for a honeymoon, and spent it at Universal Studios in Hollywood. Then we boarded a Lufthansa flight back to Germany, where we had secured government housing, quarters that were provided for married soldiers and their families. At this point in our lives—even though both of us had been down the aisle before— we were like newlyweds. Hell, we were newlyweds, filled with nothing but optimism and hope for an endless future together. Neither one of us sensed there was a time bomb ticking that could doom our relationship.

CHAPTER SIXTEEN

Another War

In January 1983 I was reassigned to Fort Sill, Oklahoma, where I eventually became the S 2/3 Operations NCO with the 100th Service and Supply Battalion. In 1984, Ellen got out of the army.

About four years after I made sergeant first class (E-7), I took the opportunity to apply for warrant officer school. I'd been in the service for seventeen years, and making the change was not done casually. Ellen and I looked at the positives and negatives, and decided that the significantly larger retirement benefits would make it worthwhile for me to apply.

After I'd been a senior NCO, warrant officer school at Aberdeen Proving Ground, Maryland, was a shock. Perhaps as much of a shock as someone going from being a civilian into basic training as a private E-nothing. But I persevered, went through six months of grief and aggravation, and graduated as "Mr. Mitchell."

The training had been intense and time-consuming—imagine basic training that lasts half a year instead of a couple of months. I did have some of my Vietnam nightmares during this period, which were exacerbated by the fact that we were living in the old WWII-style open-bay barracks.

Once we were newly minted as a warrant officer, the army sent us back to Germany. This time it was Bamberg, where I held down a variety of assignments with the 504th Maintenance Company of the 87th Maintenance Battalion. Four years later it was back to Aberdeen, where I joined the Wheeled Vehicle Department at the U.S. Army Ordnance Center, becoming a branch chief, instructor-writer, and an instructor in the Officer Basic Course. I was in charge of basic knowledge and skills (BKS)—the basics for new mechanics: This is a screwdriver; this is electricity; these are gears and their flow of power.

Life was good and we were happy, which probably is what ensured the likelihood that the army would find something different for me to do. I was sitting at Aberdeen, minding my own business, with twenty-nine instructors working for me. I had a wife, on-post housing, a new car and a new truck, a TV with cable. Oh, Lord, I had forty channels on TV, and someone said, "The boss wants to see you."

I went down and reported to the major, and she said, "I got a deal for you." I knew I was in trouble.

"What kind of deal?"

She said, "You know this thing they're calling Desert Shield? Well, you're going to be part of it."

I tried to tell her that I'd already had my turn in a war, so someone else could go, but she wasn't having any of it. So I went, but I flew over there with a feeling of dread. I had made this flight before, and was not the happiest GI on the airplane among the eleven of us who were on our way to join the American advisory group based near Riyadh. From the time I had come home from Vietnam, I'd managed to keep my commanders from being aware that I had any problems related to my service in a combat zone. I had no way of knowing how being in the line of fire once more might affect me—and there was no way I could discuss that concern with anyone.

The Iraqis had invaded Kuwait on August 2, 1990. On the fifth of September, I was in Saudi Arabia as part of OPM-SANG—acronymese for Office of the Program Manager, Saudi Arabian National Guard Modernization Program. I was one of what would become about 150

Americans officially based in the U.S. military compound in Riyadh, but farmed out to appropriate SANG units in the desert in an effort to improve their war-fighting ability.

My specialty was maintenance, and I was assigned to the maintenance company, part of the Logistics Support Battalion, King Abdul Azziz Brigade (2nd Brigade). The unit was bivouacked just outside the city of Al Khafji, which is on the Persian Gulf just a couple of miles south of the Kuwaiti–Saudi Arabian border. I shared a tent with three U.S. Army captains: two combat engineers, Everett Mc-Daniel and Steve Zeltner; and a quartermaster, Keith Nelson.

From the day I arrived, I knew that it was inevitable that I was once again going to be involved in a shooting war. The only question was when. Actually, that wasn't the only question. Sitting in the tent at night, drinking pot after pot of coffee with our tentmates, we pondered questions like "What happens to us Americans when the war starts? What if we're taken prisoner by the Iraqis? Are we expected to stay with our SANG unit no matter what happens?" Frankly, we were overwhelmed by their lack of fighting ability, but we worked to try to improve it on a daily basis, although at times it seemed as if they resisted our attempts to provide training similar to what American army units do.

The average training day went something like this. We would get up between five and six, drink a pot of coffee, and then make tapes or write home. Around seven thirty I would make contact with the commander of the maintenance company. He and I spent time nearly every day discussing such things as forward support, unit defense, deployment, and maintenance on the move.

His troops would be having breakfast about that time and would have already prayed earlier in the morning—they would get up in the predawn hours to pray, and then go back to sleep. Around eight they would be in their work area and remain there until a little after noon, when they would pray again, and then rest during the intense heat of the day. In midafternoon they would go back to work, and then close down around five or five thirty. A few of the Saudi guards-men were willing, and in fact wanted, to learn how the "American" would do it, and would not rest in the afternoon.

All of us taught classes. Because I'm a maintenance guy, my over-riding concern was to train the Saudi maintenance people to keep their equipment functioning in the midst of battle. The general heading was "battlefield damage assessment and repair," but it's a lot more creative than the manual might make it sound. I actually taught them how to use black pepper in a leaking radiator, how a uniform belt can replace a broken fan belt, and how to drive on a flat tire. We dealt with combat recovery, which meant towing a vehicle out of an ongoing firefight in order to repair it and get it back into service, and taught them how to check a vehicle for booby traps if it had been deserted for a short period of time where the enemy might have had access to it. There's an exact science to performing this task, but our mandate was to teach them what to do while the battle was still raging, so what we showed them to do with the potentially booby-trapped vehicle was to hook a cable to it and jerk it with the towing vehicle. If it exploded, it was booby-trapped. If it didn't, it wasn't. Hey, I never said it was rocket science, but unless someone teaches you these little field expedients, how would you know? We also taught defense against chemical weapons, and testing to deter-mine whether you were under chemical attack. Those were critically important topics because no one knew whether or not the Iraqis would use chemical agents.

Generally, the Saudis we were training had an aversion to live fire exercises, which wasn't surprising when you learn that each soldier was expected to account for every bullet he fired, bringing the brass back to a collection point. We looked upon it as rather lackluster preparation for battle. We also had some questions as to whether sol-diers and officers in the SANG unit would stay and fight, especially if the Iraqi army carried out the threats that Saddam Hussein had made and fired missiles into Israel. Such an act would confuse the situation exponentially, because Israel was the enemy of all the Arab nations. If Saddam attacked Israel—even while his forces were occupying Kuwait—and Israel fired back, the Saudis' natural response would be to ally with Iraq and start shooting at the Israelis. You can see the problem: On one front the Saudis could be fighting side by side with Iraq against the Jewish state, and on another front they could be going toe-to-toe with Saddam's forces.

Given that potential for battlefield confusion, we were more than a little concerned that the day would probably come when our lives were going to be on the line, and we weren't even supposed to have "offensive" weapons with which to fight. Each of us had a sidearm, which wouldn't do much good in an infantry or tank battle in the desert. Actually, the sidearm did have one function that we avoided discussing: We knew that if worse came to worst, we each had one 9mm bullet that we'd saved for ourselves. Being captured by the Iraqis, infamous for their death squads and treatment of prisoners, was not an option for me.

After a day of working with our assigned units, the four of us would meet back at our tent to compare notes on our work and our lives. We did all kinds of things that you normally do in your home. We talked about our families, we played cards and dominoes, we laughed and joked, we listened to the radio station that was owned and operated by ARAMCO, formerly the Arabian American Oil Company, and, of course, we argued, though the disagreements were few and far between. In effect, we became a close-knit family. In our own way we became as close as flesh-and-blood brothers are, and any one of us would have done anything we could for another.

All four of us had become members of the "I shit my pants in the field" club, resulting from severe cases of diarrhea. We even joked about the fact that all of us had donated a pair of "dirty" underwear to our shrine, the field latrine. Our intestinal problems could probably be blamed on CNN. No, this is not another knock on the media by a military guy. Actually, just the opposite. We didn't have a television set in our tent, so each evening we would go next door to the mainte-nance company commander's tent and watch CNN while drinking tea. In the pre–Al Jazeera era, the Arabs really enjoyed America's Ca-ble News Network, especially when honey-haired, blue-eyed Bobbie Batista was in the anchor chair.

Every time we were there, the commander, Captain Ahmed, tried to convince us to stay and eat. Dinner was served Arab-style, which means sans utensils. Aside from the fact that freshly killed goat is not my favorite meal, eating goat or lamb, or occasionally a chicken, solely with my right hand might satisfy the Arabian Miss Manners, but it doesn't do much for me. Consider the technique: Using just your right hand, you strip meat from the carcass that's sitting on a big tray in the center of the table, and eat it. If the piece is too big to swallow in one bite, you have to hold the rest of it in your hand un-til you finish it. There's no individual plate in front of you where you can set it down. Also on the communal tray are rice and sliced veg-etables like cucumber and tomato, all of which must be picked up by hand and shoved into your mouth. And everyone is picking and shoving from the same tray.

Imagine going to Sizzler and watching people help themselves at the salad bar with their hands—no tongs, no forks, no spoons. Just reaching in, grabbing a handful, shoving it into their mouths, and then reaching back in for more. Get the picture? And you thought double-dipping into the chip dip was ugly. Our American digestive systems staged a minirevolt, and more than once we came to the conclusion that a pork MRE was just what the doctor ordered.

While food was a major quality-of-life item and we'd do what we could to see that we ate what we liked as often as possible, fre-quently going into town to shop at local markets, there were other things we did to make life in a difficult environment more livable. Consider bathing. To do so regularly required that we avail ourselves of—how shall I put this?—unorthodox supply channels.

If there's one thing army veterans are good at, it's scrounging.

I was shocked recently to learn that some soldiers—officers and enlisted—had been court-martialed for scrounging abandoned army vehicles in Kuwait, to better equip their own vehicles when they finally drove into Iraq to participate in the occupation. Stealing government property? You've got to be kidding me. If it's sitting there, and no one is using it, and no one is claiming it, and no one is guarding it, then if my guys need it, we take it. If scrounging is a crime, they'd better build a lot more barracks at Leavenworth, because the entire senior NCO corps in the army, air force, navy, and marines are guilty as charged. Actually, in my humble opinion, it isn't stealing; it's just redistributing government property, and I don't believe any number of courts-martial will change that fact. But I digress.

While we were waiting for the first Gulf War to begin, we decided that what was missing from our daily lives was a hot shower. So we took my pickup truck and visited a U.S. unit that was set up south of us and liberated a field shower. We returned to our area, set it up, and borrowed a large propane burner—actually, a goat cooker— from the Arabs. Then we negotiated a deal with the Arab commander: In return for the privilege of using the shower, he ensured us that his water truck would always keep the tank filled, and that we had at least one extra propane cylinder on hand to heat the water.

January 15, 1991, dawned bright and cool in the kingdom of Saudi Arabia. We all knew that this was the final date that the United Nations resolution had set for the withdrawal from Kuwait by the Iraqi forces. But from our position in the desert outside Al Khafji, there didn't appear to be anything or anyone moving.

Our U.S. adviser element kept a few hotel rooms reserved in Al Khafji so that we could make calls, take a shower, or just "get away from it all" for a short period of time.

The rooms were not fancy, and the decor was so loud that you couldn't have slept in the room. If memory serves me correctly, the bedspreads were white with bright—and I do mean bright— blue stripes. The blue was so bright that it would almost blind you.

The walls were yellow, and hanging on them was the standard hotel-type artwork. The great thing about the rooms was the Western toilet, not just a hole in the floor with a water hose. Everyone did his best to make it into Khafji at least once a week to "crap on porcelain." This is life in a combat unit; we take our pleasures when and where we can.

We received a radio call from the senior American logistics adviser, who reminded us of the date and advised us, "If you can possibly make it into Khafji, you might want to go take a real shower." It sounded as though it might be our last opportunity to experience civilization for quite some time, so we immediately rearranged our schedules in order to scramble into town.

When we got into Khafji, it was apparent that everyone was acutely aware of the date. You could almost taste the tension in the air as we drove through the city. The residents were watching us very closely to see what we were doing or what we were going to do. We had been into Al Khafji enough times since the fall of 1990 that everyone in town recognized our vehicles and knew that we were Americans, living and working in the desert not far out of their town.

As a matter of practice, when we went into town, the little group of logistics advisers whom I was with would stop at a market and pick up some fresh vegetables and, at times, some chicken or beef to use in the preparation of our meal that evening. If you purchased chicken, you picked a live one, and the store employees slaughtered and plucked it for you while you waited. Beef, on the other hand, was frozen and usually imported from Argentina.

On this day we didn't get any meat, just vegetables, because we had decided to eat in the hotel restaurant while we were there; the meal was to be one last treat for ourselves. Saudis owned the stores, but the employees were third-country nationals, normally Filipinos.

I developed a great respect for the Filipinos. They didn't make more than about a hundred dollars a month, but they could speak Arabic as well as English. The English they spoke was not always formal English, but we could communicate with very little difficulty, and they kept the stores pretty well stocked. When we stopped on that day, we couldn't move around the store without being followed very closely by the Filipinos and the Arabs who were there.

The Filipinos liked us because we always treated them with the respect due anyone. Usually the Arabs ignored us because we were foreigners and nonbelievers. But this day was quite different. They weren't really sure what to expect from us. They had children and families whom they were justifiably concerned about. All of them were asking us when the war was going to start. They wanted to know, since Khafji was just about a kilometer from the border of Kuwait. The only thing we could tell them was the truth: We didn't know when the war was going to start. Of course, if we had known we couldn't have told them.

After the final shopping trip, we went on to the hotel, called home, and took our showers. It was while I was enjoying that last shower in the hotel in Khafji that I had a fleeting memory of Vietnam. It was just a momentary vision of monks falling. It took a couple of seconds for me to get my breath back, but that was it. I trembled for a few minutes. Fortunately I was in the shower, so none of my buddies were aware that it had occurred, and I certainly wasn't going to mention it.

Freshly showered, we went to a restaurant for what would prove to be our last meal in Khafji. One of the guys ordered a steak and, being the typical American, I said, "Make that two." We were waiting for our meal when one of the guys noted that the server had given me a very strange look when I placed my order. Sure enough, when he brought the meals, he had taken me literally and brought two complete steak dinners—steak, vegetables, and baked potatoes. All we did was thank him for the great service and give him a great big smile until he left—and then we cracked up.

As we were leaving, the servers, and even the cooks, came out and asked us when the war was going to start. They wanted to know when to get out of town. It was the same question when we turned the room keys in at the desk. As we drove out of town, there were four of us in three vehicles—my four-door, three-quarter-ton, four-wheel-drive Chevrolet pickup, and a pair of Chevys—a Suburban and a Blazer. As our little convoy drove past clusters of Saudis on the street, they'd watch us go by as though they might learn something important. I can't prove it, but I think they had figured out that this was going to be our last trip into town.

When my three roommates and I got back to our tent, it was clear that we were ready to get the show on the road. The old military doctrine of "hurry up and wait" had been in effect for weeks, and we were almost insane. In letters, tapes, and occasional phone calls, we tried to keep our wives and families from knowing that we were ready to get it over with, one way or the other. Either go north or go home, and at that point I don't think we were overly concerned about which direction our travel was to be. We just wanted to travel.

We had been waiting since mid-September 1990. Early in the evening of January 17, 1991 (in the USA), it started. That was about four thirty a.m., January 18, 1991, Saudi Arabian time. It was a shock, but at the same time a relief. On that night our "home away from home" changed.

During the initial attacks, coalition force aircraft had eliminated the electronic ability of Saddam Hussein to see what was happening in Saudi Arabia. They destroyed most of his radars that could "see south." From that point on, he had to use people on the ground to determine what we—or rather, all of the coalition forces—were doing.

Within hours of the initial bombing runs, the ground forces that had been massed in the kingdom of Saudi Arabia started moving north to staging areas for the push into Iraq and Kuwait. These units waited for weeks in the staging areas while attacks on the Iraqis were carried out by aircraft and naval forces. We didn't have to move, because the SANG units were already just a few short kilometers from the Kuwaiti border.

When the American advisers were notified by the senior logistics adviser, Lieutenant Colonel Ward, that the initial attacks in Iraq had taken place, it fell to me to awaken the Saudi maintenance company commander to inform him that Desert Shield had become Desert Storm and coalition forces were on the offensive. I knocked on the flap of his tent and called his name until he responded. He stuck his head out of the door, and I simply said, "The war has started. We are bombing Iraq." He said for us to come over and we would watch CNN, but first he needed to check in with his commander. He used radio, field phones, and runners to awaken his company. The entire encampment instantly came to life. You could see small cookers being lit as the Arab soldiers started heating water to make tea. You could also see the blue glow of television sets (the task force had many) as they tuned in to CNN to watch Peter Arnett's reporting on the bombing of Baghdad. I'm not sure about the technology involved in picking up the CNN signal, but most of the Saudi troops had their TV sets hooked to antennae like you used to see on houses before cable. In some cases, they just used rabbit ears.

Throughout the day the SANG units had staff meetings, and we attended a meeting of our adviser group. Our concerns were many. Would we move, how long before we would move, where would we move to, but most important, would the coalition stay together? Saddam Hussein had threatened to launch Scud missiles into Israel should he be attacked. We did not know how the Arabs would react if that happened. Would they remain in the coalition or would they decide that they could not fight against their "Arab brother"? If the latter, we would be in a somewhat uncomfortable position, there being only about 150 of us American advisers scattered throughout the area.

In planning for the possible dissolution of the Arab Task Force, rendezvous points were identified. All of us programmed the rendezvous points into the ground positioning systems that were mounted in our vehicles so we could travel more quickly. We had two types scattered across the advisory group: Loran, commonly used by ships at that time that used beacons; and Magellan, a satellite GPS. My pickup had both mounted in it.

Periodically throughout the day, my tentmates would contact one another via radio, and on various channels we could hear other advisers also contacting one another. Everyone seemed to understand the critical nature of our position and was understandably concerned about the people we had lived with for the past few months. The tone of conversation was quite subdued.

Each of us found some time during the day to write or make a tape home. We all knew that our wives and families were now the ones going crazy. At this point the wait for us was over. For our families the wait had changed and become even more terrifying. They, and we, always had the hope that we would return home without having had to go into Iraq or Kuwait, but now that hope was gone.

That evening, we ate and then had pot after pot of coffee. All of the coffee as well as the situation had us running around like sugared-up ten-year-olds at a sleepover. Late in the evening we settled down and began to talk.

I was the only one in the group who had been in a combat zone before. To say the least, I was not the happiest camper in the tent. One of the guys asked me if I was as scared that day as I was in Vietnam. And I said that the difference was, when I was in Vietnam I was nineteen, twenty years old. And I was just sure in my own mind then that I was indestructible. In Desert Storm I was forty years old, married with three kids, and I knew that I was an old man. I couldn't run as fast as I used to. I knew that I had a low threshold of pain, I cried easily, and I just had a completely different outlook on life. All of these are things that a grown, married person thinks about that a kid doesn't. Do I have enough life insurance? Is Ellen going to have enough money to continue or start a new life? Have I taken care of the kids like I should with the will? Am I going to be killed? Am I going to be captured? Am I going to survive the captivity? The Iraqis had killer teams that were sent down from Baghdad—*infiltrated* was the word we used, because they were put into the regular army squads that were out. And their job was, You start to surrender—no, you don't. So we knew they were there. All of us had been briefed on or had heard from CNN about the "death squads" that were being sent into the Iraqi forces across the border. Were they going to take kindly to us if they captured us?

Our concerns were somewhat simple. We had confidence in ourselves and in the people we were serving with. But there were several lingering concerns. No, they were fears that each of us was trying to deal with individually and within the group. Would we be wounded, would we be captured, would we be killed? And a question that was discussed at length was whether we would surrender if forced to, or would we go down fighting, so to speak? At this point, we had no idea how the Iraqis would treat prisoners or if they would be summarily executed.

We were all concerned about our families and how they were reacting to the start of hostilities (it would be over a week before we received our first letter or tape from home).

Our families back in the States had become close, if only telephonically, since we had been in Southwest Asia. If I told my wife something, I was telling all of the wives. If the others told their wives something, all of the wives would know within a few short hours. At times we were sure they had a better information network than we did.

We talked a great deal among us about our fears. We confessed things to one another that at any other time would have been taboo. We spoke of our wives and our love for them. We wondered aloud if we had invested in enough life insurance—would they have enough money to set themselves up in a "life after death"? How would we conduct ourselves in combat? Would we freeze or react properly? We discussed the fact that we were advisers and were supposed to carry only self-defense weapons, which meant a 9mm automatic sidearm.

The maintenance commander and I had reached an agreement during that day: Screw the rules—he was going to "loan" a rifle, magazines, and ammunition to me.

We also took a closer look at the supplies and equipment that we kept loaded in our vehicles at all times. We increased the quantity of water and rations. We opted to keep all of our clothes in our vehicles and remove them only when we changed, putting the worn clothes back into the vehicles. At that time I was still a smoker, and like all smokers in that moment, I was concerned about how many cartons of cigarettes I needed to stockpile in order to make it through the war or until I could resupply. Two of us had Chevrolet Blazers, one had a Chevrolet Suburban, and I had a Chevrolet pickup (long wheel base with four doors). We each had a teapot and a propane stove with extra fuel tanks so that we could heat water for instant coffee or tea. In a moment of weakness or overcompensation on the preparedness level, we requested extra first-aid kits from the rear for each of us. We discussed our interpreters and what we would do if they declined to go into Kuwait with us because they were civilians and did not have to go if they did not want to.

We decided that we should have one last pot of coffee, and then go to bed. Each of us, without saying anything to the others, took our pistols out of the holsters and began to disassemble and clean them. We even took all of the rounds out of the magazine and blew the magazines out and wiped the ammunition off.

Finally one of the captains brought up faith, a subject that we had not discussed before. He was curious, since he was the only one who went to church services regularly, whether we believed in God. We assured him that, at that moment, all of us were fervent believers. He asked if he could say a prayer for us and for our families. We immediately agreed. All four of us then joined hands and bowed our heads, and he prayed that each of us received guidance and protection if it was in the divine plan, but mostly he prayed for the comfort of our families, whatever the future outcome.

Then, each of us deep in his own thoughts and without another word to one another, we went to bed, knowing that our futures were changed at best and unsure at worst. All of us slept restlessly, even though it was almost midnight when we went to bed, and we were all up drinking coffee again by four o'clock or four thirty in the morning.

I do not recall our speaking of that night again, but I assure you that it was one of the most intimate joining of soldiers that one can imagine.

During the battle fought at Al Khafji, the Logistics Support Battalion commander, Lt. Col. Abdul Rachman Mughem, opted to employ some of the forward support concepts that we as advisers, and the contracted civilian company the Vinnell Corporation, working with the brigade, had been providing training on. When the support element moved forward, I had the distinct honor of moving with them, driving my Chevy pickup as the trail vehicle in the convoy. This battle took place several days after the start of hostilities, but well before the coalition forces began the ground attack against the Iraqis.

We set up in an area near a deserted school just on the outskirts of the city, close enough to see laundry hanging from the balconies of apartment buildings inside Khafji, which meant we were also close enough to hear small arms and heavy weapons from the infantry battalions that were involved in urban warfare.

The forward support team (FST) was almost ready to start evacuating equipment from the streets of the city to the FST area in order to begin repairs or cannibalize equipment that was damaged beyond repair. The object was to recover the equipment, repair it, and get it back to the using unit as quickly as possible under the theory that a gun in the shop is a gun that is useless.

I moved my truck to the south side of the FST (away from the town) and fired up the small two-burner propane stove to heat some water for a cup of instant coffee for myself and tea for my interpreter. Before the water was ready, I saw the unit's officers talking in very excited tones. I was unable to understand Arabic, but my interpreter quickly said that the FST was under fire from the city.

The question was, did we stay or move? After discussion with the battalion HQ, the decision was made to move back. The unit clearly did not have the personnel or weapons to mount a successful defense of the area they presently occupied.

The intensity of fire, along with the level of my blood pressure, had increased significantly. I do not know how many rounds were fired at us—all were small arms—before we moved the support element a little farther away from the city.

The Saudi soldiers were calm, or at least not panicked, as they were tearing down and loading. I helped one soldier load a couple of oxygen and acetylene cylinders onto his truck. Within moments we loaded the bottles, and the interpreter and I were running back to our truck when a round struck the truck we had just loaded the cylinders on. None of us was injured, and none of the equipment on the truck was damaged enough to hinder movement, so we pulled out quickly. Again, I was the last vehicle in the convoy.

Ultimately, U.S. Marines and the Saudi National Guard drove the Iraqis out of Khafji, and back across the border into Kuwait.

After the battle at Al Khafji, things more or less settled down to some semblance of "normalcy." The Saudis held decoration ceremonies, and they did have some genuine heroes to reward.

Once the ground war started, it was over in about one hundred hours. As the coalition forces moved forward, the Logistics Support Battalion, or at least elements of the battalion, moved forward supporting the combat elements. At age forty, I was more than uncomfortable; I was scared out of my wits. I can't speak for the other advisers, but I was not a happy guy. I thought back to Vietnam, and how things had happened there, and realized that each and every war, or even each individual firefight or battle, is different. Each person reacts differently each time.

As the war moved across the border into Kuwait, elements of the battalion moved forward rearming and repairing without much rest, just as did all members of the coalition forces. There was very little, if any, sleep for anyone. The combat units fought and captured a large number of the Iraqi forces, although I'm not sure the Iraqis really had the heart to fight. I was told that in interrogation the Iraqis said that they had not been paid in months, their officers had departed unannounced, leaving them alone, and their water and rations were at a premium. They were demoralized and hungry. They also had the same fears that we had: How would they be treated as prisoners of war? They had been told they would be killed or that any number of horrible things would happen to them if they surrendered.

Finally we received word that it was all over. After looking myself over to make sure that I didn't have any new orifices in my body, I said a prayer of thanks.

However, in Vietnam I learned that it's never over until it's over. Or you're not out of the woods till you're out of the woods. I should have remembered those lessons for Desert Storm. Because just when we thought it was over, my buddies and I were given an assignment that could easily have gotten us blown to kingdom come: We were told to take ground positioning equipment and map the precise coordinates of the massive minefields the Iraqis had laid in Kuwait.

This was not in my contract! Over twenty years in the army, a couple of wars—and now they wanted me to walk and drive around a minefield? Whose bright idea was this? I guess I understand the need to trace the minefield, but I wasn't enamored with the selection of personnel to do it: a couple of engineer captains and yours truly to assist.

When the Iraqis laid the minefields, it had been done quickly, and many of the mines had not been well camouflaged. For us, that was a good thing. But it had rained heavily over the last couple of weeks, and we wondered if the mines had been moved or covered completely with all of that water and sand washing around.

The thought of the mines made for an uneasy trip across the desert. We traveled two in the lead vehicle and one in the trail vehicle. When we got to where the minefield started on the road, we flipped a coin to see who would walk, who would drive the marker vehicle, and who would drive the trail vehicle to start. We'd agreed on half-hour shifts. The guy walking had to physically walk along the edge of the minefield to keep the vehicle from drifting one way or the other and crossing into the minefield. The marker vehicle had a ground positioning system in it that would give ten-digit military grid coordinates.

We were dealing with a variety of mines. There were the little toe poppers, just a couple of inches across, that weren't meant to kill you—just screw you up. Then there were other mines that were twelve and fourteen inches in diameter. And there were also the big thirty-three-inch Russian antitank mines.

The Iraqis also used something like the Bouncing Betty that Americans had faced in Vietnam, but they laid them in sequences of five. If you set off a trip wire over here, the charge would blow that mine about waist-high into the air, and then the main charge would explode at a height designed to tear a soldier apart. But when the first mine blew into the air it pulled a trip wire on the second mine in the chain, and that kept going until all five of them had blown.

We would walk and drive, listing the grid coordinates every time the minefield border changed directions. At the end of the minefield, or at the end of the day, we would list the coordinates again. By the end of it all we had precise points and directions that the minefield traveled that could be shown on a map for intelligence purposes.

We started off and went about a half a kilometer west, and then the minefield took a ninety-degree turn to the south. We followed it south for a ways, and then it turned west again. This went on for almost half a day, turning one way and then another. We were tired, pissed off, and, more important, terrified. We had been out here doing this for nearly four hours and we hadn't reached the end of one side yet. How big was this thing, anyway?

We stopped and had a great MRE meal with Kool-Aid and coffee.

Then we started again, keeping our eyes on a storm cloud slowly heading in our direction. When it began to sprinkle forty minutes later, we recorded the last coordinate of the day and started back to the highway. All of us were shocked to discover that we'd plotted minefield coordinates that stretched almost ten kilometers before we had to stop.

It had been made clear that we needed to finish the assignment, no matter how long it took or what the weather was doing, but we didn't dare go back out there until it had dried up some. We didn't want to get stuck in our vehicles, but more important, we wanted to give the earth time to settle before we started the trek again.

We would make three more trips to the minefield before we completed the trace. When all was said and done, the minefield was about forty kilometers long and ranged in depth from about a hundred meters to a kilometer. It was a sight to see once it was plotted and marked on the map.

At the end of each day we'd sit and drink coffee, wish for something a little stronger, and silently thank God in our own way for another safe trip through the minefield and another safe day.

When it was all over and I was due to leave, I had one ceremonial task that I took care of all by myself. I'd saved a 9mm round from the first day of Desert Storm, kept it in my pocket. That one was for me if worse really came to worst. Would I have had nerve enough to use it? I can't tell you. I don't know. Fortunately it never reached that point. But just before I left for home I walked out into the desert and shot that round. That one wasn't going to be turned in. Was there something symbolic about the act, or was I just acting the fool? I don't know. But after walking the edge of a minefield for days on end, I figured I was entitled.

CHAPTER SEVENTEEN

Get a Lawyer or Get a Shrink

The only real clues I'd given Ellen about what was going on in Desert Storm were vague ones in audiocassettes that I mailed home. Lines like "We had some pretty tense times." My fear—aside from not wanting to alarm her—was that I didn't want specific details to fall into the wrong hands. It's a war zone; stuff happens. But by not letting her know that it wasn't a walk in the park for those of us involved in the battle for Al Khafji, I didn't give her any reason to prepare for the fact that I might be seriously stressed-out when I got back home. I was also dealing with the notion that my homecoming was just going to be temporary.

When the powers that be no longer had any immediate tasks for me to perform, they said I could go back home to Aberdeen Proving Ground. But it was sort of like playing Monopoly—the "Gary" marker was "just visiting." OPM-SANG wasn't ready to release me back to Maryland. I came home just long enough to clear quarters, clear my unit, and then I was going back to Saudi Arabia, only this time Ellen would be permitted to go with me. But first we had to adjust to being back together, and to hear her tell it, that didn't go so well.

"I went to Baltimore/Washington International Airport to pick him up in a limo with champagne. But I could tell immediately that he wasn't comfortable at all. He came out of the terminal wearing his desert camouflage uniform, and he was a different man. He wasn't the Gary that I was in love with.

"I could tell right off the bat that he'd changed. He was really quiet, not really saying a whole lot. At first I thought it had to do with my expectations. You pick someone up at the airport, you expect they're going to be all exuberant. 'Oh, I'm so excited, I'm home!' Y'know? And he wasn't that way. It wasn't that he was upset to see me; it just wasn't the reaction I expected. So I just tried to put it aside—best-laid plans. 'Oh, well, that's just the way it is.' I'd never met my husband after he'd just gone through a war, so everything was brand-new.

"Gary had lost quite a bit of weight in the desert. He'd gone back to his rail-thin self. But he just didn't react to anything the way he had in the past. His sense of humor was gone. He rarely smiled. I'd ask him a question and get two-word answers. He was very pensive, somewhat morose all of the time. I figured I'd give it some time, but after about a week I could see that the behavior was just continuing, not smiling, not joking, not really there. And the aberrant behaviors were starting back up.

"He wasn't hitting himself like he'd done during that period of time in Germany. But he would hit the wall, or he'd throw something across the room. He'd pick up whatever he could get his hands on—a can of food, his keys, fruit, it didn't make any difference. If he was angry and upset, that's what he'd do.

"So I knew we were starting over from scratch. This war had just screwed him up again, but we had no time to try to deal with it because we had to clear quarters, he had to clear his unit, we had to get the household packed up. There are a lot of things that you just kind of let go because you can only deal with so many things on your plate at one time. And then we flew home to see my family in California and his in Texas before flying to Saudi Arabia."

I was blissfully unaware that Ellen had figured out that our old problems were cropping up again. Nevertheless, we both looked forward to my next assignment in the Middle East as a shared adventure.

We were booked on Saudi Arabian Airlines for the flight to Riyadh, and every few hours during the flight the Muslim passengers would check the compass in the cabin that pointed toward Mecca, spread their prayer rugs in the aisle, and pray. But that was just the beginning of a very foreign odyssey.

Being an American in Saudi Arabia after the war was undoubtedly more difficult for Ellen than for me. The notion of living in the fairyland of *Arabian Nights* wore off in a couple of weeks, and whenever we would venture outside the American compound in Riyadh, the medieval treatment of women tended to make life unbearable. Immediately after the war, many of the *Muttawah*—the religious police—had not yet returned to Riyadh, so the rules weren't as strict off post. Ellen wore what the wives called a "paki" outfit—probably because they were imported from Pakistan—which are big, baggy pants that are tight around the ankles and waist, but loose everywhere else. The paki top had a high collar and long sleeves. It also was long enough that it hung almost to the knees. The sides had slits to facilitate movement. On her feet she wore sandals.

But then the *Muttawah* came back, and as a way to reassert their authority and enforce the radical *Wahhabi* form of Islam, they went nuts. She was no longer allowed to wear the paki outfit in public, because women were not supposed to reveal that they had breasts. So they required American women off the compound to wear a black abaya that covered them from the neck down to the ankles, with long sleeves, and a scarf over the head because no hair could be showing.

Ellen was allowed to show her face for the oddest of reasons— because only whores could show their faces, and they considered non-Muslim women to be whores. You could tell they wanted to call her that on the streets of Riyadh. And one time when we were on R & R in Bahrain, a member of the royal family of Saudi Arabia (there are thousands of them) thought nothing of offering a million dollars to take her up to his room. She was a light-haired, non-Muslim female and, therefore, for sale. The fact that she was sitting with her husband didn't stop him; he was ignoring my presence. When she rejected the offer, he returned to hypocritically sipping his liquor through a straw so as not to violate the Koran's dictate that alcohol not touch his lips.

The *Muttawah,* whose official organization is known as the Authority for the Promotion of Virtue and Prevention of Vice, carried heavy camel quirts on the streets, and when they encountered someone who offended them—irrespective of nationality—they'd beat them. One day we'd gone shopping with another American couple in the gold souk of Riyadh. My friend's wife, who was Puerto Rican and darker skinned than Ellen, wasn't feeling well, and remained in the truck by herself. Because of her skin color, the *Muttawah* took her to be a Saudi woman—I guess they chose to ignore the license plates that identified us as foreigners—and began beating on the truck with their sticks, trying to force her to get out of the vehicle. As you can imagine, she was terrified. When we got there, her husband stepped into the fray, and as they usually do when a man is involved, they backed down. But it was an ugly scene.

During prayer call, everything stops. If you're in a restaurant they turn off the lights and pull metal gates down in front of the windows, and you just have to sit there and wait about forty-five minutes, locked in the place, until they're allowed to reopen. One time I had stopped my truck when the call to prayer was made, but I got out and stood there smoking a cigarette, which I shouldn't have done. The *Muttawah* decided he was going to make an issue of it. He came up to me and raised his stick, and I said, "You hit me with that stick, old man, and I'll take it away from you and stick it up your ass! When I do, they're going to take me down to the mosque and cut my head off, but you're still gonna have that stick up your ass." I'm not sure why, but he chose not to pursue the issue any further.

After an incident involving a Canadian woman, men from the Canadian embassy went *Muttawah* hunting and severely beat the ones that they could find in retaliation for the attack on that particular woman and other attacks that had taken place on Western women and men.

Just getting used to the calls to prayer was difficult for Ellen. At first the sounds were exotic, but after a week, five times a day, it was just a pain in the butt. It's loud and intrusive, and you just want to scream, "Shut up!"

Adjusting to the manner in which the Saudi women were treated was also an ordeal. The American military referred to them as BMOs—black moving objects, or "moving eggplants." The only outfit they were permitted to wear was the abaya, with a heavy black veil that completely covered their heads, a mask over their eyes and mouths, black elbow-length gloves, and black socks with sandals. And the temperature, without exaggeration, was 140 degrees.

There was a Baskin-Robbins ice-cream store that had an air-conditioned room for men to go to eat their cones, but women had to order from an outside window and sit on the curb. They'd pull out their veil and shove the ice-cream cone underneath it, sitting on the curb in 140-degree weather.

Our tour in Saudi Arabia lasted a very long year. When I was passed over for CWO-3 a second time, Ellen and I decided that we were going to get out of the army on our own terms, rather than wait for a letter telling me my services were no longer needed—after all, I had already given them twenty-four years. While my officer evaluation reports were top-notch and recommended me for promotion, mentioning my performance under fire with the SANG during the war, what I couldn't overcome was my age. I was forty-two, and with a flood of younger warrant officers moving up, they just didn't need a dinosaur like me. Had I gone to warrant officer school when I was an E-5 rather than an aging E-7, the story might have been different.

In July 1992, after a year in Saudi following the end of the war, I retired from the service. What to do next? The choice I made was the same one that a lot of retirees made: I got myself a job with a company that contracts to the military. I joined the Vinnell Corporation. While Ellen was working for the Bradley program during our tour in Riyadh, a former battalion commander of mine showed up for a scheduled meeting with the Bradley program manager in Saudi Arabia. He recognized Ellen from our days in Germany and started talking to her about me. She told him that I had submitted my retirement paperwork, and he immediately invited us out to dinner that evening. That's when I was recruited for Vinnell in Saudi Arabia. They had a program with the Saudi military involving the Bradley Fighting Vehicle, and while Ellen settled in California with family, I spent two years working for Vinnell in Tabuk, north of Jidda, assisting with and training soldiers for their maintenance program.

The advantage of working for Vinnell is that it was kind of like being in the army. Nearly everyone working there was retired military, and was used to a very structured way of life. So that sort of cushioned the blow of returning to civilian life. But when I finally came back to the States, I went through culture shock. For almost a quarter of a century, everyone around me had been like family. There was always someone around to help if you needed them, for any kind of circumstance.

As a civilian I felt like I'd been thrown to the wolves, and retiring to California it was even worse. Southern California is a place where you don't know your next-door neighbor, and they don't want to know you. That's not the kind of environment I was coming from. Ellen used to say that all of the military is just like living in the South, where everybody's a neighbor and everybody helps one another. So to be out of the military, and in the LA area to boot, was a double blow. It was a lot to get used to.

We experienced quite a bit of shifting around. I'd start one job, be there awhile, and then go somewhere else. What I was trying to do was find my footing and figure out exactly how civilian life worked. In the army, if you did A, you'd get B and C. Rewards or punishments for deeds done or not done were structured; there were no surprises. There was no such promise in civilian life. For me, it was very confusing and difficult to handle, and I clearly had problems with authority figures whose rules I didn't understand. Ellen had a better perspective on what was going on with me than I did.

"I think Gary's difficulties adjusting triggered everything. All the issues he'd been able to kind of put aside to some degree while he was in the military and his time with Vinnell came tumbling out. He went from rarely having outbursts to always having them. The Vietnam nightmares started to come back. He'd wake up in the middle of the night soaking wet with sweat, as though he'd just been through the war in Vietnam all over again. His pillows weren't lasting three months.

"It was like having a cocked gun around; you never knew when he was going to go off. We could be having a perfectly lovely day, and I'd say one thing that somehow set him off. We'd be driving down the street and talking about what we were going to do that night—a perfectly innocent conversation. And things would escalate out of control.

"He might ask me what restaurant I wanted to go to, and I'd make a suggestion, and he'd say, 'Well, that sounds really good.' We'd be laughing and talking, and I'd notice that the stoplight was yellow, ready to turn red. And by the time he'd go through it, it would be red, and I'd say, 'Honey, you just ran through a red light,' and that did it. Now he'd turn the car into a weapon. He'd slam his foot on the gas pedal and shoot forward, and I was taken aback.

" 'What're you doing?' I'd say, and that made him madder, and he'd start swinging in and out of lanes. 'You wanna drive the fucking car?' he'd scream. That sort of thing, until he'd finally calm down. He was the poster boy for road rage—but it didn't even take another driver to set him off. It was just awful.

"As the months went on, things got worse and worse and worse. He'd mostly quit drinking, so that wasn't the problem. Alcohol didn't add to or take away from the rage. It was the same intensity, whether or not he was drinking. And he was having one of these episodes every three or four days."

Ellen talked to me until she was blue in the face, crying, yelling, pounding her fist on the table. I remember her screaming at me, saying, "You've got to hear what you're saying. Can't you hear what you're saying?" But I didn't want to talk about it. I really didn't want to talk about anything. She told me that anger was the only form of expression I had. And she was right. It wasn't about anything concrete; it was just anger for the sake of being angry. I'd be like a race car, going from zero to one hundred in one second. That's how it would go.

By Christmas Day in 1996, Ellen was at her wits' end. She'd tried everything to the point that she was feeling as though she were going crazy, wondering if she was the one doing something to cause my violent mood swings. We'd moved to Azusa, a suburb of Los Angeles, and I was working for Waste Management, doing truck maintenance, when I really snapped. The nightmares had come back full force, and I just wasn't fit to live with. On Christmas Day—a pretty crappy time to act a fool—I started in on her, and it was the straw that broke the camel's back. When I went a little bit nuts because I couldn't easily open the cellophane-wrapped package of dinner rolls, she'd had enough.

She *couldn't* take it anymore, and she'd finally decided she *wouldn't* take it anymore. She told me, "You either get some help now, or you get a lawyer. It's as simple as that. I'm not putting up with it anymore, none of it. You get yourself some help, and if you don't want that, then you can find yourself a new wife."

It was like throwing a glass of cold water in my face. For the first time she said something that actually sank in and got my attention. It took my breath away, and I broke down and started to cry.

The next day when I went into work, I talked to the human resources people and signed up for their employee-assistance program. It would get me only six visits with a psychologist, but it was a start.

A couple of weeks later I showed up at the office of Phoebe Cervantes, a Ph.D. psychologist in West Covina, where my employee-assistance program had referred me. Dr. Cervantes was waiting to get my age, description, etc. I walked in and sat on a couch, while she took a chair off to one side, so as not to block the path between me and the door. I later found out that this was standard shrink operating procedure.

"I know that you're a self-referral through your EAP, so tell me what's going on," she said.

And I began, "Well, my wife thinks I've got a—" And I caught myself, stopped, and started again. "Well, not just my wife. I've got a problem." I began giving her a description of what had been going on, but she interrupted me, and asked me to tell her about myself.

"I work a night shift. I run the maintenance shop for a trash company." She stopped me again.

"I need to know that, but let's go back a ways." By the time the end of the fifty-minute session rolled around, she told me that she was prepared to say tentatively that I was suffering from post-traumatic stress disorder.

I was horrified. Not just because I suddenly had a label, but because I was still seeing things on the news about guys—vets—who couldn't work, didn't work, wouldn't work. They were burdens on society. They were insane. And I was terrified at the thought of being *insane*—that's my word for it, definitely not Dr. Cervantes's. And now I was being told that I'd been insane for years, and didn't know it.

At that first session on the couch I hadn't really gone into the details of what I'd done, or discussed the specifics of what I was reliving in my nightmares. I spent a lot of time talking about my anger-management problem, because I knew that in order not to lose Ellen, that's what I had to fix.

I had no idea of what to expect from a psychologist. What I wanted from her was a miracle. I wanted her to wave the magical psychological wand and say, "Heal," and it would be over. I didn't know if she would send me to a psychiatrist for drugs, or what was going to happen. I was on the verge of losing the woman whom I truly loved, and still do love. I was willing to crawl naked through downtown LA if that was what it took to save our marriage. Did I think it would be a quick fix? Probably so. What I found was the beginning of a journey that is still in progress today.

Toward the end of that first session, Dr. Cervantes asked, "Have you ever written anything about your experiences or dreams?"

The only thing I'd written in the army were reports and evaluations, that sort of thing. I didn't think that was what she meant, so I told her that I hadn't.

She said, "Okay, every time you have a dream or a flashback, I want you to immediately—right then, while it's fresh in your memory—sit down and write about it. Don't worry about spelling; don't worry about grammar. Just let it go. Then bring that back here and we'll go over it together."

I had no idea what she meant by us going over it together. I was still a little bit stunned by the assignment. I'd never really told anyone the whole story. Even when Ellen sat me down in Germany, when our relationship was just starting, I pretty much self-censored. And while I'd swapped war stories with my buddies in the army, those sessions weren't intended to be introspective. Even in that first session with the psychologist, I'd held back; I'd understated things. And she caught me. She said, "Are you being honest with me?" And I knew that I wasn't telling her everything; I was holding back.

At that first session I told her about Dave's death, and how I waved off the Dustoff because we'd started taking fire again. If I recall correctly, I told the story in a pretty mechanical way. "By the time the helicopter came back in, he was already dead." Period. End of discussion. But she didn't go for it. Again, she asked me not only if I was being honest, but if I was being honest with myself.

She told me that I tend to "talk around" incidents, and I didn't really comprehend what she was saying. So she threw my words back at me; she said, "You 'take care of things,' or you 'did the deed,' or you 'took the appropriate action.' What does that mean?"

And I said, "I killed someone." And that was the first time I had said it like that. It had been almost twenty-five years, and I had never really said it out loud, just like that. And I thought, *Okay, I'm gonna write about it, I'll bring it back here, and we'll go over it together.* In my mind, she was going to read it while I sat there looking out the window. I didn't know that wasn't the way she played this game.

I remember coming home and telling Ellen that the shrink wanted me to start writing down my nightmares. We talked about it a little bit, and I told her it scared me. It would've been okay to write it down if nobody were ever going to see it, but now all these things I'd held inside of me, things I'd never really told anyone, were going to be on paper for someone else to actually read.

The next time I had a nightmare, I got up, went to the computer, and wrote it out stream-of-consciousness style. The experience wasn't nearly as bad as I thought it might be, and eventually I would just come home from work, sit down, and begin writing more of the nightmares and memories from Vietnam.

On my second appointment, I walked into Dr. Cervantes's office and handed her a three-ring binder with my writings. She opened it up and began paging through it while I just sat there watching her. For a minute it looked as though she were just going to read it with me sitting there, but then she stopped, looked at me, closed the binder, and handed it back to me. She said, "Why don't you pick one and read it to me?"

It was a terrifying moment. It's one thing to write it. It's one thing to see it in the privacy of your own mind. But it's another thing to

share it and read it with a complete outsider. We had no relationship, and I knew that this therapy with her was not going to be a
long-term thing. The company paid for six sessions, and this was the
second.

I flipped through the pages of the binder and chose to read her
my memories of how my buddy Dave had died before I could get a
Dustoff in. I don't recall deliberately avoiding reading one of the
sniper missions to her, but it's a pretty good bet that it was a sub-
conscious decision not to go there—at least not yet.

I tried watching her face while I was reading my memory of what
happened to Dave. I was looking for a reaction. Let me tell you, I
wouldn't want to play poker with that woman. She didn't show any
emotion at all. In fact, the only time she showed any emotion was at
the end of our last session, when I was leaving. She asked me if she
could make a copy of what I'd written so she could share it with the
other members of her staff.

Anyway, I finished reading to her and sat there waiting for a reaction. She said, "Have you ever told your wife anything?"

"Not really," I said, knowing that when Ellen had made me talk in
Germany about the nightmares, I'd kept a lot of the truth from her.

Cervantes was pretty blunt, saying, "Well, she's hung around for
all these years. Don't you think she has a right to know? These things
helped form the person whom she fell in love with and married, and
has been with, and put up with. You should let her read it."

At first I was dumbstruck with that notion. And then panic began
to set in. I'd been keeping this stuff from Ellen for almost twenty
years, and now there would be no way to maintain my secrecy any
longer. But I was caught between the classic rock and a hard place.
Sharing my memories with her was difficult, but the alternative was
that if I didn't do what my therapist was asking me to do, the consequences of that choice were even worse. Because if Ellen saw that I
wasn't taking the therapy seriously, I'd be sitting in a lawyer's office
right quick.

The first story I gave her to read was about me shooting the water buffalo. But it was really about me being scared stiff. We were living in a house in Azusa at the time, and I didn't want to be around her while she was reading. So she took the binder and went out and sat by the pool. Ellen says, "It was funny and poignant at the same time. He'd never told me that before. But I could feel what it was like for him to be brand-new in country, out on his first patrol, and terrified. From reading it, I could sense what it was like to hear that strange sound coming toward him in the dark, with no one else making any noise, and the fog is settling in, and he's thinking that everybody around him has been slaughtered and he's the only one left to deal with it. It's easy to laugh about it now—too easy. But it began to give me some insight into what was going in Gary's head.

"After the water buffalo story, I kept right on reading, and that's when I got into the bad stuff—one of the sniper stories, and then the tunnel story, then another sniper story. When we talked about them, he said something about feeling like a Mafia hit man, standing up there, not really in any danger yourself. And there for the purpose of killing a specific person. That was really hard for him to deal with, and it was difficult for me to figure out how I felt about it.

"When I read about his second mission, killing the woman, I knew that for Gary, that cut him more than anything. I know my husband, and deliberately hurting women or children was something that would be virtually impossible for him to do. I saw how he reacted to the mistreatment of women in Saudi Arabia. I honestly would have thought that he'd be incapable of deliberately killing a woman.

"But it was war, and you just don't have the choice. I know that from my own time in the army. The only choice that he would have had was to say no, and then be court-martialed. And I don't believe that as a nineteen-year-old kid he thought he could do that. We've talked about it, and I believe that once he got the training, it never entered his mind to say, 'I'm not going to do it.' He wasn't happy when he found out what he'd been sent to school for. When he was there, he just thought it was a good time. 'Oh, boy, they're teaching me how to shoot better.' They didn't slap him upside the head and say, 'Boy, this is what you're going to school to learn how to do.'

"At nineteen, you're just a stupid kid who's expected to be an adult. That's the problem. I think guys like my Gary were rushed out of childhood so fast and into a weird kind of adulthood, that I don't know that the rest of your psyche catches up with you. And now, much later, we see that it has taken an awful toll."

After she'd had a chance to read what I'd written, Ellen and I sat down to talk. She told me that what she'd read hadn't changed her feelings for me one bit. I cried when she said it. I'd been terrified that reading my journal would make her hate me.

The following week I went back to see Dr. Cervantes. She said, "Okay, did you let Ellen read it?"

"Yes."

"Well, what was her reaction?"

I sort of grinned and said, "Well, she's still here." She didn't push me more for Ellen's reaction. She did something that, at the time, I thought was worse.

"Well," she said, "I think it's time to share it with someone else. Pick a couple other people in your family and let them read it, too."

That was one of the hardest things I ever had to do. I knew Ellen loved me, and I had a sense that she wouldn't throw things at me after she read it. But I couldn't be sure about anyone else. I discussed it with Ellen, and together we picked her mother and her younger sister. I was terrified, literally terrified, because up until that time I had just been Gary, the guy Ellen married who had dragged her all over the world. I didn't know how they were going to react, what it was going to do to my relationship with them or theirs with me. Was it going to change their perception of me, because perceptions are real? It may not make sense, but I was probably more scared of that than I was of giving it to Ellen to read. Ellen had been there when I was having the nightmares; she'd experienced the temper tantrums—nobody else had.

"But he truly was horrified at the notion of giving the journal to my mother and my sister, for them to know what kind of monster he thought he was. It was probably the bravest thing he's ever done. I think he would've rather faced a firing squad."

My fears turned out to be unfounded. Ellen's family reacted with support and loving kindness, and when I finally gave it to my own sister to read, she was loving and supportive as well. As a footnote, I would add that my mother and father both went to their graves without ever knowing about their "baby boy." I really don't think my mother would have been surprised, because I remember that when I was home during my thirty-day leave after Vietnam, she made a point of telling me that I'd changed. I guess mothers really do have a sixth sense, an intuition about their children.

By the end of my sixth and final session with Dr. Cervantes, I was not a happy camper. I didn't think that we had the money to continue paying for therapy on my own, so it was over, and I didn't know what other resources were available. Additionally, I was on my way to Alabama for a job interview. I really didn't have a good grasp on how what happened to me and what I had done in Vietnam related to my anger-management problems twenty-five years later. I just knew it wasn't a straight line. Besides that, I felt like I had met my promise to Ellen to get some help. Dredging up, writing about, and sharing what I felt was "my hurt" was not something that I really wanted to do any more than I was absolutely forced to do.

Dr. Cervantes gave me some education about PTSD when she first diagnosed it in me. The way I recall it, she said that when a person is exposed to a traumatic event—whether it's a car wreck, a family member being kidnapped or murdered, witnessing the death of a child—PTSD can result. Everyone reacts differently to these traumatizing events. Some people aren't bothered, other people get bothered a little bit, and some people end up with a lifelong disability.

(See the appendix for a series of information sheets provided by the VA explaining PTSD, its symptoms, diagnosis, and treatment, as well as where to go for help.)

Cervantes said, "You've got a very mild case of PTSD," and I'm thinking, *If this is mild—my God*... because by that time I had realized that my problems with anger control, the temper tantrums, nightmares, and just being an ass were a result of my trying to manipulate myself. In other words, it's a way of escaping the problems that I have, while trying to convince myself and those around me that I am as normal as everyone else—nothing that has happened has had an effect or has changed me.

Even though I had only half a dozen sessions with Dr. Cervantes, I feel that I got a lot out of it. My instant reaction to her diagnosis was that it meant I was insane. She took the time to tell me that I wasn't. She basically said, "This is what the problem is; we may not be able to cure it, but there are tools to help you manage it."

In retrospect, what I should have done was figure out a way to stay in therapy. Instead, I opted for a change of scenery. An opportunity had arisen to move to Huntsville, Alabama, and work for a company that a guy I'd been in the service with was starting. Both Ellen and I wanted out of California, and this seemed like the perfect move. I promised her that once we got to Alabama, I'd find a way to continue therapy—but I didn't.

We loved Huntsville, but the startup company didn't expand or progress as fast as they expected it to, so I was laid off. And unless you're a farmer or a rocket scientist, it's hard to find a job there. We struggled for six or eight months and nothing developed, so we moved back to California, and I went back to work for the same company I'd been working for when we left. Once again, Ellen and I had problems. My anger was out of control.

She says, "We got to the same point again where I had to threaten him with divorce in order to get him to seek help. And that's when he went to the Vet Center in Sepulveda and got himself into a group."

Even though the group wasn't run by a licensed therapist, he was a trained readjustment counselor. In the beginning I felt like I was getting help from the group therapy sessions. A little later I realized that a core group of guys wanted to spend the entire session talking about the great drugs they'd done during the war. Others just bitched and moaned and griped and complained about the same damn things over and over and over again. I put up with it for nearly a year, hoping that my complaints to the group's facilitator would result in constructive change. Unfortunately nothing improved. It seemed that some members of the group felt that the army was responsible for their use of drugs, alcohol, or whatever they chose to use in their efforts to relieve the pain—some mental, some physical.

One night, after what I felt was another useless group session, Ellen and I went online and found a Web site dedicated to Vietnam veterans, where families could leave notes on a message board. A typical note said, "Could someone from my dad's unit please contact me?" And they'd give the unit. "We'd like to know what my dad did in Vietnam. He would never talk about it."

And that phrase echoed. "Never talk about it, never talk about it, never talk about it." That's what they all seemed to say. And almost every dad, brother, or husband on that list had either died of cancer or suicide or drug- or alcohol-related overdoses. But the suicides far outnumbered everything else, and Ellen and I were looking at the screen as I was scrolling through it, and it's "committed suicide, committed suicide, committed suicide." So many of them. And then there were the guys who died of cancer from Agent Orange.

Ellen recalled the moment we found that Web site. "It was so horrifying that they're still killing themselves over a war that's been over for so many years. The number of people they say were killed in Vietnam—the 58,000-plus whose names are on the Wall—is so far off because they're still being killed, and they're still dying because of Vietnam.

"It was so upsetting, we both just broke down into tears and sobbed for about half an hour, just going through that list and seeing how hopeless it could be. And I believe that was a huge turning point for Gary. It's when he realized that he had to get a grip on what had happened to him, on what was happening to him, and try to understand that there were things he could do to control his feelings, his responses to triggers that were way out of proportion to whatever was going on at the moment."

Over the past few years I've tried everything from food supplements to hypnotherapy to help control the outbursts. And they seem to have helped. I've spent more time just feeling normal again—normal like before I went to Vietnam. Frankly, I'd forgotten what that was like, because the craziness had become my new normal, and that clearly wasn't conducive to a happy, ordinary life.

And that's basically where I am right now. I told you at the start that this was the story of my journey. I'm still on the road, still finding my way, occasionally stumbling, but much more optimistic than I've been in years. I still haven't reconciled with all three of my sons, although I have hope that they will one day find time in their lives to forgive me for not being there when needed. To this point, I've still not spoken to them about the things that have happened. Maybe this writing will be, in some small way, an explanation. I hope so.

Ellen and I are still together, still planning on being together forever. I can't forget that my road to recovery really started when she told me to get some help. That was like a slap in the face, warning me that I was getting ready to lose the best thing that had ever happened to me if I didn't make some changes.

I think that in a way it's like alcoholism: Even though it is never cured, you simply have to learn how to coexist with it. First you have to admit you have a problem before you realize that you need help. Since I stood up and said, "Hi, my name is Gary," Ellen has been right there with me. She's laughed with me, cried with me, fussed at me, and put up with my fussing at her. She's always realized that I didn't choose to become the way I am; it's just something that happened. Although she has never condescended to or withdrawn from my pain, she also has never let me off the hook. She made me face who I was, made me see the value in trying to change, and helped me try to use the tools that I have learned to try to get through it. What more could I ask of her?

APPENDIX

The following fact sheets are adapted from the Web site of the National Center for Post-Traumatic Stress Disorder of the Department of Veterans Affairs.

For additional information:
- Visit http://www.ncptsd.org/facts/index.html. References and research citations for the information reprinted here may be found at the Web site.
- Call the PTSD Information Line at (802) 296-6300
- Send e-mail to ncptsd@ncptsd.org

What Is Post-traumatic Stress Disorder?

Post-traumatic stress disorder, or PTSD, is a psychiatric disorder that can occur following the experience or witnessing of life-threatening events such as military combat, natural disasters, terrorist incidents, serious accidents, or violent personal assaults like rape. People who suffer from PTSD often relive the experience through nightmares and flashbacks, have difficulty sleeping, and feel detached or estranged, and these symptoms can be severe enough and last long enough to significantly impair the person's daily life.

PTSD is marked by clear biological changes as well as psychological symptoms. PTSD is complicated by the fact that it frequently occurs in conjunction with related disorders such as depression, substance abuse, problems of memory and cognition, and other problems of physical and mental health. The disorder is also associated with impairment of the person's ability to function in social or family life, including occupational instability, marital problems and divorces, family discord, and difficulties in parenting.

Understanding PTSD

PTSD is not a new disorder. There are written accounts of similar symptoms that go back to ancient times, and there is clear documentation in the historical medical literature starting with the Civil War, when a PTSD-like disorder was known as "Da Costa's Syndrome." There are particularly good descriptions of post-traumatic stress symptoms in the medical literature on combat veterans of World War II and on Holocaust survivors.

Careful research and documentation of PTSD began in earnest after the Vietnam War. The National Vietnam Veterans Readjustment Study estimated in 1988 that the prevalence of PTSD in that group was 15.2 percent at that time, and that 30 percent had experienced the disorder at some point since returning from Vietnam.

PTSD has subsequently been observed in all veteran populations that have been studied, including World War II, the Korean conflict, and the Persian Gulf populations, and in United Nations peacekeeping forces deployed to other war zones around the world. There are remarkably similar findings of PTSD in military veterans in other countries. For example, Australian Vietnam veterans experience many of the same symptoms that American Vietnam veterans experience.

PTSD is not only a problem for veterans, however. Although there are unique cultural- and gender-based aspects of the disorder, it occurs in men and women, adults and children, Western and non-Western cultural groups, and all socioeconomic strata. A national study of

American civilians conducted in 1995 estimated that the lifetime prevalence of PTSD was 5 percent in men and 10 percent in women.

How Does PTSD Develop?

Most people who are exposed to a traumatic, stressful event experience some of the symptoms of PTSD in the days and weeks following exposure. Available data suggest that about 8 percent of men and 20 percent of women go on to develop PTSD, and roughly 30 percent of these individuals develop a chronic form that persists throughout their lifetimes.

The course of chronic PTSD usually involves periods of symptom increase followed by remission or decrease, although some individuals may experience symptoms that are unremitting and severe. Some older veterans, who report a lifetime of only mild symptoms, experience significant increases in symptoms following retirement, severe medical illness in themselves or their spouses, or reminders of their military service (such as reunions or media broadcasts of the anniversaries of war events).

How Is PTSD Assessed?

In recent years, a great deal of research has been aimed at developing and testing reliable assessment tools. It is generally thought that the best way to diagnose PTSD—or any psychiatric disorder, for that matter—is to combine findings from structured interviews and questionnaires with physiological assessments. A multimethod approach especially helps address concerns that some patients might be either denying or exaggerating their symptoms.

How Common Is PTSD?

An estimated 7.8 percent of Americans will experience PTSD at some point in their lives, with women (10.4 percent) twice as likely as men (5 percent) to develop PTSD. About 3.6 percent of U.S. adults aged 18 to 54 (5.2 million people) have PTSD during the course of a given year. This represents a small portion of those who have experienced at least one traumatic event; 60.7 percent of men and 51.2 percent of women reported at least one traumatic event. The traumatic events most often associated with PTSD for men are rape, combat exposure, childhood neglect, and childhood physical abuse. The most traumatic events for women are rape, sexual molestation, physical attack, being threatened with a weapon, and childhood physical abuse.

About 30 percent of the men and women who have spent time in war zones experience PTSD. An additional 20 to 25 percent have had partial PTSD at some point in their lives. More than half of all male Vietnam veterans and almost half of all female Vietnam veterans have experienced "clinically serious stress reaction symptoms." PTSD has also been detected among veterans of the Gulf War, with some estimates running as high as 8 percent.

Who Is Most Likely to Develop PTSD?

1. Those who experience greater stressor magnitude and intensity, unpredictability, uncontrollability, sexual (as opposed to nonsexual) victimization, real or perceived responsibility, and betrayal.
2. Those with prior vulnerability factors such as genetics, early age of onset and longer-lasting childhood trauma, lack of functional social support, and concurrent stressful life events.
3. Those who report greater perceived threat or danger, suffering, upset, terror, and horror or fear.
4. Those with a social environment that produces shame, guilt, stigmatization, or self-hatred.

What Are the Consequences Associated with PTSD?

PTSD is associated with a number of distinctive neurobiological and physiological changes. PTSD may be associated with stable neurobiological alterations in both the central and autonomic nervous systems, such as altered brain-wave activity, decreased volume of the hippocampus, and abnormal activation of the amygdala. Both the hippocampus and the amygdala are involved in the processing and integration of memory. The amygdala has also been found to be involved in coordinating the body's fear response.

Psychophysiological alterations associated with PTSD include hyperarousal of the sympathetic nervous system, increased sensitivity of the startle reflex, and sleep abnormalities.

People with PTSD tend to have abnormal levels of key hormones involved in the body's response to stress. Thyroid function also seems to be enhanced in people with PTSD. Some studies have shown that cortisol levels in those with PTSD are lower than normal, and epinephrine and norepinephrine levels are higher than normal. People with PTSD also continue to produce higher-than-normal levels of natural opiates after the trauma has passed. An important finding is that the neurohormonal changes seen in PTSD are distinct from, and actually opposite to, those seen in major depression. The distinctive profile associated with PTSD is also seen in individuals who have both PTSD and depression.

PTSD is associated with the increased likelihood of co-occurring psychiatric disorders. In a large-scale study, 88 percent of men and 79 percent of women with PTSD met criteria for another psychiatric disorder. The co-occurring disorders most prevalent for men with PTSD were alcohol abuse or dependence (51.9 percent), major depressive episodes (47.9 percent), conduct disorders (43.3 percent), and drug abuse and dependence (34.5 percent). The disorders most frequently comorbid with PTSD among women were major depressive disorders (48.5 percent), simple phobias (29 percent), social phobias (28.4 percent), and alcohol abuse/dependence (27.9 percent).

PTSD also significantly impacts psychosocial functioning, independent of comorbid conditions. For instance, Vietnam veterans with PTSD were found to have profound and pervasive problems in their daily lives. These included problems in family and other interpersonal relationships, problems with employment, and involvement with the criminal justice system.

Headaches, gastrointestinal complaints, immune system problems, dizziness, chest pain, and discomfort in other parts of the body are common in people with PTSD. Often medical doctors treat the symptoms without being aware that they stem from PTSD.

How Is PTSD Treated?

PTSD is treated by a variety of forms of psychotherapy and drug therapy. There is no definitive treatment, and no cure, but some treatments appear to be quite promising, especially cognitive-behavioral therapy, group therapy, and exposure therapy. Exposure therapy involves having the patient repeatedly relive the frightening experience under controlled conditions to help him or her work through the trauma. Studies have also shown that medications help ease associated symptoms of depression and anxiety and help with sleep. The most widely used drug treatments for PTSD are the selective serotonin reuptake inhibitors, such as Prozac and Zoloft. At present, cognitive-behavioral therapy appears to be somewhat more effective than drug therapy. However, it would be premature to conclude that drug therapy is less effective overall, since drug trials for PTSD are at a very early stage. Drug therapy appears to be highly effective for some individuals and is helpful for many more. In addition, the recent findings on the biological changes associated with PTSD have spurred new research into drugs that target these biological changes, which may lead to much increased efficacy.

Help for Veterans with PTSD and Help for Their Families

Veterans experiencing the symptoms of post-traumatic stress disorder (PTSD) often request several types of assistance, as do their families. As a research and education organization, the National Center for PTSD cannot provide this assistance, but we can refer you to the people who can provide assistance. Here are the answers to some questions about PTSD and service-connected disability that are frequently asked by veterans and their families.

Do I Have PTSD?

A natural first question is whether the symptoms really are due to PTSD. Stress symptoms are not always due to PTSD, and it is helpful to know if they are specifically the result of psychological trauma and if they are the full condition of PTSD. Such symptoms may be due to other conditions created by stressors other than trauma (for example, work or financial pressures), medical problems (such as heart conditions or diabetes), or other psychological conditions (such as depression or anxiety).

Resources

The VA Medical Center system's specialized PTSD clinics and programs can provide to eligible veterans educational information and diagnostic evaluations concerning PTSD. The Readjustment Counseling Service's community-based Vet Centers can provide educational information and diagnostic evaluations concerning PTSD to any veteran who served in a war zone or in a military conflict (such as in Panama, Grenada, or Somalia).

If I Have Other Stress, Medical, or Psychological Problems, Do I Also Have PTSD?

Veterans with PTSD often have other types of stress, medical, or psychological problems in addition to PTSD. Sometimes PTSD is unintentionally overlooked when other problems seem particularly pressing, and it can be helpful to know if PTSD also needs to be treated.

Resources

VA Medical Center specialized PTSD programs and VA Readjustment Counseling Service Vet Centers.

What Kinds of Education and Treatment Can Help Me (or My Veteran Family Member)?

There are several types of education and treatment for PTSD that have proven helpful to veterans and their family members. These include classes on dealing with PTSD symptoms, stress, anger, sleep, and personal relationships. Individual, group, and family counseling and selected medications have also been helpful.

Resources

You may wish to begin by reviewing the general information on PTSD provided on our Web site. For specific options for education and treatment in your local area, contact the closest VA Medical Center specialized PTSD program or VA Readjustment Counseling Service Vet Center.

How Can I Establish That I Am Disabled Due to PTSD Caused by Military Service?

A determination of service-connected disability for PTSD is made by the Compensation and Pension Service, an arm of VA's Veterans Benefits Administration. The clinicians who provide care for veterans in VA's specialized PTSD clinics and Vet Centers do not make this decision. A formal request (claim) must be filed by the veteran using forms provided by the VA's Veterans Benefits Administration. After all the forms are submitted, the veteran must complete interviews concerning her or his social history (a review of family, work, and educational experiences before, during, and after military service) and psychiatric status (a review of past and current psychological symptoms and of traumatic experiences during military service). The forms and information about the application process can be obtained by benefits officers at any VA medical center, outpatient clinic, or regional office.

The process of applying for a VA disability for PTSD can take several months and can be both complicated and quite stressful. The Veterans Service Organizations provide service officers at no cost to help veterans and family members pursue VA disability claims. Service officers are familiar with every step in the application and interview process and can provide both technical guidance and moral support. In addition, some service officers particularly specialize in assisting veterans with PTSD disability claims. Even if a veteran has not been a member of a specific veterans service organization, the veteran still can request the assistance of a service officer working for that organization. In order to get representation by a qualified and helpful service officer, you can directly contact the local office of any veterans service organization. You may also wish to ask for recommendations from other veterans who have applied for VA disability or from a PTSD specialist at a VA PTSD clinic or a Vet Center.

My Claim for a VA PTSD Disability Has Been Turned Down by the Benefits Office, but I Believe I Have PTSD Due to Military Service. What Can I Do?

Contact a veterans service officer, who can explain how to file an appeal and who can help you gather the information necessary to make a successful appeal. You may want to contact a service officer who has extensive experience in helping veterans file and appeal claims specifically for PTSD.

I Can't Get Records from the Military That I Need for My Disability Claim. What Can I Do?

Veterans service officers can help you file the specific paperwork required to obtain your military records. If your service officer is not able to help you get necessary records, ask him or her to refer you to another service officer who has more experience in getting records.

Partners of Veterans with PTSD: Caregiver Burden and Related Problems

By Jennifer L. Price, Ph.D., and Susan P. Stevens, Psy.D.

Introduction

A number of studies have found that veterans' PTSD symptoms can negatively impact family relationships and that family relationships may exacerbate or ameliorate a veteran's PTSD and comorbid conditions. This fact sheet provides information about the common problems experienced in relationships in which one (or both) of the partners has PTSD. This sheet also provides recommendations for how one can cope with these difficulties. The majority of this research involved female partners (typically wives) of male veterans; however, there is much clinical and anecdotal evidence to suggest that these problems also exist for couples where the identified PTSD patient is female.

What Are Common Problems in Relationships with PTSD-Diagnosed Veterans?

Research that has examined the effect of PTSD on intimate relationships reveals severe and pervasive negative effects on marital adjustment, general family functioning, and the mental health of partners. These negative effects result in such problems as compromised parenting, family violence, divorce, sexual problems, aggression, and caregiver burden.

- *Marital adjustment and divorce rates.* Male veterans with PTSD are more likely to report marital or relationship problems, higher levels of parenting problems, and generally poorer family adjustment than veterans without PTSD. Research has shown that veterans with PTSD are less self-disclosing and expressive with their partners than veterans without PTSD. PTSD veterans and their wives have also reported a greater sense of anxiety around intimacy. Sexual dysfunction also tends to be higher in combat veterans with PTSD than in veterans without PTSD. It has been posited that diminished sexual interest contributes to decreased couple satisfaction and adjustment.

Related to impaired relationship functioning, a high rate of separation and divorce exists in the veteran population (those with PTSD and those without PTSD). Approximately 38 percent of Vietnam veteran marriages failed within six months of the veteran's return from Southeast Asia (President's Commission on Mental Health, 1978). The overall divorce rate among Vietnam veterans is significantly higher than for the general population, and rates of divorce are even higher for veterans with PTSD. The National Vietnam Veterans Readjustment Study (NVVRS) found that both male and female veterans without PTSD tended to have longer-lasting relationships with their partners than their counterparts with PTSD. Rates of divorce for veterans with PTSD were two times greater than for veterans without PTSD. Moreover, veterans with PTSD were three times more likely than veterans without PTSD to divorce two or more times.

- *Interpersonal violence.* Studies have found that, in addition to more general relationship problems, families of veterans with PTSD have more family violence, more physical and verbal aggression, and more instances of violence against a partner. In these studies, female partners of veterans with PTSD also self-reported higher rates of perpetrating family violence than did the partners of veterans without PTSD. In fact, these female partners of veterans with PTSD reported perpetrating more acts of family violence during the previous year than did their partner veteran with PTSD.

Similarly, Byrne and Riggs (1996) found that 42 percent of the fifty Vietnam veterans in their study had engaged in at least one act of violence against their partner during the preceding year, and 92 percent had committed at least one act of verbal aggression in the preceding year. The severity of the veteran's PTSD symptoms was directly related to the severity of relationship problems and physical and verbal aggression against the partner.

- *Mental health of partners.* PTSD can also affect the mental health and life satisfaction of a veteran's partner. Numerous studies have found that partners of veterans with PTSD or other combat stress reactions have a greater likelihood of developing their own mental health problems compared to partners of veterans without these stress reactions. For example, wives of Israeli veterans with PTSD have been found to report more mental health symptoms and more impaired and unsatisfying social relations compared to wives of veterans without PTSD. In at least two studies, partners of Vietnam veterans with PTSD reported lower levels of happiness, markedly reduced satisfaction in their lives, and more demoralization compared to partners of Vietnam veterans not diagnosed with PTSD. About half of the partners of veterans with PTSD indicated that they had felt "on the verge of a nervous breakdown." In addition, male partners of female Vietnam veterans with PTSD reported poorer subjective well-being and more social isolation than partners of female veterans without PTSD.

  Nelson and Wright (1996) indicate that partners of PTSD-diagnosed veterans often describe difficulty coping with their partner's PTSD symptoms, describe stress because their needs are unmet, and describe experiences of physical and emotional violence. These difficulties may be explained as secondary traumatization, which is the indirect impact of trauma on those in close contact with victims. Alternatively, the partner's mental health symptoms may be a result of his or her own experiences of trauma, related to living with a veteran with PTSD (e.g., increased risk of domestic violence) or related to a prior trauma.

- *Caregiver burden.* Limited empirical research exists that details the specific relationship challenges that couples must face when one of the partners has PTSD. However, clinical reports indicate that significant others are presented with a wide variety of challenges related to their veteran partner's PTSD. Wives of PTSD-diagnosed veterans tend to assume greater responsibility for household tasks (e.g., finances, time management, house upkeep) and the maintenance of relationships (e.g., children, extended family). Partners feel compelled to care for the veteran and to attend closely to the veteran's problems. Partners are keenly aware of cues that precipitate symptoms of PTSD, and partners take an active role in managing and minimizing the effects of these precipitants. *Caregiver burden* is one construct used to categorize the types of difficulties associated with caring for someone with a chronic illness, such as PTSD. Caregiver burden includes the objective difficulties of this work (e.g., financial strain) as well as the subjective problems associated with caregiver demands (e.g., emotional strain).

Why Are These Problems So Common?

Because of the dearth of research that examines the connection between PTSD symptoms and intimate-relationship problems, it is difficult to discern the exact correspondence between them. Some symptoms, like anger, irritability, and emotional numbing, may be direct pathways to relationship dissatisfaction. For example, a veteran who cannot feel love or happiness (emotional numbing) may have difficulty feeling loving toward a spouse. Alternatively, the relationship discord itself may facilitate the development or exacerbate the course of PTSD. Perhaps the lack of communication, or combative communication, in discordant relationships impedes self-disclosure and the emotional processing of traumatic material, which leads to the onset or maintenance of PTSD.

What Are the Treatment Options for Partners of Veterans with PTSD?

The first step for partners of veterans with PTSD is to gain a better understanding of PTSD and the impact on families by gathering information. Resources on the National Center for PTSD Web site (http://www.ncptsd.org) and in the reference list for this fact sheet may be useful. Particularly helpful are the National Center for PTSD fact sheets about the definition of PTSD, effects of traumatic experiences, and frequently asked questions relevant to veterans and their families. Fact sheets on PTSD and the family and PTSD and relationships may also be useful.

With regard to specific treatment strategies, Nelson and Wright (1996) suggest, "[E]ffective treatment should involve family psychoeducation, support groups for both partners and veterans, concurrent individual treatment, and couple or family therapy." Psychoeducational groups teach coping strategies and educate veterans and their partners about the effects of trauma on individuals and families. Often these groups function as self-help support groups for partners of veterans. Preliminary research offers encouragement for the use of group treatment for female partners of Vietnam veterans. Individual therapy for both the veteran and his or her partner is an important treatment component, especially when PTSD symptoms are prominent in both individuals. Couples or family therapy may also be highly effective treatment for individuals' symptoms and problems within the family system. Several researchers have begun exploring the benefits of family or couples therapy for both the veteran and other family members. In light of the recent research on the negative impact of PTSD on families, Veterans Affairs PTSD programs (http://www.va.gov) and Vet Centers (http://www.va.gov/rcs/) across the country are beginning to offer group, couples, and individual programs for families of veterans.

Overall, it seems that the most important message for partners is that relationship difficulties and social and emotional struggles are common when living with a traumatized veteran. The treatment options listed earlier are but a few of the available approaches that partners may find useful in their search for improved family relationships and mental health.

Additional Resources

Vietnam Veteran Wives (VVW http://www.vietnamveteranwives.com), established in 1996, is an organization designed to meet the needs of veterans and their families. The specific and primary purpose of VVW is the advancement of research and the distribution of information about PTSD, Agent Orange, and Gulf War diseases. VVW publishes a variety of literature, including newspapers, magazines, and brochures. VVW provides PTSD counseling, safe retreats for wives during times of crisis, a national hotline, and assistance to the families of incarcerated veterans. Membership is open to all family members and significant others of anyone that served in the military during any period.

Avoidance

by Laura E. Gibson, Ph.D., The University of Vermont

Why Have a Fact Sheet on Avoidance?

Avoidance is a common reaction to trauma, and it can interfere with emotional recovery and healing. It is understandable that individuals who have experienced stressful events want to avoid thinking about or feeling emotions related to those events. Research with a wide variety of populations (e.g., survivors of sexual abuse, rape, assault, and motor vehicle accidents) indicates that those individuals who try to cope with their trauma by avoiding thoughts and feelings about it tend to have more severe psychological symptoms. Because the research clearly suggests that avoidance can interfere with recovery and healing, this fact sheet provides an overview of this common reaction to trauma.

What Does Emotional Avoidance Mean?

Emotional avoidance in the context of trauma refers to people's tendency to avoid thinking or having feelings about a traumatic event. For example, a rape survivor may try to suppress thoughts about her rape by forcing herself to think about other things whenever the thoughts arise, or by simply trying to push away thoughts about the rape. She may use emotional avoidance by stopping herself every time she begins to feel sadness about the rape, or by bringing her attention to something that makes her feel less sad. She may say things to herself like "Don't go there" or "Don't think about it."

What Does Behavioral Avoidance Mean?

Behavioral avoidance generally refers to avoiding reminders of a trauma. An extreme example of behavioral avoidance would be for someone who lived in Manhattan to move out of the city after the 9/11 terrorist attacks to avoid reminders of the trauma. Less extreme examples might involve remaining in Manhattan but making sure to avoid Ground Zero to avoid difficult emotional reminders. Other examples would include individuals who try to avoid driving after they have been in car accidents, or assault survivors who go out of their way to avoid the scene of their attack.

Doesn't Avoidance Help People Cope with Trauma?

Not when it is extreme or when it is the primary coping strategy. Many people were raised hearing advice like "Just try not to think about it," "Try to think about positive things," or "Don't dwell on it." These suggestions seem very logical—especially if you grew up hearing them regularly. However, although the desire to turn one's attention away from painful thoughts and feelings is completely natural, research indicates that the more people avoid their thoughts and feelings about difficult life stressors, the more their distress seems to increase and the less likely they are to be able to move on with their lives.

Is All Avoidance Bad?

No, not all avoidance is bad. If you have experienced a traumatic event in your life, it can be extremely useful to learn ways to focus your thoughts and feelings on things that are not related to the trauma. This is typically referred to as "distraction." Distraction is a useful and necessary skill that allows us to get on with our daily routines even when we are feeling very distressed. If it weren't for our ability to distract ourselves, we would have difficulty getting on with our lives after traumatic life events. Our ability to use distraction skills allows us to go to school or work, buy groceries, etc.—even in the face of difficult life events.

While distraction and avoidance can be very useful in the short term, they become problematic when they are the primary means of coping with trauma. When we caution against the use of avoidance, we are really cautioning against the use of avoidance or distraction as the primary means of coping with a trauma. If an individual were to avoid thinking about or having feelings about a trauma all of the time, they would likely have a much harder time recovering from the trauma.

"But If I Let Myself Experience My Emotions, I Would Be Overwhelmed by Them. . . ."

One common reaction to the suggestion that people should allow themselves to feel difficult emotions is a fear that those emotions will overwhelm them. Sometimes people are afraid that if they start crying, they'll cry forever. Other people worry that if they let themselves experience the anger inside them, they will lose control. Attending therapy with someone who is knowledgeable about trauma can be very useful for individuals who harbor these fears. For suggestions on how to locate a therapist in your area, go to the FAQ page at http://neptsd.org. This page contains information about contacting specialists and support groups for PTSD.

Nightmares
by Laura E. Gibson, Ph.D., The University of Vermont

What Are Nightmares?

Nightmares refer to elaborate dreams that cause high levels of anxiety or terror. In general, the content of nightmares revolves around imminent harm being caused to the individual (e.g., being chased, threatened, injured, etc.). When nightmares occur in the context of post-traumatic stress disorder (PTSD), they tend to involve the original threatening or horrifying set of circumstances that was involved during the traumatic event. For example, someone who was in the Twin Towers on September 11, 2001, might experience frightening dreams involving terrorists, airplane crashes, collapsing buildings, fires, people jumping from buildings, etc. A rape survivor might experience disturbing dreams about the rape itself or some aspect of the experience that was particularly frightening (e.g., being held at knifepoint).

Nightmares can occur multiple times in a given night, or one might experience them very rarely. Individuals may experience the same dream repeatedly, or they may experience different dreams with a similar theme. When individuals awaken from nightmares, they can typically remember them in detail. Upon awakening from a nightmare, individuals typically report feelings of alertness, fear, and anxiety. Nightmares occur almost exclusively during rapid eye movement (REM) sleep. Although REM sleep occurs on and off throughout the night, REM sleep periods become longer and dreaming tends to become more intense in the second half of the night. As a result, nightmares are more likely to occur during this time.

How Common Are Nightmares?

The prevalence of nightmares varies by age group and by gender. Nightmares are reportedly first experienced between the ages of three and six years. From 10 percent to 50 percent of children between the ages of three and five have nightmares that are severe enough to cause their parents concern. This does not mean that children with nightmares necessarily have a psychological disorder. In fact, children who develop nightmares in the absence of traumatic events typically grow out of them as they get older. Approximately 50 percent of adults report having at least an occasional nightmare. Estimates suggest that between 6.9 percent and 8.1 percent of the adult population suffer from chronic nightmares.

Women report having nightmares more often than men do. Women report two to four nightmares for every one nightmare reported by men. It is unclear at this point whether men and women actually experience different rates of nightmares, or whether women are simply more likely to report them.

Nightmares and Cultural Differences

The interpretation of and significance given to nightmares varies tremendously by culture. While some cultures view nightmares as indicators of mental health problems, others view them as related to supernatural or spiritual phenomena. Clinicians should keep this in mind during their assessments of the impact that nightmares have on clients.

How Are Nightmares Related to PTSD?

Nightmares are one of seventeen possible symptoms of PTSD. One does not have to experience nightmares in order to have PTSD. However, nightmares are one of the most common of the "reexperiencing" symptoms of PTSD, seen in approximately 60 percent of individuals with PTSD. A recent study of nightmares in female sexual assault survivors found that a higher frequency of nightmares was related to increased severity of PTSD symptoms. Little is known about the typical frequency or duration of nightmares in individuals with PTSD.

Are There Any Effective Treatments for Nightmares?

Yes. There are both psychological treatments (involving changing thoughts and behaviors) and psychopharmacological treatments (involving medicine) that have been found to be effective in reducing nightmares.

Psychological Treatment

In recent years, Barry Krakow and his colleagues at the University of New Mexico have conducted numerous studies regarding a promising psychological treatment for nightmares. This research group found positive results in applying this treatment to individuals suffering from nightmares in the context of PTSD. Krakow and colleagues found that crime victims and sexual assault survivors with PTSD who received this treatment showed fewer nightmares and better sleep quality after three group-treatment sessions. Another group of researchers applied the treatment to Vietnam combat veterans and found similarly promising results in a small pilot study.

The treatment studied at the University of New Mexico is called "Imagery Rehearsal Therapy" and is classified as a cognitive-behavioral treatment. It does not involve the use of medications. In brief, the treatment involves helping the clients change the endings of their nightmares, while they are awake, so that the ending is no longer upsetting. The client is then instructed to rehearse the new, nonthreatening images associated with the changed dream. Imagery Rehearsal Therapy also typically involves other components designed to help clients with problems associated with nightmares, such as insomnia. For example, clients are taught basic strategies that may help them to improve the quality of their sleep, such as refraining from caffeine during the afternoon, having a consistent evening wind-down ritual, or refraining from watching TV in bed.

Psychologists who use cognitive-behavioral techniques may be familiar with Imagery Rehearsal Therapy, or may have access to research literature describing it. If you need help locating a cognitive-behavioral therapist in your area, try using the clinical referral directory of the Association for the Advancement of Behavior Therapy.

Psychopharmacological Treatment

Researchers have also conducted studies of medications for the treatment of nightmares. However, it should be noted that the research findings in support of these treatments are more tentative than findings from studies of Imagery Rehearsal Therapy. Part of the reason for this is simply that fewer studies have been conducted with medications at this point in time. Also, the studies that have been conducted with medications have generally been small and have not included a comparison control group (that did not receive medication). This makes it difficult to know for sure whether the medication is responsible for reducing nightmares, or whether the patient's belief or confidence that the medication will work was responsible for the positive changes (a.k.a., a placebo effect).

Some medications that have been studied for treatment of PTSD-related nightmares and may be effective in reducing nightmares include topiramate, prazosin, nefazodone, trazodone, and gabapentin. Because medications typically have side effects, many patients choose to try a behavioral treatment first. If that does not help improve their symptoms, they may choose to try medication.

What Happens If Nightmares Are Left Untreated?

Nightmares can be a chronic mental health problem for some individuals, but it is not yet clear why they plague some people and not others. One thing that is clear is that nightmares are common in the early phases after a traumatic experience. However, research suggests that most people who have PTSD symptoms (including nightmares) just after a trauma will recover without treatment. This typically occurs by about the third month after a trauma. However, if PTSD symptoms (including nightmares) have not decreased substantially by about the third month, these symptoms can become chronic. If you have been suffering from nightmares for more than three months, you are encouraged to contact a mental health professional and discuss with him or her the behavioral treatments described above.

Sleep and Post-Traumatic Stress Disorder
By Pamela Swales, Ph.D.

Many people suffer from problems with their sleep. This can be especially true for those who have witnessed or experienced one or more traumatic events such as rape, military combat, natural disasters, beatings, or neighborhood violence. Some individuals exposed to traumatic physical or psychological events develop a condition known as post-traumatic stress disorder (PTSD). It is well-known that a problem with sleep is one of many problems for those with PTSD. Sleep problems, such as difficulty falling asleep, waking frequently, and having distressing dreams or nightmares, are common to those with PTSD. In fact, sleep disturbance can be a normal response to past trauma or anticipated threat.

What Are the Major Reasons Why People with PTSD Have Problems with Sleep?

Severe psychological or physical trauma can cause changes in a person's basic biological functioning. As a result of being traumatized, a person with PTSD may be constantly hypervigilant, or "on the look-out," to protect him- or herself from danger. It is difficult to have restful sleep when you feel the need to be always alert.

What Are Some Sleep Problems Commonly Associated with PTSD?

Difficulty Falling Asleep

- **Basic Biological Changes**: Actual biological changes may occur as a result of trauma, making it difficult to fall asleep. In addition, a continued state of hyperarousal or watchfulness is usually present. It is very hard for people to fall asleep if they think and feel that they need to stay awake and alert to protect themselves (and possibly others) from danger.
- **Medical Problems**: There are medical conditions commonly associated with PTSD. They can make going to sleep difficult. Such problems include: chronic pain, stomach and intestinal problems, and pelvic-area problems (in women).
- **Your Thoughts**: A person's thoughts can also contribute to problems with sleep. For example, thinking about the traumatic event, thinking about general worries and problems, or just thinking, "Here we go again, another night, another terrible night's sleep," may make it difficult to fall asleep.
- **Use of Drugs or Alcohol**: These substances are often associated with difficulty going to sleep.

Difficulty Staying Asleep

- **Distressing Dreams or Nightmares**: Nightmares are typical for people with PTSD. Usually the nightmares tend to be about the traumatic event or some aspect of it. For example, in Vietnam veterans, nightmares are usually about traumatic things that happened in combat. In dreams, the person with

PTSD may also attempt to express the dominant emotions of the traumatic event; these are usually fear and terror. For example, it is not uncommon to dream about being overwhelmed by a tidal wave or swept up by a whirlwind.

- **Night Terrors**: These are events such as screaming or shaking while asleep. The person may appear awake to an observer, but he or she is not responsive.
- **Thrashing Movements**: Because of overall hyperarousal, active movements of the arms or legs during bad dreams or nightmares may cause awakening. For example, if one were having a dream about fleeing an aggressor, one might wake up because of the physical movements of trying to run away.
- **Anxiety (Panic) Attacks**: Attacks of anxiety or outright panic may interrupt sleep. Symptoms of such attacks may include:

  - Feeling your heart beating very fast
  - Feeling that your heart is "skipping a beat"
  - Feeling light-headed or dizzy
  - Having difficulty breathing (e.g., tight chest, pressure on chest)
  - Sweating
  - Feeling really hot ("hot flashes")
  - Feeling really cold (cold sweat)
  - Feeling fearful
  - Feeling disoriented or confused
  - Fearing that you may die (as a result of these symptoms)
  - Thinking and feeling that you may be "going crazy"
  - Thinking and feeling that you may "lose control"

- **Hearing the Slightest Sound and Waking Up to Check for Safety**: Many people with PTSD, especially combat veterans, wake up frequently during the night. This can be for various reasons. However, once awake, a "perimeter check," or a check of the area, is often made. For example, a vet may get up, check the sleeping area, check the locks on windows and doors, and even go outside and walk around to check for danger. Then the vet may stay awake and vigilant and "stand guard;" he (or she) may not return to sleep that night.

What Can You Do If You Have Problems Sleeping Due to PTSD?

Talk to Your Doctor

Let your doctor know that you have trouble sleeping. Tell your doctor exactly what the problems are; he or she can help you best if you share this information about yourself.

Let your doctor know that you have (or think you have) PTSD. It is not your fault that you have these symptoms. Tell your doctor exactly what they are.

Let your doctor know about any physical problems that you think are contributing to your sleep problems. For example, chronic pain associated with traumatic injuries can make it difficult to sleep.

Let your doctor know about any other emotional problems you have—these may also be contributing to your sleep problems. For example, depression or panic attacks can make it hard to fall asleep or to stay asleep.

There are a number of medications that are helpful for sleep problems in PTSD. Depending on your sleep symptoms and other factors, your doctor may prescribe some medication for you.

Your doctor may recommend that you work with a therapist skilled in dealing with emotional and behavioral problems. Psychologists, social workers, and psychiatrists fall into this category. They can help you take a closer look at, and possibly change, the variety of factors that may be preventing you from sleeping well. They can help you with PTSD and other problems.

Do Not Use Alcohol or Other Drugs

These substances disturb a variety of bodily processes. They impair a person's ability to get a good night's sleep. For example, alcohol may help a person fall asleep, but it interferes with one's ability to stay asleep.

If you are dependent on drugs or alcohol, let your doctor know, and seek assistance for this problem.

Other Strategies

- Limit substances that contain caffeine (e.g., soda, coffee, some over-the-counter medicines).
- Try to set a regular sleep/wake schedule:
  A consistent sleep schedule helps to regulate and set the body's "internal clock," which tells us when we are tired and when it is time to sleep, among other things.
- Make your sleeping area as free from distractions as possible:
  Aim for quiet surroundings; keep the room darkened; keep the television out of the bedroom.
- Consider a light nighttime snack:
  A light snack after dinner may prevent hunger from waking you up in the middle of the night.
- Avoid overarousal for at least two to three hours prior to going to sleep:
  Try not to get your body and mind in "arousal mode." Things that may tend to do this are: heavy meals, strenuous exercise, heated arguments, paying bills, and action-packed movies.
- Don't worry that you can't sleep:
  Remember, there may be a number of reasons for your sleep problems. The first step is to talk to your doctor.

The information on this Web site is presented for educational purposes only. It is not a substitute for informed medical advice or training.

Do not use this information to diagnose or treat a mental health problem without consulting a qualified health professional.

Self-Harm

by Laura E. Gibson, Ph.D., The University of Vermont

What Is Self-Harm?

"Self-harm" refers to the deliberate, direct destruction of body tissue that results in tissue damage. When someone engages in self-harm, they may have a variety of intentions. However, the person's intention is *not* to kill themselves. You may have heard self-harm referred to as "parasuicide," "self-mutilation," "self-injury," "self-abuse," "cutting," "self-inflicted violence," and so on.

How Common Is Self-Harm?

Self-harm is not well understood and has not yet been extensively studied. The rates of self-harm revealed through research vary tremendously depending on how researchers pose their questions about this behavior. One widely cited estimate of the incidence of impulsive self-injury is that it occurs in at least one person per one thousand annually. A recent study of psychiatric outpatients found that 33 percent reported engaging in self-harm in the previous three months. A recent study of college undergraduates asked study participants about specific self-harm behaviors and found alarmingly high rates. Although the high rates may have been due in part to the broad spectrum of self-harm behaviors that were assessed (e.g., severe scratching and interfering with the healing of wounds were included), the numbers are certainly cause for concern:

- 18 percent reported having harmed themselves more than ten times in the past,

- 10 percent reported having harmed themselves more than a hundred times in the past, and
- 38 percent endorsed a history of deliberate self-harm.
- The most frequently reported self-harm behaviors were needle sticking, skin cutting, and scratching, endorsed by 16 percent, 15 percent, and 14 percent of the participants, respectively.

It is important to note that research on self-harm is still in the early stages, and these rates may change as researchers begin to utilize more consistent definitions of self-harm and more studies are completed.

Who Engages in Self-Harm?

Only a handful of empirical studies have examined self-harm in a systematic, sound manner. Self-harm appears to be more common in females than in males, and it tends to begin in adolescence or early adulthood. While some people may engage in self-harm a few times and then stop, others engage in it frequently and have great difficulty stopping the behavior. Several studies have found that individuals who engage in self-harm report unusually high rates of histories of:

- Childhood sexual abuse
- Childhood physical abuse
- Emotional neglect
- Insecure attachment
- Prolonged separation from caregivers

At least two studies have attempted to determine whether particular characteristics of childhood sexual abuse place individuals at greater risk for engaging in self-harm as adults. Both studies reported that more severe, more frequent, or a longer duration of sexual abuse was associated with an increased risk of engaging in self-harm in one's adult years.

Also, individuals who self-harm appear to have higher rates of the following psychological problems.

- High levels of dissociation
- Borderline personality disorder
- Substance abuse disorders
- Post-traumatic stress disorder
- Intermittent explosive disorder
- Antisocial personality
- Eating disorders

Why Do People Engage in Self-Harm?

While there are many theories about why individuals harm themselves, the answer to this question varies from individual to individual.

Some Reasons Why People Engage in Self-Harm:

- To distract themselves from emotional pain by causing physical pain
- To punish themselves
- To relieve tension
- To feel real by feeling pain or seeing evidence of injury
- To feel numb, zoned out, calm, or at peace
- To experience euphoric feelings (associated with release of endorphins)
- To communicate their pain, anger, or other emotions to others
- To nurture themselves (through the process of healing the wounds)

How Is Self-Harm Treated?

Self-harm is a problem that many people are embarrassed or ashamed to discuss. Often, individuals try to hide their self-harm behaviors and are very reluctant to seek needed psychological or even medical treatment.

Psychological Treatments

Because self-harm is often associated with other psychological problems, it tends to be treated under the umbrella of a co-occurring disorder like a substance abuse problem or an eating disorder. Sometimes the underlying feelings that cause the self-harm are the same as those that cause the co-occurring disorder. For example, a person's underlying feelings of shame may cause them to abuse drugs *and* cut themselves. Often the self-harm can be addressed in the context of therapy for an associated problem. For example, if people can learn healthy coping skills to help them deal with their urges to abuse substances, they may be able to apply these same skills to their urges to harm themselves.

There are also some treatments that specifically focus on stopping the self-harm. A good example of this is Dialectical Behavior Therapy (DBT), a treatment that involves individual therapy and group skills training. DBT is a therapy approach that was originally developed for individuals with borderline personality disorder who engage in self-harm or "parasuicidal behaviors." Now the treatment is also being used for self-harming individuals with a wide variety of other psychological problems, including eating disorders and substance dependence. The theory behind DBT is that individuals tend to engage in self-harm in an attempt to regulate or control their strong emotions. DBT teaches clients alternative ways of managing their emotions and tolerating distress. Research has shown that DBT is helpful in reducing self-harm. To learn more about DBT, or to locate a DBT therapist in your area, go to: http://www.behavioraltech.com/basics.html.

Pharmacological Treatments

It is possible that psychopharmacological treatments would be helpful in reducing self-harm behaviors, but this has not yet been rigorously studied. As yet, there is no consensus regarding whether or not psychiatric medications should be used in relation to self-harm behaviors. This is a complicated issue to study because self-harm can occur in many different populations and co-occur with many different kinds of psychological problems. If you are wondering about the use of medications for the emotions related to your self-harm behaviors, we recommend that you discuss this with your doctor or psychiatrist.

How to Find a Qualified Psychologist or Psychiatrist

If you are trying to find a psychologist or psychiatrist, we advise you to ask them whether they are familiar with self-harm. Consider which issues are important to you, and make sure you can talk to the potential therapist about them. Remember that you are the consumer—you have the right to interview therapists until you find someone with whom you feel comfortable. You may want to ask trusted friends or medical professionals for referrals to psychologists or psychiatrists. Consider asking your potential provider questions such as:

- How do you treat self-harm?
- What do you think causes self-harm?
- Do you have experience in treating self-harm?

For tips on communicating with medical providers in a medical context (including communicating with professionals in an emergency room), go to http://www.palace.net/~llama/psych/injury.html, click the icon on the left side of the screen that reads "first aid," and then click the icon "what to expect in the emergency room." For more ideas on finding a therapist who is familiar with the treatment of self-harm, go to http://www.palace.net/~llama/psych/injury.html, and then click on "offline resources" on the left side of the screen.

Self-Help Resources

There are a variety of self-help books on the market for people who engage in self-harm. Most of these provide practical advice, support, and coping skills that may be helpful to individuals who engage in self-harm. These approaches have not been studied in research trials, so it is not known how effective they are for individuals who self-harm.

My Friend or Relative Self-Harms. What Should I Do to Be Supportive?

If you have a friend or relative who engages in self-harm, it can be very distressing and confusing for you. You may feel guilty, angry, scared, powerless, or any number of things. Some general guidelines are:

- Take the self-harm seriously by expressing concern and encouraging the individual to seek professional help.
- Don't get into a power struggle with the individual— ultimately they need to make the choice to stop the behavior. You cannot force them to stop.
- Don't blame yourself. The individual who is self-harming initiated this behavior and needs to take responsibility for stopping it.
- If the individual who is self-harming is a child or adolescent, make sure the parent or a trusted adult has been informed and is seeking professional help for them.
- If the individual who is engaging in self-harm does not want professional help because he or she doesn't think the behavior

is a problem, inform them that a professional is the best person to make this determination. Suggest that a professional is a neutral third party who will not be emotionally invested in the situation and so will be able to make the soundest recommendations.

Why Seek Help for PTSD?

Most people experience considerable distress and avoidance after being exposed to a severely traumatic experience. This is a normal and adaptive response and often includes reliving the event in thoughts, images, and dreams. This initial rumination of the event may in fact contribute to the healing process and provide a way of achieving mastery over the event. For most people, these symptoms usually become less severe and gradually disappear over time. For others, the symptoms persist and become chronic, leading to PTSD. About 8 percent of men and 20 percent of women develop PTSD after experiencing a traumatic event, and roughly 30 percent of these individuals develop a chronic form that persists throughout their lifetimes.

The symptoms and problems associated with PTSD can interfere with a person's life and become difficult to manage. Turning to someone for help is the first step in addressing the impact of PTSD in your life. Psychologists and other appropriate mental-health providers help educate people about reactions to extreme stress and ways of processing the event and dealing with the emotional impact.

With children, continual and aggressive emotional outbursts, serious problems at school, preoccupation with the traumatic event, continued and extreme withdrawal, and other signs of intense anxiety or emotional difficulties all point to the need for professional assistance. A qualified mental-health professional can help such children and their parents understand and deal with thoughts, feelings, and behaviors that result from trauma.

Knowing what kind of help is available, where to look for help, and what kind of questions to ask might make the process of seeking help easier and lead to more successful outcomes.

How Is PTSD Assessed and Treated?

In recent years, a great deal of attention has been aimed at developing reliable assessment tools to aid in the diagnosis of PTSD. Today there is a range of available measures that clinicians can use to diagnose PTSD.

PTSD is treated with a variety of forms of psychotherapy and medication. Today there are some promising treatments that include cognitive-behavioral interventions such as cognitive restructuring and exposure.

How Do I Get an Evaluation?

While it may be tempting to identify PTSD for yourself or someone you know, the diagnosis generally is made by a mental-health professional. This will usually involve a formal evaluation by a psychiatrist, psychologist, or clinical social worker specifically trained to assess psychological problems.

What Can I Expect from an Evaluation for PTSD?

The nature of an evaluation for PTSD can vary widely, depending on how the evaluation will be used and the training of the professional evaluator. As part of a screening, an interviewer may take as little as fifteen minutes to get a sense of your traumatic experiences and its effects. On the other hand, a specialized PTSD assessment can last several hours and involve detailed, structured interviews and questionnaires. Whatever the particulars of your situation, you should always be able to find out in advance from the professional conducting the evaluation what the assessment will involve and what information they will be looking for to determine a diagnosis.

How Is PTSD Treated?

The many therapeutic approaches offered to PTSD patients are presented in Foa, Keane, and Friedman's (2000) comprehensive book on treatment. The most successful interventions are cognitive-behavioral therapy (CBT) and medication. Excellent results have been obtained with some CBT combinations of exposure therapy and cognitive restructuring, especially with female victims of childhood or adult sexual trauma. Sertraline (Zoloft) and Paroxetine (Paxil) are selective serotonin reuptake inhibitors (SSRI) that are the first medications to have received FDA approval as indicated treatments for PTSD. Success has also been reported with Eye Movement Desensitization and Reprocessing (EMDR), although rigorous scientific data are lacking and it is unclear whether this approach is as effective as CBT.

What Is Psychotherapy and How Can It Help Treat PTSD?

Psychotherapy is meant to help with a person's emotional, behavioral, or mental distress. In practice, psychotherapy is the relationship between a professional psychotherapist and a client who work together to make changes in the client's thoughts, feelings, and behaviors. How the psychotherapist goes about helping a client will depend upon the client's goals and the therapist's training and theoretical orientation. Theoretical underpinnings can determine what techniques a therapist uses and the focus of therapy, and they can affect the psychotherapist's style of interaction.

However, sometimes a person's diagnosis will influence the decision about what type of therapeutic orientation the person should engage in. PTSD is a good example of this type of diagnosis, because there are many psychotherapeutic treatments that have been designed specifically to treat PTSD. A client's response to treatment will have a lot to do with the unique values, hopes, and personality factors of that individual, but there are some treatments that have been rigorously studied and shown to be helpful for PTSD.

Who Is Available to Provide Psychotherapy?

There are many different types of professionals qualified to practice psychotherapy. These types can be divided into three basic groups: clinical psychologists, clinical social workers, and psychiatrists.

Clinical Psychologists

Clinical psychologists have doctoral degrees (Ph.D., Psy.D., Ed.D.) from graduate programs that specialize in the study of clinical, research, and educational psychology. Programs that are approved by the American Psychological Association (APA) must meet specific teaching and training requirements that adhere to ethical, academic, and clinical standards. In addition to four years of course work, clinical psychologists must complete one year of supervised clinical training. After the fifth year of training, clinical psychologists must have another one to two years of supervised clinical experience to be eligible for licensure. Licensure is granted after passing an examination given by the American Board of Professional Psychology. Licensure allows the psychologist to practice psychotherapy without formal supervision. Although psychologists are doctors, they cannot prescribe medications.

Clinical Social Workers

Certified social workers have a master's degree or doctoral degree in social work (MSW, DSW, or Ph.D.). Graduate training for the master's level requires at least two years of schooling beyond the four years necessary for the undergraduate degree. To be licensed, clinical social workers must pass an exam given by the Academy of Certified Social Workers (ACSW).

Psychiatrists

Psychiatrists attend medical school and have a medical degree (MD). As with other medical specialties, psychiatrists participate in a three- to four-year residency training in psychiatry after they complete four years of medical school. Child psychiatrists must complete at least one year of concentrated clinical experience with children. Board-certified psychiatrists have also passed a written and oral examination given by the American Board of Psychiatry and Neurology. Psychiatrists, like medical doctors, prescribe medications. Some also provide psychotherapy.

Psychotherapeutic Approaches Commonly Used to Treat PTSD

There are a number of different therapeutic approaches used to treat PTSD. We will briefly explain some of the more effective approaches.

Cognitive-Behavioral Treatment (CBT)

Cognitive-behavioral strategies have been the most frequently studied and most effective form of psychotherapy treatment for PTSD. The essential feature in all cognitive therapies is an understanding of PTSD in terms of the workings of the mind. Implicit in this approach is the idea that PTSD is, in part, caused by the way we think. CBT helps people understand the connection between their thoughts and feelings. CBT can help change the way we think ("cognitive restructuring") by exploring alternative explanations, and assessing the accuracy of our thoughts. Even if we are not able to change the situation, we can change the way we think about a situation.

CBT is based on the understanding that many of our emotional and behavioral reactions to situations are learned. The goal of therapy is to unlearn the unhelpful reactions to certain events and situations and learn new ways of responding. CBT relies on evaluating thoughts to see whether they are based on fact or on assumptions. Often we get upset because we think something is occurring when it is not. CBT encourages us to look at our thoughts as hypotheses to be questioned and tested. CBT for trauma includes strategies for processing thoughts about the event and challenging negative or unhelpful thinking patterns.

Exposure Therapy

Exposure is one form of CBT. Exposure uses careful, repeated, detailed imagining of the trauma (exposure) in a safe, controlled context to help the survivor face and gain control of the fear and distress that was overwhelming during the trauma. In some cases, trauma memories or reminders can be confronted all at once ("flooding"). For other individuals or traumas, it is preferable to work up to the most severe trauma gradually by using relaxation techniques and by starting with less upsetting life stresses or by taking the trauma one piece at a time ("desensitization"). When exposure is conducted by having the person imagine the trauma (such as a rape), it is called "imaginal exposure." When it is done in real life, such as having the person go into a feared situation such as a crowded place, it is called "in vivo exposure." In most cases, both forms of exposure are used.

CBT often involves reading assignments and homework so that clients can practice on their own the techniques they have learned in therapy.

Pharmacotherapy (Medication)

Medications can reduce the anxiety, depression, and insomnia often experienced with PTSD, and in some cases they may help relieve the distress and emotional numbness caused by trauma memories.

Several kinds of antidepressant drugs have contributed to patient improvement in most (but not all) clinical trials, and some other classes of drugs have shown promise. The FDA has approved two medications, paroxetine and sertraline, for use in the treatment of PTSD. Although no medication has been proven to cure PTSD, medications are clearly useful for symptom relief, which makes it possible for survivors to participate in psychotherapy.

Eye Movement Desensitization and Reprocessing (EMDR)

EMDR is a relatively new treatment for traumatic memories that involves elements of exposure therapy and CBT combined with techniques (eye movements, hand taps, sounds) that create an alternation of attention back and forth across the person's midline. While the theory and research are still evolving for this form of treatment, evidence suggests that it is the exposure and cognitive components of EMDR that make it effective, rather than the attentional alternation.

Group Treatment

Group therapy is often an ideal therapeutic setting because trauma survivors are able to share traumatic material within the safety, cohesion, and empathy of other survivors. In such a setting, the PTSD patient can discuss traumatic memories, PTSD symptoms, and functional deficits with others who have had similar experiences. As group members achieve greater understanding and resolution of their individual traumas, they often feel more confident and able to trust. As they discuss and share how they cope with trauma-related shame, guilt, rage, fear, doubt, and self-condemnation, they prepare themselves to focus on the present rather than the past. Telling one's story (the "trauma narrative") and directly facing the grief, anxiety, and guilt related to trauma enables many survivors to cope with their symptoms, memories, and other aspects of their lives.

How Can I Tell If Therapy Is Working Well?

When you begin psychotherapy, you and your therapist should decide together what goals you hope to reach in therapy. Not every person with PTSD will have the same treatment goals. For instance, not all people with PTSD are concerned with lessening their symptoms. Some people want to learn instead the best way to live with existing symptoms and how to cope with other problems associated with PTSD. Perhaps you want to lessen your feelings of guilt and sadness. Perhaps you would like to work on more tangible aspects of your distress, like your relationships at work, or communication issues with your friends and family. Your therapist should help you decide which of these goals seem most important to you, and he or she should discuss with you which goals might take a long time to achieve.

Your therapist should also provide you with a good rationale for the therapy. That is, you should understand why your therapist is choosing a specific treatment for you, how long they expect the therapy to last, and how they will evaluate its effectiveness. The two of you should agree at the outset that this plan makes sense for you and what you will do if it does not seem to be working. If you have any questions about the treatment your therapist should be able to answer them.

Another aspect important to the course of good therapy is the relationship you have with your therapist. If you feel comfortable with your therapist and feel you are working as a team to tackle your problems, it is likely that the therapy will go well. If you have concerns about your therapist, or concerns about the therapy, you should speak with your therapist about them. Therapy is not easy. It can be difficult to talk about painful situations in your life, or about traumatic experiences that you have had. Feelings that emerge during therapy can be frightening and challenging. Talking with your therapist about the process of therapy, and about your hopes and fears in regards to therapy, will help make therapy successful.

If you have concerns about your therapy or concerns about your therapist that have not been successfully worked out with your therapist, it might be helpful to consult another professional. It is recommended, however, that you let your therapist know you are seeking a second opinion.

How Do I Find a Qualified Therapist?

Selecting a therapist is a highly personal matter. A professional who works very well with one individual may not be a good choice for another person. There are several ways to get referrals to qualified therapists such as licensed psychologists.

Listed below are some ways to find help. When you call, tell whomever you speak to that you are trying to find a mental-health provider who specializes in helping people who have been through traumatic events. Check the National Center for Post-Traumatic Stress Disorder Web site (http://ncptsd.org) regularly for updated information on how to get help. We will be listing more ways to get help as they become available.

For Veterans

VA medical centers and Vet Centers provide veterans with mental-health services that health insurance will cover or that cost little or nothing, according to a veteran's ability to pay. VA medical centers and Vet Centers are listed in the phone book in the blue Government pages. Under "United States Government Offices," look in the section for "Veterans Affairs, Dept. of." In that section look for VA Medical Centers and Clinics listed under "Medical Care" and for "Vet Centers—Counseling and Guidance," and call the one nearest to where you live. On the Internet, go to http://www.va.gov/ and look for the VHA Facilities Locator link under "Health Benefits and Services," or go to www.va.gov/rcs.

For more information see Specialized PTSD Treatment Programs in the U.S. Department of Veterans Affairs.

For Nonveterans

Some local mental-health services are listed in the phone book in the blue Government pages. In the "County Government Offices" section for the county where you live, look for a "Health Services, Dept. of" or "Department of Health Services" section. In that section, look for listings under "Mental Health." In the Yellow Pages, services and mental-health professionals are listed under "counseling," "psychologists," "social workers," "psychotherapists," "social and human services," or "mental health." Health insurance may pay for mental-health services, and some are available at low cost according to your ability to pay.

For Anyone

Call your doctor's office or ask friends if they can recommend any mental-health providers.

If you work for a large company or organization, call the human resources or personnel office to find out if they provide mental-health services or make referrals.

If you are a member of a Health Maintenance Organization (HMO), call to find out if mental-health services are available.

Call the National Center for Victims of Crime's toll-free information and referral service at 1-800-FYI-CALL. This is a comprehensive database of more than 6,700 community service agencies throughout the country that directly support victims of crime.

Contact your local mental-health agencies or family physician.

Online Resources

The Anxiety Disorders Association of America offers a referral network of professional therapists, as well as a self-help group network.

The Association for Advancement of Behavior Therapy (AABT) is a professional organization that maintains a database of CBT therapists at https://aabt.org/members/Directory/Clinical_Directory.cfm.

The National Institute of Mental Health Anxiety Disorders has published an extensive list of mental health organizations to help the consumer find more information about anxiety disorders and related issues, as well as to obtain referrals for specialists in different geographical areas.

The National Alliance for Mental Illness (NAMI) has a Web site (http://www.nami.org) with information on advocacy for those with mental illness, including affiliates who provide family support groups in different states.

About.com's trauma resource page (http://mentalhealth.about.com/od/traumaptsd)offers a comprehensive listing of information, resources, links, and support groups on a wide array of topics related to trauma, particularly incest and child abuse.

Facts for Health (http://www.factsforhealth.org) offers a referral database for clinicians based on clinicians who have completed a continuing-education course on PTSD or clinicians who have been identified by the directors of the Madison Institute of Medicine as being specialists in PTSD.

The Holistic Health Yellow Pages (http://www.findhealer.com) offer a referral network of holistic practitioners.

For more information call the PTSD Information Line at (802) 296-6300, or send e-mail to ncptsd@ncptsd.org.

ACKNOWLEDGMENTS

We wish to thank our agent, Matt Bialer, at Sanford J. Greenburger Associates, for his creative support, business acumen, and assistance in nurturing our collaboration. Matt's assistant, Anna Bierhaus, also deserves acknowledgment for handling our anxious phone calls with aplomb.

Our appreciation also goes to the editor at New American Library who bought *A Sniper's Journey*, Doug Grad, and the editor who saw it to completion, Mark Chait, and their assistant, Brent Howard.

The unsung heroes in bringing *A Sniper's Journey* to the bookshelves are NAL associate managing editor Sally Franklin and copy editor Tiffany Yates, who has a *really* annoying eye for inconsistencies, echoed words and substandard English. But we *really* do thank her for making our book more readable. The cover design, unique for its avoidance of sniper clichés, is by NAL's chief of graphic design, Anthony Ramondo. We're grateful for his creativity.

The subtext of this book deals with the mental health of those who are called upon to fight our nation's wars, and the emotional price they can pay for following the orders they're given. For the insight they've provided during the writing of *A Sniper's Journey*, the authors are grateful to Elizabeth Heron, Ph.D., whose work with the air force is aimed at preventing emotional trauma in troops about to be deployed in combat, and Roger Melton, MFCC, a therapist and Vietnam veteran who has specialized in the treatment of PTSD.

Debra Johnson Knox at MilitaryUSA.com (and author of *How to Locate Anyone Who Is or Has Been in the Military*) graciously assisted in our attempt to locate service members with whom Gary Mitchell served.

Former army snipers in Vietnam Howard Kramer, Neil Korbas, Deano Miller, Chester Clarke, and Brian K. Sain, founder of American-Snipers.org, provided insight and assistance. No matter what your position on the wars our troops are currently committed to, all agree that asking soldiers to do their job without enough of the right equipment is wrong. AmericanSnipers.org has raised hundreds of thousands of dollars to purchase equipment requested by sniper units in Iraq and Afghanistan, equipment that is unavailable on a timely basis through regular supply channels.

While we consulted a number of books about Vietnam and the Gulf War in writing *A Sniper's Journey,* one unique volume is worth a special mention: *Where We Were in Vietnam* by Michael P. Kelley is the definitive reference work for anyone who served in that war and who might still be wondering where he or she really was. Michael also took the time to share considerable information about rifle ranges not necessarily belonging to American forces where sniper training such as Gary Mitchell underwent may have taken place.

It's always useful to have writer friends who are willing to be brutally honest. In this case, thanks go to John Corcoran and Ira Furman for their moral support, and their time and energy in critiquing the work in progress. Kathy Kirkland typed the interview transcripts, and was first to provide valuable feedback on their content.

Finally, thanks to our wives, Ellen Mitchell and Karen Hirsh, for their unflagging support during this uphill marathon.

Gary D. Mitchell entered the U.S. Army in 1968 and retired in 1992. He served a combat tour in Vietnam from 1969 to 1970. He also participated in Operation Desert Shield and Operation Desert Storm, where he was an adviser to the Saudi Arabian National Guard and fought in the battle of Al Khafji. During his twenty-four-year career, he was stationed in Korea, Vietnam, Germany, and Saudi Arabia, as well as numerous installations in the continental United States. Starting as a private, he retired as a chief warrant officer. He and his wife, Ellen, reside in California.

Michael Hirsh was a combat correspondent with the 25th Infantry Division at Cu Chi, Vietnam, in 1966, where he earned the CIB. In 2002 he was embedded with Air Force Combat Search and Rescue forces in Operation Enduring Freedom on bases in Afghanistan, Pakistan, and Uzbekistan to write *None Braver: U.S. Air Force Pararescuemen in the War on Terrorism.* He is also the author of *Your Other Left: Punch Lines from the Front Lines.* Hirsh is a George Foster Peabody Award and Writers Guild Award winner, as well as an Emmy Award–winning television documentary producer and investigative reporter. He lives in Punta Gorda, Florida.